Student Solutions Manual

Financial Accounting
An Introduction to Concepts, Methods, and Uses

THIRTEENTH EDITION

Clyde P. Stickney
Dartmouth College

Roman L. Weil
University of Chicago

Katherine Schipper
Duke University

Jennifer Francis
Duke University

SOUTH-WESTERN
CENGAGE Learning

Australia • Brazil • Japan • Korea • Mexico • Singapore • Spain • United Kingdom • United States

SOUTH-WESTERN
CENGAGE Learning™

ISBN-13: 978-0-324-78900-3
ISBN-10: 0-324-78900-9

South-Western Cengage Learning
5191 Natorp Boulevard
Mason, OH 45040
USA

Cengage Learning is a leading provider of customized learning solutions with office locations around the globe, including Singapore, the United Kingdom, Australia, Mexico, Brazil, and Japan. Locate your local office at: **international.cengage.com/region**.

Cengage Learning products are represented in Canada by Nelson Education, Ltd.

For your course and learning solutions, visit **www.cengage.com**.

Purchase any of our products at your local college store or at our preferred online store **www.ichapters.com**.

Printed in the United States of America
3 4 5 6 7 13 12 11 10

PREFACE

This book presents odd-numbered answers and solutions for the questions, exercises, and problems contained in each chapter of the textbook *Financial Accounting: An Introduction to Concepts, Methods and Uses* Thirteenth Edition. We do not attempt to give all possible ways to work a problem, showing the multiple paths to the correct solution. We do not even try to give the most commonly chosen one, even if we know what that is, which is rare. Our students often ask the equivalent of, "Why can't I work the problem this way?" or "Is it OK to work the problem this other way?" In a word, yes. You can work most problems in several different ways. If you get the right final answer, then do not worry if you reached it via a path different from the one we show.

If you have any suggestions as to how this book might be improved in subsequent editions, please feel free to bring them to our attention.

C.P.S.

R.L.W.

K.S.

J.F.

This page is intentionally left blank

CONTENTS

CHAPTER 1

INTRODUCTION TO BUSINESS ACTIVITIES AND
OVERVIEW OF FINANCIAL STATEMENTS
AND THE REPORTING PROCESS

Questions, Exercises, and Problems: Answers and Solutions

1.1   The first question at the end of each chapter asks the student to review the important terms and concepts discussed in the chapter. Students may wish to consult the glossary at the end of the book in addition to the definitions and discussions in the chapter.

1.3   The balance sheet shows assets, liabilities and shareholders' equity as of a specific date (the balance sheet date), similar to a snapshot. The income statement and statement of cash flows report changes in assets and liabilities over a period of time, similar to a motion picture.

1.5   Management, under the oversight of the firm's governing board, prepares the financial statements.

1.7   Accounts receivable represent amounts owed by customers for goods and services they have already received. The customer, therefore, has the benefit of the goods and services before it pays cash. The length of the financing period is the number of days between when the customer receives the goods and services and when the customer pays cash to the seller of those goods and services.

1.9   A calendar year ends on December 31. A fiscal year ends on a date that is determined by the firm, perhaps based on its business model (for example, many retailers choose a fiscal year end that is close to the end of January). A firm can choose the calendar year as its fiscal year, and many do. Both calendar years and fiscal years have 12 months.

1.11   A current item is expected to result in a cash receipt (assets such as accounts receivable) or a cash payment (liabilities such as accounts payable) within approximately one year or less. A noncurrent item is expected to generate cash over periods longer than a year (assets, such as factory buildings that will be used to produce goods for sale over many years) or use cash over periods longer than a year (liabilities such as long term debt). Users of financial statements would likely be interested in this distinction because the distinction provides information about short term cash flows separately from long term cash flows).

1.13   An income statement connects two successive balance sheets through its
        effect on retained earnings. Net income that is not paid to shareholders as
        dividends increases retained earnings. A statement of cash flows connects
        two successive balance sheets because it explains the change in cash (a
        balance sheet account) from operating, financing, and investing activities.
        The statement of cash flows also shows the relation between net income
        and cash flows from operations, and changes in assets and liabilities that
        involve cash flows.

1.15   U.S. GAAP must be used by U.S. SEC registrants and may be used by
        other firms as well. International Financial Reporting Standards (IFRS)
        may be used by non-U.S. firms that list and trade their securities in the
        U.S, and these firms may also use U.S. GAAP.

1.17   The accrual basis of accounting is based on assets and liabilities, not on
        cash receipts and disbursements. It provides a better basis for measuring
        performance because it is based on revenues (inflows of assets from
        customers) not cash receipts from customers, and on expenses (outflows of
        assets from generating revenues) not cash payments. It matches
        revenues with the costs associated with earning those revenues and is not
        sensitive to the timing of expenditures.

1.19   (Mayr Melnhof Karton; understanding the income statement.)

        a. Cost of Goods Sold = €1,331,292.1 thousand.

        b. Selling and distribution expenses = €172,033.4 thousand.

        c. Gross margin percentage = 23.4% (= €405,667.1/€1,736,959.2).

        d. Operating profit = €169,418.2 thousand.

            Profit before tax = €170,863.9 thousand.

            Difference equals €1,445.7 thousand (= €169,418.2 − €170,863.9).
            The items comprising this difference are sources of income (expense) of
            a nonoperating nature for Mayr Melnhof.

        e. Effective tax rate = €54,289.9/€170,863.9 = 31.8%.

        f. Profit = €116,574.0 thousand.

1.21 (Alcatel-Lucent; balance sheet relations.) (Amounts in Millions)

Current Assets	+	Noncurrent Assets	=	Current Liabilities	+	Noncurrent Liabilities	+	Share-holders' Equity
€20,000	+	€29,402	=	€15,849	+	?	+	€17,154

Noncurrent liabilities total €16,399 million.

1.23 (Rolls Royce Group Plc.; income statement relations.)

Sales	£ 7,435
Less Cost of Sales	(6,003)
Gross Margin	£ 1,432
Less Other Operating Expenses	(918)
Loss on Sale of Business	(2)
Net Financing Income	221
Profit before Taxes	£ 733
Less Tax Expense	(133)
Net Income	£ 600

1.25 (Gold Fields; retained earnings relations) (Amounts in Millions of Rand)

Retained Earnings at End of 2006	+	Net Income for 2007	−	Dividends Declared for 2007	=	Retained Earnings at End of 2007
R4,640.9	+	R2,362.5	−	?	=	R5,872.4

Dividends declared during 2007 totaled R1,131.0 million.

1.27 (Target Corporation; cash flow relations.) (Amounts in Millions)

Cash at Feb. 3, 2007	+	Cash Flow from Operations	+	Cash Flow from Investing	+	Cash Flow from Financing	=	Cash at Feb. 2, 2008
$813	+	$4,125	+	$(6,195)	+	$3,707	=	?

Cash balance at February 3, 2008 = $2,450 million.

1.29 (Kenton Limited; preparation of simple balance sheet; current and noncurrent classifications.)

Assets

Cash	£ 2,000
Inventory	12,000
Prepaid Rent	24,000
Total Current Assets	£ 38,000
Prepaid Rent	£ 24,000
Total Noncurrent Assets	£ 24,000
Total Assets	£ 62,000

Liabilities and Shareholders' Equity

Accounts Payable	£ 12,000
Total Current Liabilities	£ 12,000
Total Noncurrent Liabilities	--
Total Liabilities	£ 12,000
Common Stock	£ 50,000
Total Shareholders' Equity	£ 50,000
Total Liabilities and Shareholders' Equity	£ 62,000

1.31 Boeing Company; accrual versus cash basis of accounting.)

a. Net Income = Sales Revenue − Expenses

$$= \$66,387 \text{ million} - \$62,313 \text{ million} = \$4,074 \text{ million.}$$

Net Cash Flow = Cash Inflows − Cash Outflows

$$= \$65,995 \text{ million} - \$56,411 \text{ million} = \$9,584 \text{ million.}$$

b. Cash collections may differ from revenues for several reasons.

Cash collected might exceed revenues if
(1) Boeing collected in 2007 for customer credit sales made in 2006; or
(2) Boeing may have collected cash from customers in advance of providing the goods and services, or both.

Cash collected might be less than revenues if
(1) Customers purchased products or services on credit; or
(2) Boeing delivered on products/services for which it had received cash, in advance, in prior years, or both.

c. Cash payments may be less than expenses for at least two reasons. First, Boeing may have received goods and services from suppliers, but not yet paid for those items (i.e., the amounts are to be paid in the next year). Second, Boeing may have accrued expenses in 2007 that will be paid in cash in future periods; an example would be the accrual of interest expense on a bond that will be paid the next year.

1.33   (Dragon Group International Limited; balance sheet relations.) (Amounts in Millions)

The missing items appear in **boldface** type below.

	2007	2006
Assets		
Current Assets	$ 170,879	$ 170,234
Noncurrent Assets	**28,945**	17,368
Total Assets	$ 199,824	$ **187,602**
Liabilities and Shareholders' Equity		
Current Liabilities	$ 139,941	$ 126,853
Noncurrent Liabilities	7,010	**7,028**
Total Liabilities	$ **146,951**	$ **133,881**
Shareholders' Equity	$ **52,873**	$ 53,721
Total Liabilities and Shareholders' Equity	$ **199,824**	$ **187,602**

1.35   (Colgate Palmolive Company; income statement relations.)

The missing items appear in **boldface** type below.

	2007	2006	2005
Sales	$ 13,790	$ **12,238**	$ 11,397
Cost of Goods Sold	**(6,042)**	(5,536)	(5,192)
Selling and Administrative Expenses	(4,973)	(4,355)	(3,921)
Other (Income) Expense	(121)	(186)	(69)
Interest Expense, Net	(157)	(159)	(136)
Income Tax Expense	(759)	(648)	(728)
Net Income	$ 1,738	$ 1,354	$ **1,351**

1.37   (Ericsson; statement of cash flows relations.)

ERICSSON
Statement of Cash Flows
(Amounts in SEK Millions)

	2007	2006	2005
Operations:			
Revenues, Net of Expenses..........	SEK 19,210	SEK 18,489	SEK 16,669
Cash Flow from Operations..............	SEK 19,210	SEK 18,489	SEK 16,669
Investing:			
Acquisition of Property and Equipment.....................................	SEK (4,319)	SEK (3,827)	SEK (3,365)
Acquisition of Businesses	(26,292)	(18,078)	(1,210)
Sale Property and Equipment	152	185	362
Sale of Short-Term Investments	3,499	6,180	6,375
Other Investing Activities............	(573)	663	(1,131)
Cash Flow from Investing.................	SEK(27,533)	SEK(14,877)	SEK 1,031
Financing:			
Proceeds from Borrowings............	SEK 15,587	SEK 1,290	SEK 657
Repayment of Borrowings............	(1,291)	(9,510)	(2,784)
Sale of Common Stock...................	94	124	174
Dividends Paid.................................	(8,132)	(7,343)	(4,133)
Other Financing Activities	406	58	(288)
Cash Flow from Financing................	SEK 6,664	SEK(15,381)	SEK (6,374)
Change in Cash.................................	SEK (1,659)	SEK(11,769)	SEK 11,326
Cash, Beginning of Year	29,969	41,738	30,412
Cash, End of Year.............................	SEK 28,310	SEK 29,969	SEK 41,738

1.39   (JetAway Airlines; preparing a balance sheet and an income statement.)

a.
JETAWAY AIRLINES
Balance Sheet
(Amounts in Thousands)

	Sept. 30, 2008	Sept. 30, 2007
Assets		
Cash..	$ 378,511	$ 418,819
Accounts Receivable	88,799	73,448
Inventories...	50,035	65,152
Other Current Assets......................................	56,810	73,586
Total Current Assets................................	$ 574,155	$ 631,005
Property, Plant and Equipment (Net)..........	4,137,610	5,008,166
Other Noncurrent Assets................................	4,231	12,942
Total Assets..	$ 4,715,996	$ 5,652,113

1.39 a. continued.

Liabilities and Shareholders' Equity

Accounts Payable	$ 157,415	$ 156,755
Current Maturities of Long-Term Debt	11,996	7,873
Other Current Liabilities	681,242	795,838
Total Current Liabilities	$ 850,653	$ 960,466
Long-Term Debt	623,309	871,717
Other Noncurrent Liabilities	844,116	984,142
Total Liabilities	$ 2,318,078	$ 2,816,325
Common Stock	$ 352,943	$ 449,934
Retained Earnings	2,044,975	2,385,854
Total Shareholders' Equity	$ 2,397,918	$ 2,835,788
Total Liabilities and Shareholders' Equity	$ 4,715,996	$ 5,652,113

b.

JETAWAY AIRLINES
Income Statement
(Amounts in Thousands)

For the Year Ended:	Sept. 30, 2008
Sales	$ 4,735,587
Salaries and Benefits Expense	(1,455,237)
Fuel Expense	(892,415)
Maintenance Expense	(767,606)
Other Operating Expenses	(1,938,753)
Interest Expense	(22,883)
Interest Income	14,918
Net Income	$ (326,389)

c.

Retained Earnings, September 30, 2007	$ 2,385,854
Plus Net Loss for 2008	(326,389)
Less Dividends Declared during 2008 (Plug)	(15,390)
Retained Earnings, September 30, 2008	$ 2,044,075

1.41 (Stationery Plus; cash basis versus accrual basis accounting.)

a. **Income for November, 2008:**

(1) **Cash Basis Accounting**

Sales	$ 23,000
Cost of Merchandise	(20,000)
Rent	(9,000)
Salaries	(10,000)
Utilities	(480)
Income (Loss)	$ (16,480)

1.41 a. continued.

(2) Accrual Basis Accounting

Sales	$ 56,000
Cost of Merchandise	(29,000)
Rent	(1,500)
Salaries	(10,000)
Utilities	(480)
Interest	(1,000)
Income (Loss)	$ 14,020

b. Income for December, 2008:

(1) Cash Basis Accounting

Sales Made in November, Collected in December	$ 33,000
Sales Made and Collected in December	34,000
Cost of Merchandise Acquired in November and Paid in December	(20,000)
Cost of Merchandise Acquired and Paid in December	(27,500)
Salaries	(10,000)
Utilities	(480)
Interest	(2,000)
Income (Loss)	$ 7,020

(2) Accrual Basis Accounting

Sales	$ 62,000
Cost of Merchandise	(33,600)
Rent	(1,500)
Salaries	(10,000)
Utilities	(480)
Interest	(1,000)
Income (Loss)	$ 15,420

1.43 (Balance sheet and income statement relations.)

a. Bushels of wheat are the most convenient in this case with the given information. This question emphasizes the need for a common measuring unit.

1.43 continued.

b.

IVAN AND IGOR
Comparative Balance Sheets
(Amounts in Bushels of Wheat)

	IVAN		IGOR	
Assets	**Beginning of Period**	**End of Period**	**Beginning of Period**	**End of Period**
Wheat.............................	20	223	10	105
Fertilizer......................	2	--	1	--
Ox..................................	40	36	40	36
Plow..............................	--	--	--	2
Land.............................	100	100	50	50
Total Assets...........	162	359	101	193
Liabilities and Owner's Equity				
Accounts Payable.....	--	3	--	--
Owner's Equity...........	162	356	101	193
Total Liabilities and Owner's Equity..................	162	359	101	193

Questions will likely arise as to the accounting entity. One view is that there are two accounting entities (Ivan and Igor) to whom the Red Bearded Baron has entrusted assets and required a periodic reporting on stewardship. The "owner" in owner's equity in this case is the Red Bearded Baron. Another view is that the Red Bearded Baron is the accounting entity, in which case financial statements that combine the financial statements for Ivan and Igor are appropriate. Identifying the accounting entity depends on the intended use of the financial statements. For purposes of evaluating the performance of Ivan and Igor, the accounting entities are separate—Ivan and Igor. To assess the change in wealth of the Red Bearded Baron during the period, the combined financial statements reflect the accounting entity.

1.43 continued.

c.

IVAN AND IGOR
Comparative Income Statement
(Amounts in Bushels of Wheat)

	IVAN	IGOR
Revenues	243	138
Expenses:		
Seed	20	10
Fertilizer	2	1
Depreciation on Ox	4	4
Plow	3	1
Total Expenses	29	16
Net Income	214	122

Chapter 1 does not expose students to the concept of depreciation. Most students, however, grasp the need to record some amount of expense for the ox and the plow.

d. (Amounts in Bushels of Wheat)

	IVAN	IGOR
Owner's Equity, Beginning of Period	162	101
Plus Net Income	214	122
Less Distributions to Owner	(20)	(30)
Owner's Equity, End of Period	356	193

e. We cannot simply compare the amounts of net income for Ivan and Igor because the Red Bearded Baron entrusted them with different amounts of resources. We must relate the net income amounts to some base. Several possibilities include:

	IVAN	IGOR
Net Income/Average Total Assets	82.2%	83.0%
Net Income/Beginning Total Assets	132.1%	120.8%
Net Income/Average Noncurrent Assets	155.1%	137.1%
Net Income/Beginning Noncurrent Assets	152.9%	135.6%
Net Income/Average Owner's Equity	82.6%	83.0%
Net Income/Beginning Owner's Equity	132.1%	120.8%
Net Income (in bushels)/Acre	10.70	12.20

This question has no definitive answer. Its purpose is to get students to think about performance measurement. The instructor may or may not wish to devote class time at this point discussing which base is more appropriate.

CHAPTER 2

THE BASICS OF RECORD KEEPING AND FINANCIAL STATEMENT PREPARATION

Questions, Exercises, and Problems: Answers and Solutions

2.1   See the text or the glossary at the end of the book.

2.3   A T-account is used to record the effects of events and transactions that affect a specific asset, liability, shareholders' equity, revenue or expense account. It captures both the increases and decreases in that specific account, without reference to the effects on other accounts. It also shows the beginning and ending balances of balance sheet accounts. A journal entry shows all the accounts affected by a single event or transaction; each debit and each credit in a journal entry will affect a specific T-account. Journal entries provide a record of transactions, and T-accounts summarize the effects of transactions on specific accounts.

2.5   The distinction is based on time. Current assets are expected to be converted to cash within a year, for example, Accounts Receivable. Noncurrent assets are expected to be converted to cash over longer periods.

2.7   The purpose of the income statement is to show the user of the financial statements the components of net income, that is, the causes of net income. A user of financial statements can calculate net income by analyzing the change in retained earnings, but this analysis does not reveal the specific factors that combine to produce the net income number.

2.9   Contra accounts provide disaggregated information concerning the net amount of an asset, liability, or shareholders' equity item. For example, the account, Property, Plant and Equipment net of Accumulated Depreciation, does not indicate separately the acquisition cost of fixed assets and the portion of that acquisition cost written off as depreciation since acquisition. If the firm used a contra account, it would have such information. The alternative to using contra accounts is to debit or credit directly the principal account involved (for example, Property, Plant and Equipment). This alternative procedure, however, does not permit computation of disaggregated information about the net balance in the account. Note that the use of contra accounts does not affect the total of assets, liabilities, shareholders' equity, revenues, or expenses, but only the balances in various accounts that comprise the totals for these items.

2.11   (Fresh Foods Group; dual effects on balance sheet equation.) (Amounts in Millions)

Transaction	Assets	=	Liabilities	+	Shareholders' Equity
(1)	+$ 678		+$ 678		
(2)	−$ 45		−$ 45		
(3)	−$ 633		−$ 633		

2.13   (Braskem S.A.; analyzing changes in accounts receivable.) (Amounts in Millions)

Accounts Receivable, Beginning of 2007	R$ 1,594.9
Plus Sales on Account during 2007	12,134.5
Less Cash Collections during 2007	(?)
Accounts Receivable, End of 2007	R$ 1,497.0

Cash collections during 2007 total R$12,232.4 million.

2.15   (Ericsson; analyzing changes in inventory and accounts payable.) (Amounts in Millions)

Inventory, Beginning of 2007	SEK 21,470
Plus Purchases of Inventory during 2007	?
Less Cost of Goods Sold for 2007	(114,059)
Inventory, End of 2007	SEK 22,475

Purchases during 2007 total SEK115,064 million.

Accounts Payable, Beginning of 2007	SEK 18,183
Plus Purchases of Inventory on Account during 2007 from above	115,064
Less Cash Payments to Suppliers during 2007	(?)
Accounts Payable, End of 2007	SEK 17,427

Cash payments to suppliers during 2007 total SEK115,820 million.

2.17   (Eaton Corporation; analyzing changes in retained earnings.) (Amounts in Millions)

Retained Earnings, Beginning of 2007	$ 2,796
Plus Net Income for 2007	?
Less Dividends Declared and Paid during 2007	(251)
Retained Earnings, End of 2007	$ 3,257

Net Income for 2007 totals $712 million.

2.19   (Beyond Petroleum; relations between financial statements.)   (Amounts in Millions)

a.   a + $288,951 − $289,623 = $38,020; a = $38,692.

b. $2,635 + $10,442 − b = $3,282; b = $9,795.

c. $42,236 + $15,162 + c = $43,152; c = $14,246.

d. $88,453 + $21,169 − $8,106 = d; d = $101,516.

2.21   (Monana Company; journal entries for insurance.)   (Amounts in Millions)

April 30, 2008
Insurance Expense.. 12
    Prepaid Insurance 12

Assets	=	Liabilities	+	Shareholders' Equity	(Class.)
−12				−12	IncSt → RE

Adjusting entry required for prepaid insurance consumed during April, 2008.

May 30, 2008
Insurance Expense.. 12
    Prepaid Insurance 12

Assets	=	Liabilities	+	Shareholders' Equity	(Class.)
−12				−12	IncSt → RE

Adjusting entry required for prepaid insurance consumed during May, 2008.

June 1, 2008
Prepaid Insurance.. 156
    Cash 156

Assets	=	Liabilities	+	Shareholders' Equity	(Class.)
+156					
−156					

To record payment of insurance for next 12 months.

2.21 continued.

June 30, 2008

Insurance Expense... 13
    Prepaid Insurance   13

Assets	=	Liabilities	+	Shareholders' Equity	(Class.)
−13				−13	IncSt → RE

Adjusting entry required for prepaid insurance consumed during June, 2008 ($13 = $156/12 months).

July 31, 2008

Insurance Expense... 13
    Prepaid Insurance   13

Assets	=	Liabilities	+	Shareholders' Equity	(Class.)
−13				−13	IncSt → RE

Adjusting entry required for prepaid insurance consumed during July, 2008.

2.23   (Sappi Limited; journal entries for borrowing.) (Amounts in Millions)

a.   Sappi repaid liabilities in fiscal 2007, in the amount of $1,634 + $1,200 − $1,828 = $1,006 million. To record the repayment, Sappi made the following journal entry:

Date of Repayment, Fiscal 2007

Noncurrent Financial Liabilities................................. 1,006
    Cash..   1,006

Assets	=	Liabilities	+	Shareholders' Equity	(Class.)
−1,006		−1,006			

2.23 continued.

b. **Journal Entries:**

Fiscal Year 2007:
March 31, 2007

Cash 1,200

   Bank Loan Payable.. 1,200

Assets	=Liabilities	+	Shareholders' Equity	(Class.)
+1,200	+1,200			

To record the loan from the local bank.

September 30, 2007

Interest Expense [= $1,200 Million x .075 x
   (180/360)].. 45

   Interest Payable.. 45

Assets	=Liabilities	+	Shareholders' Equity	(Class.)
	+45		−45	IncSt → RE

Adjusting entry to record interest expense earned but not yet paid at the end of fiscal year 2007.

Fiscal Year 2008:
March 31, 2008

Interest Payable.. 45

Interest Expense 45

   Cash.. 90

Assets	=Liabilities	+	Shareholders' Equity	(Class.)
−90	−45		−45	IncSt → RE

To record payment of interest for the first year.

2.23 b. continued.

September 30, 2008
Interest Expense [= $1,200 Million x .075 x
   (180/360)]... 45
     Interest Payable... 45

Assets	=	Liabilities	+	Shareholders' Equity	(Class.)
		+45		−45	IncSt → RE

Adjusting entry to record interest expense earned but
not yet paid at the end of fiscal year 2008.

Fiscal Year 2009:
March 31, 2009
Interest Payable.. 45
Interest Expense 45
   Cash.. 90

Assets	=	Liabilities	+	Shareholders' Equity	(Class.)
−90		−45		−45	IncSt → RE

To record payment of interest for the second year.

March 31, 2009
Bank Loan Payable..................................... 1,200
   Cash.. 1,200

Assets	=	Liabilities	+	Shareholders' Equity	(Class.)
−1,200		−1,200			

To record repayment of the principal.

No further entries required as borrower has repaid note in full.

2.25   (Teva Pharmaceutical; journal entries related to the income statement.)
    (Amounts in Millions)

2007
Accounts Receivable................................... 9,408
   Revenues.. 9,408

Assets	=	Liabilities	+	Shareholders' Equity	(Class.)
+9,408				+9,408	IncSt → RE

To record product sales on account.

2.25 continued.

Cost of Goods Sold... 6,531
   Inventories...   6,531

Assets	=	Liabilities	+	Shareholders' Equity	(Class.)
−6,531				−6,531	IncSt → RE

To record the cost of sales.

Cash... 2,659
   Accounts Receivable..   2,659

Assets	=	Liabilities	+	Shareholders' Equity	(Class.)
−2,659					
+2,659					

To record the cash collected on sales made on account.

2.27   (Bullseye Corporation; dual effects of transactions on balance sheet equation and journal entries.) (Amounts in Millions)

a.

Transaction Number		Assets	=	Liabilities	+	Shareholders' Equity
(1)		+ $ 960			+	$ 960
	Subtotal	$ 960	=			$ 960
(2)		+ 1,500		+ $ 1,500		
	Subtotal	$ 2,460	=	$ 1,500	+	$ 960
(3)		+ 3,200				
		+ 930				
		− 4,130				
	Subtotal	$ 2,460	=	$ 1,500	+	$ 960
(4)		+ 860	=	+ 860		
	Subtotal	$ 3,320	=	$ 2,360	+	$ 960
(5)		− 1,500		− 1,500		
	Subtotal	$ 1,820	=	$ 860	+	$ 960
(6)		− 430		− 860	+	430
	Total	$ 1,390	=	-0-	+	$ 1,390

2.27 continued.

b. (1) Cash.. 960.0
       Common Stock.. 1.7
       Additional Paid-in Capital 958.3

Assets	=	Liabilities	+	Shareholders' Equity	(Class.)
+960.0				+1.7	ContriCap
				+958.3	ContriCap

Issue 20 million shares of $0.0833 par value common stock for $960 million.

(2) Merchandise Inventory... 1,500
    Accounts Payable.. 1,500

Assets	=	Liabilities	+	Shareholders' Equity	(Class.)
+1,500		+1,500			

Purchase $1,500 million of inventory on account.

(3) Building... 3,200
    Land.. 930
    Cash 4,130

Assets	=	Liabilities	+	Shareholders' Equity	(Class.)
+3,200					
+930					
−4,130					

Acquires building costing $3,200 million and land costing $930 million, and pays in cash.

(4) Building Fixtures 860
    Accounts Payable.. 860

Assets	=	Liabilities	+	Shareholders' Equity	(Class.)
+860		+860			

Acquires building fixtures costing $860 million on account.

2.27 b. continued.

(5) Accounts Payable.. 1,500
     Cash   1,500

Assets	=	Liabilities	+	Shareholders' Equity	(Class.)
−1,500		−1,500			

Pays suppliers in Transaction (2).

(6) Accounts Payable.. 860.0
     Cash 430.0
     Common Stock..   0.7
     Additional Paid-in Capital 429.3

Assets	=	Liabilities	+	Shareholders' Equity	(Class.)
−430.0		−860.0		+0.7	ContriCap
				+429.3	ContriCap

Pays suppliers of fixtures cash of $430 million in shares of common stock. Bullseye Corporation shares are trading at $50 per share, so it gave the supplier 8.6 million shares of common stock (= $430 million/$50 per share).

2.29   (Callen Incorporated; preparing a balance sheet and an income statement.) (Amounts in Thousands of Euros)

a.   **CALLEN, INCORPORATED**
Balance Sheet

	Jan. 31, 2008	Jan. 31, 2007
Assets		
Cash..	€ 30,536	€ 2,559
Merchandise Inventory	114,249	151,894
Other Current Assets....................................	109,992	134,916
Total Current Assets	€ 254,777	€ 289,369
Property, Plant and Equipment (Net).........	98,130	149,990
Other Noncurrent Assets	56,459	88,955
Total Assets..	€ 409,366	€ 528,314

2.29 a. continued.

Liabilities and Shareholders' Equity

Accounts Payable	€ 16,402	€ 14,063
Notes Payable to Banks	15,241	43,598
Other Current Liabilities	84,334	109,335
Total Current Liabilities	€ 115,977	€ 166,996
Long-Term Debt	31,566	38,315
Other Noncurrent Liabilities	19,859	27,947
Total Liabilities	€ 167,402	€ 233,258
Common Stock	€ 72,325	€ 72,325
Retained Earnings	169,639	222,731
Total Shareholders' Equity	€ 241,964	€ 295,056
Total Liabilities and Shareholders' Equity	€ 409,366	€ 528,314

b.

CALLEN, INCORPORATED
Income Statement

For the Year Ended:	Dec. 31, 2008
Sales	€ 695,623
Cost of Goods Sold	(382,349)
Selling Expenses	(72,453)
Administrative Expenses	(141,183)
Interest Expense	(2,744)
Income Taxes	(24,324)
Net Income	€ 72,570

c. Retained Earnings, December 31, 2007	€ 222,731
Plus Net Income for 2008	72,570
Less Dividends Declared during 2008 (Plug)	(125,662)
Retained Earnings, December 31, 2008	€ 169,639

2.31   (LBJ Group; miscellaneous transactions and adjusting entries.) (Amounts in Millions)

a.   (1)   Inventories 180,000

          Notes Payable 180,000

Assets	=	Liabilities	+	Shareholders' Equity	(Class.)
+180,000		+180,000			

2.31 a. continued.

    (2)   Interest Expense [= $180,000 x .08 x
            (60/360)]...   2,400
              Interest Payable..   2,400

Assets	=	Liabilities	+	Shareholders' Equity	(Class.)
		+2,400		−2,400	IncSt → RE

b. (1) Cash 842,000
           Advances from Customers   842,000

Assets	=	Liabilities	+	Shareholders' Equity	(Class.)
+842,000		+842,000			

c. (1) Equipment...1,400,000
           Cash...   1,400,000

Assets	=	Liabilities	+	Shareholders' Equity	(Class.)
+1,400,000					
−1,400,000					

    (2)   Depreciation Expense [= 3/12 x ($1,400,000
           − $160,000)/10] 31,000
              Accumulated Depreciation   31,000

Assets	=	Liabilities	+	Shareholders' Equity	(Class.)
−31,000				−31,000	IncSt → RE

d. (1) Accounts Receivable....................................... 565,000
           Revenues   565,000

Assets	=	Liabilities	+	Shareholders' Equity	(Class.)
+565,000				+565,000	IncSt → RE

    (2)   Cost of Goods Sold 422,000
             Merchandise Inventory.....................................   422,000

Assets	=	Liabilities	+	Shareholders' Equity	(Class.)
−422,000				−422,000	IncSt → RE

2.31 continued.

e. (1) Prepaid Insurance 360,000
        Cash 360,000

Assets	=	Liabilities	+	Shareholders' Equity	(Class.)
+360,000					
−360,000					

(2) Insurance Expense [= (4/12) x $360,000] 120,000
        Prepaid Insurance 120,000

Assets	=	Liabilities	+	Shareholders' Equity	(Class.)
−120,000				−120,000	IncSt → RE

f. (1) Cash 1,040,000
        Common Stock Par Value 40,000
        Additional Paid-in Capital 1,000,000

Assets	=	Liabilities	+	Shareholders' Equity	(Class.)
+1,040,000				+40,000	ContriCap
				+1,000,000	ContriCap

(2) Accounts Payable 1,040,000
        Cash 1,040,000

Assets	=	Liabilities	+	Shareholders' Equity	(Class.)
−1,040,000		−1,040,000			

2.33 (Hansen Retail Store; preparing income statement and balance sheet using accrual basis.)

a.
HANSEN RETAIL STORE
Income Statement
For the Year Ended December 31, 2008

Sales ($52,900 + $116,100)	$ 169,000
Cost of Goods Sold ($125,000 − $15,400)	(109,600)
Salary Expense ($34,200 + $2,400)	(36,600)
Utility Expense ($2,600 + $180)	(2,780)
Depreciation Expense ($60,000/30)	(2,000)
Interest Expense (.10 x $40,000)	(4,000)
Net Income before Income Taxes	$ 14,020
Income Taxes at 40%	(5,608)
Net Income	$ 8,412

b.
HANSEN RETAIL STORE
Balance Sheet
December 31, 2008

Assets

Cash ($50,000 + $40,000 − $60,000 − $97,400 + $52,900 + $54,800 − $34,200 − $2,600)	$ 3,500
Accounts Receivable ($116,100 − $54,800)	61,300
Inventories	15,400
Total Current Assets	$ 80,200
Building ($60,000 − $2,000)	58,000
Total Assets	$138,200

Liabilities and Shareholders' Equity

Accounts Payable ($125,000 − $97,400)	$ 27,600
Salaries Payable	2,400
Utilities Payable	180
Income Taxes Payable	5,608
Interest Payable	4,000
Loan Payable	40,000
Total Current Liabilities	$ 79,788
Common Stock	$ 50,000
Retained Earnings	8,412
Total Shareholders' Equity	$ 58,412
Total Liabilities and Shareholders' Equity	$138,200

2.35 (Regaldo Department Stores; analysis of transactions and preparation of income statement and balance sheet.)

a. T-accounts.

Cash (A)			
√	247,200		
(3a)	62,900	32,400	(4)
(6)	84,600	2,700	(5)
		205,800	(7a)
		29,000	(7b)
√	124,800		

Accounts Receivable (A)			
√	0		
(3a)	194,600	84,600	(6)
√	110,000		

Inventory (A)			
√	188,800		
(2)	217,900	162,400	(3b)
		4,200	(7a)
√	240,100		

Prepaid Rent (A)			
√	60,000		
		30,000	(11)
√	30,000		

Prepaid Insurance (A)			
√	12,000	1,000	(12)
√	11,000		

Equipment (A)			
√	0		
(1)	90,000		
√	90,000		

Accumulated Depreciation (XA)			
		0	√
		1,500	(10)
		1,500	√

Patent (A)			
√	24,000		
		400	(13)
√	23,600		

Accounts Payable (L)			
		32,000	√
(7a)	210,000	217,900	(2)
(7b)	29,000		
		10,900	√

Note Payable (L)			
		0	√
		90,000	(1)
		90,000	√

Compensation Payable (L)			
		0	√
		6,700	(8)
		6,700	√

Utilities Payable (L)			
		0	√
		800	(9)
		800	√

2.35 a. continued.

Interest Payable (L)			
	0	√	
	900	(14)	
	900	√	

Income Tax Payable (L)			
	0	√	
	5,610	(15)	
	5,610	√	

Common Stock (SE)			
	500,000	√	
	500,000	√	

Retained Earnings (SE)			
	0	√	
	13,090	(16)	
	13,090	√	

Sales Revenue (SE)			
(16)	257,500	257,500	(3a)

Cost of Goods Sold (SE)			
(3b)	162,400	162,400	(16)

Compensation Expense (SE)			
(4)	32,400		
(8)	6,700	39,100	(16)

Utilities Expense (SE)			
(5)	2,700		
(9)	800	3,500	(16)

Depreciation Expense (SE)			
(10)	1,500	1,500	(16)

Rent Expense (SE)			
(11)	30,000	30,000	(16)

Insurance Expense (SE)			
(12)	1,000	1,000	(16)

Patent Amortization Expense (SE)			
(13)	400	400	(16)

Interest Expense (SE)			
(14)	900	900	(16)

Income Tax Expense (SE)			
(15)	5,610	5,610	(16)

2.35 continued.

b.

REGALDO DEPARTMENT STORES
Income Statement
For the Month of February 2008

Sales Revenue	$ 257,500
Expenses:	
Cost of Goods Sold	$ 162,400
Compensation ($32,400 + $6,700)	39,100
Utilities ($2,700 + $800)	3,500
Depreciation	1,500
Rent	30,000
Insurance	1,000
Patent Amortization	400
Interest	900
Total Expenses	$ 238,800
Net Income before Income Taxes	$ 18,700
Income Tax Expense at 30%	(5,610)
Net Income	$ 13,090

c.

REGALDO DEPARTMENT STORES
Comparative Balance Sheet

	January 31, 2008	February 28, 2008
Assets		
Cash	$ 247,200	$ 124,800
Accounts Receivable	0	110,000
Inventories	188,800	240,100
Prepaid Rent	60,000	30,000
Prepaid Insurance	12,000	11,000
Total Current Assets	$ 508,000	$ 515,900
Equipment (at Cost)	$ 0	$ 90,000
Less Accumulated Depreciation	0	(1,500)
Equipment (Net)	$ 0	$ 88,500
Patent	24,000	23,600
Total Noncurrent Assets	$ 24,000	$ 112,100
Total Assets	$ 532,000	$ 628,000

2.35 c. continued.

Liabilities and Shareholders' Equity

Accounts Payable	$ 32,000	$ 10,900
Notes Payable	0	90,000
Compensation Payable	0	6,700
Utilities Payable	0	800
Interest Payable	0	900
Income Tax Payable	0	5,610
Total Liabilities	$ 32,000	$ 114,910
Common Stock	$ 500,000	$ 500,000
Retained Earnings	0	13,090
Total Shareholders' Equity	$ 500,000	$ 513,090
Total Liabilities and Shareholders' Equity	$ 532,000	$ 628,000

2.37 (Zealock Bookstore; analysis of transactions and preparation of comparative income statements and balance sheet.)

a. T-accounts.

	Cash (A)				Accounts Receivable (A)		
√	24,350			√	5,800		
(3)	75,000	1,320	(1)	(7)	327,950	320,600	(9)
(4)	8,000	31,800	(2)				
(7)	24,900	20,000	(5)				
(9)	320,600	29,400	(10)				
		281,100	(11)				
		4,000	(12)				
√	85,230			√	13,150		

	Merchandise Inventory (A)				Prepaid Rent (A)		
√	5,400			√	10,000		
(6)	310,000	286,400	(7)	(5)	20,000	20,000	(13)
		22,700	(8)				
√	6,300			√	10,000		

	Deposit with Suppliers (A)				Equipment (A)	
√	8,000			√	14,000	
		8,000	(4)			
√	0			√	14,000	

2.37 a. continued.

Accumulated Depreciation (XA)		
	1,900	√
	800	(14)
	3,000	(15)
	5,700	√

Note Payable (L)				
			30,000	√
(2)	30,000		75,000	(3)
			75,000	√

Accounts Payable (L)				
			5,600	√
(8)	22,700		310,000	(6)
(11)	281,100			
			11,800	√

Advance from Customers (L)				
			850	√
(7)	850			
			0	√

Interest Payable (L)				
			900	√
(2)	900		3,000	(16)
			3,000	√

Income Tax Payable (L)				
			1,320	√
(1)	1,320		4,080	(17)
			4,080	√

Common Stock (SE)		
	25,000	√
	25,000	√

Retained Earnings (SE)				
			1,980	√
(12)	4,000		6,120	(18)
			4,100	√

Sales Revenue (SE)				
(18)	353,700		353,700	(7)

Cost of Goods Sold (SE)				
(7)	286,400		286,400	(18)

Compensation Expense (SE)				
(10)	29,400		29,400	(18)

Interest Expense (SE)				
(2)	900			
(16)	3,000		3,900	(18)

Rent Expense (SE)				
(13)	20,000		20,000	(18)

Depreciation Expense (SE)				
(14)	800			
(15)	3,000		3,800	(18)

2.37 a. continued.

Income Tax Expense (SE)

(17)	4,080	4,080	(18)

b.
ZEALOCK BOOKSTORE
Comparative Income Statement
For 2008 and 2009

	2008	2009
Sales Revenue	$353,700	$172,800
Less Expenses:		
Cost of Goods Sold	$286,400	$140,000
Compensation Expense	29,400	16,700
Interest Expense	3,900	900
Rent Expense	20,000	10,000
Depreciation Expense	3,800	1,900
Income Tax Expense	4,080	1,320
Total Expenses	$347,580	$170,820
Net Income	$ 6,120	$ 1,980

c.
ZEALOCK BOOKSTORE
Comparative Balance Sheet
December 31, 2008 and 2009

	2009	2008
Assets		
Current Assets:		
Cash	$ 85,230	$ 24,350
Accounts Receivable	13,150	5,800
Merchandise Inventories	6,300	5,400
Prepaid Rent	10,000	10,000
Deposit with Suppliers	--	8,000
Total Current Assets	$114,680	$ 53,550
Noncurrent Assets:		
Equipment	$ 14,000	$ 14,000
Less Accumulated Depreciation	(5,700)	(1,900)
Equipment (Net)	$ 8,300	$ 12,100
Total Assets	$122,980	$ 65,650

2.37 c. continued.

Liabilities and Shareholders' Equity

Current Liabilities:		
Accounts Payable...	$ 11,800	$ 5,600
Note Payable	75,000	30,000
Advances from Customers	--	850
Interest Payable..	3,000	900
Income Tax Payable....................................	4,080	1,320
Total Current Liabilities.........................	$ 93,880	$ 38,670
Shareholders' Equity:		
Common Stock..	$ 25,000	$ 25,000
Retained Earnings	4,100	1,980
Total Shareholders' Equity	$ 29,100	$ 26,980
Total Liabilities and Shareholders' Equity...	$122,980	$ 65,650

2.39 (Computer Needs, Inc.; reconstructing the income statement and balance sheet.)

T-accounts.

	Cash					Accounts Receivable		
√	15,600				√	32,100		
(A)	37,500	164,600	(D)		(C)	159,700	151,500	(B)
(B)	151,500	21,000	(G)					
		3,388	(H)					
		4,800	(I)					
		6,000	(J)					
√	4,812				√	40,300		

	Inventory					Prepayments	
√	46,700				√	1,500	
(E)	172,100	158,100	(F)		(G)	300	
√	60,700				√	1,800	

	Property, Plant and Equipment			Accumulated Depreciation		
√	59,700				2,800	√
(J)	6,000				3,300	(K)
√	65,700				6,100	√

	Accounts Payable—Merchandise				Income Tax Payable		
		37,800	√			3,388	√
(D)	164,600	172,100	(E)	(H)	3,388	3,584	(L)
		45,300	√			3,584	√

Other Current Liabilities				Mortgage Payable		
	2,900	√			50,000	√
(G)	1,700		(I)	800		
	1,200	√			49,200	√

Common Stock				Retained Earnings		
	50,000	√			8,712	√
					9,216	(M)
	50,000	√			17,928	√

Sales				Cost of Goods Sold		
	37,500	(A)	(F)	158,100	158,100	(M)
(M) 197,200	159,700	(C)				

Selling and Administrative Expense				Depreciation Expense		
(G)	19,000	19,000	(M)	(K)	3,300	3,300	(M)

Interest Expense				Income Tax Expense		
(I)	4,000	4,000	(M)	(L)	3,584	3,584	(M)

COMPUTER NEEDS, INC.
Income Statement
For the Years Ended December 31, 2007 and 2008

	2008	2007
Sales	$197,200	$152,700
Cost of Goods Sold	(158,100)	(116,400)
Selling and Administrative Expense	(19,000)	(17,400)
Depreciation Expense	(3,300)	(2,800)
Interest Expense	(4,000)	(4,000)
Income Taxes	(3,584)	(3,388)
Net Income	$ 9,216	$ 8,712

2.39 continued.

COMPUTER NEEDS, INC.
Balance Sheet
For the Years Ended December 31, 2007 and 2008

	2008	2007
Assets		
Cash..	$ 4,812	$ 15,600
Accounts Receivable...	40,300	32,100
Inventories...	60,700	46,700
Prepayments..	1,800	1,500
Total Current Assets.......................................	$ 107,612	$ 95,900
Property, Plant and Equipment:		
At Cost...	$ 65,700	$ 59,700
Less Accumulated Depreciation.......................	(6,100)	(2,800)
Net..	$ 59,600	$ 56,900
Total Assets...	$ 167,212	$ 152,800
Liabilities and Shareholders' Equity		
Accounts Payable—Merchandise...........................	$ 45,300	$ 37,800
Income Tax Payable..	3,584	3,388
Other Current Liabilities.......................................	1,200	2,900
Total Current Liabilities................................	$ 50,084	$ 44,088
Mortgage Payable..	49,200	50,000
Total Liabilities..	$ 99,284	$ 94,088
Common Stock...	$ 50,000	$ 50,000
Retained Earnings..	17,928	8,712
Total Shareholders' Equity............................	$ 67,928	$ 58,712
Total Liabilities and Shareholders' Equity...	$ 167,212	$ 152,800

2.41 (Forgetful Corporation; effect of recording errors on financial statements.)

Note: The actual and correct entries appear below to show the effect and amount of the errors, but are not required.

a. **Actual Entry:**

Cash 1,400

    Sales Revenue.. 1,400

Assets	=	Liabilities	+	Shareholders' Equity	(Class.)
+1,400				+1,400	IncSt → RE

2.41 a. continued.

Correct Entry:

Cash 1,400

    Advance from Customer 1,400

Assets	=	Liabilities	+	Shareholders' Equity	(Class.)
+1,400		+1,400			

Liabilities understated by $1,400 and shareholders' equity overstated by $1,400.

b. **Actual Entry:**

Cost of Goods Sold 5,000

    Cash 5,000

Assets	=	Liabilities	+	Shareholders' Equity	(Class.)
−5,000				−5,000	IncSt → RE

Correct Entries:

Machine 5,000

    Cash 5,000

Assets	=	Liabilities	+	Shareholders' Equity	(Class.)
+5,000					
−5,000					

Depreciation Expense 500

    Accumulated Depreciation 500

Assets	=	Liabilities	+	Shareholders' Equity	(Class.)
−500				−500	IncSt → RE

Assets understated by $4,500 and shareholders' equity understated by $4,500.

2.41 continued.

c. **Actual Entry:**
None for accrued interest.

Correct Entry:

Interest Receivable ($2,000 x .12 x 60/360).............   40

    Interest Revenue   40

Assets	=Liabilities +	Shareholders' Equity	(Class.)
+40		+40	IncSt → RE

Assets understated by $40 and shareholders' equity understated by $40.

d. The entry is correct as recorded.

e. **Actual Entry:**
None for declared dividend.

Correct Entry:

Retained Earnings...   1,500

    Dividend Payable..   1,500

Assets	=Liabilities +	Shareholders' Equity	(Class.)
	+1,500	−1,500	Dividend

Liabilities understated by $1,500 and shareholders' equity overstated by $1,500.

f. **Actual Entries:**

Machinery   50,000

    Accounts Payable..   50,000

Assets	=Liabilities +	Shareholders' Equity	(Class.)
+50,000	+50,000		

Accounts Payable..   50,000

    Cash..   49,000

    Miscellaneous Revenue..   1,000

Assets	=Liabilities +	Shareholders' Equity	(Class.)
−49,000	−50,000	+1,000	IncSt → RE

2.41 f. continued.

Maintenance Expense 4,000
   Cash..   4,000

Assets	=	Liabilities	+	Shareholders' Equity	(Class.)
−4,000				−4,000	IncSt → RE

Correct Entries:

Machinery 50,000
   Accounts Payable..   50,000

Assets	=	Liabilities	+	Shareholders' Equity	(Class.)
+50,000		+50,000			

Accounts Payable... 50,000
   Cash..   49,000
   Machinery...   1,000

Assets	=	Liabilities	+	Shareholders' Equity	(Class.)
−49,000		−50,000			
−1,000					

Machinery 4,000
   Cash..   4,000

Assets	=	Liabilities	+	Shareholders' Equity	(Class.)
+4,000					
−4,000					

Assets understated by $3,000 and shareholders' equity understated by $3,000.

2.43   (The Secunda Company; working backwards to cash receipts and disbursements.)

A T-account method for deriving the solution appears on the following two pages. After Entry (6), we have explained all revenue and expense account changes. Plugging for the unknown amounts determines the remaining, unexplained changes in balance sheet accounts. A "p" next to the entry number designates these entries. Note that the revenue and expense accounts are not yet closed to retained earnings, so dividends account for the decrease in the Retained Earnings account during the year of $10,000.

2.43 continued.

Cash

Bal.	20,000		
(7)	85,000		
		2,000	(9)
		81,000	(10)
		3,000	(11)
		10,000	(12)
Bal.	9,000		

Accounts Receivable

Bal.	36,000		
(1)	100,000	85,000	(7p)
Bal.	51,000		

Merchandise Inventory

Bal.	45,000		
(8p)	65,000	50,000	(2)
Bal.	60,000		

Prepayments

Bal.	2,000		
		1,000	(5)
Bal.	1,000		

Land, Buildings, and Equipment

Bal.	40,000		
Bal.	40,000		

Cost of Goods Sold

Bal.	0		
(2)	50,000		
Bal.	50,000		

Interest Expense

Bal.	0		
(3)	3,000		
Bal.	3,000		

Other Operating Expenses

Bal.	0		
(4)	2,000		
(5)	1,000		
(6p)	26,000		
Bal.	29,000		

Accumulated Depreciation

		16,000	Bal.
		2,000	(4)
		18,000	Bal.

Interest Payable

		1,000	Bal.
(9p)	2,000	3,000	(3)
		2,000	Bal.

Accounts Payable

		30,000	Bal.
(10p)	81,000	26,000	(6)
		65,000	(8)
		40,000	Bal.

Mortgage Payable

		20,000	Bal.
(11p)	3,000		
		17,000	Bal.

2.43 continued.

Common Stock				Retained Earnings			
	50,000	Bal.				26,000	Bal.
			(12p)	10,000			
	50,000	Bal.				16,000	Bal.

Sales		
	0	Bal.
	100,000	(1)
	100,000	Bal.

SECUNDA COMPANY
Cash Receipts and Disbursements Schedule

Receipts:		
Collections from Customers.............................		$85,000
Disbursements:		
Suppliers of Merchandise and Other Services..	$81,000	
Mortgage..	3,000	
Dividends	10,000	
Interest..	2,000	
Total Disbursements...............................		96,000
Decrease in Cash		$11,000
Cash Balance, December 31, 2007......................		20,000
Cash Balance, December 31, 2008......................		$ 9,000

2.43 continued.

Transactions spreadsheet.

Transactions, By Number and Description

Balance Sheet Accounts	Balance: Beginning of Period	1 Recog. Sales on Acct.	2 Cash Collect. From Cus.	3 Recog. COGS	4 Pur. Of Mer. On Acct.	5 Cash Pay. For Merchn.	6 Recog. Int. Exp.	7 Int. Paid	8 Recog. Depre. Exp.	8 Recog. Of Oper. Exp.	9 Cash Paid for Prepay.	10 Recog. Mort. Paid	11 Recog. Div. Dec. & Paid	12 Check on Ending Bal. Sheet Amts.	Balance: End of 2008
ASSETS															
Current Assets:															
Cash	20,000		85,000			-55,000		-2,000			-26,000	-3,000	-10,000	9,000	9,000
Accounts Receivable	36,000	100,000	-85,000											51,000	51,000
Merchandise Inventory	45,000			-50,000	65,000									60,000	60,000
Prepayments	2,000									-27,000	26,000			1,000	1,000
Total Current Assets	103,000													121,000	121,000
Noncurrent Assets:															
Land, Buildings, & Equip.	40,000													40,000	40,000
Accumulated Depreciation	-16,000								-2,000					(18,000)	(18,000)
Total Noncurrent Assets	24,000													22,000	22,000
Total Assets	127,000													143,000	143,000
LIABILITIES AND SHAREHOLDERS' EQUITY															
Current Liabilities:															
Interest Payable	1,000						3,000	-2,000						2,000	2,000
Accounts Payable	30,000				65,000	-55,000								40,000	40,000
Total Current Liabilities	31,000													42,000	42,000
Noncurrent Liabilities:															
Mortgage Payable	20,000											-3,000		17,000	17,000
Total Noncurrent Liabilities	20,000													17,000	17,000
Total Liabilities	51,000													59,000	59,000
Shareholders' Equity:															
Common Stock	50,000													50,000	50,000
Retained Earnings	26,000	100,000		-50,000			-3,000		-2,000	-27,000			-10,000	34,000	34,000
Total Shareholders' Equity	76,000													84,000	84,000
Total Liabilities and Shareholders' Equity	127,000													143,000	143,000
Imbalance, if Any	-	-	-	-	-	-	-	-	-	-	-	-	-	-	-
Income Statement Accounts		Sales Rev.	-	COGS	-	-	Int. Exp.	-	Ot. Oper. Exp.	Ot. Oper. Exp.	-	-	-	-	

2.45 (Preparing adjusting entries.)

a. The Prepaid Rent account on the year-end balance sheet should represent eight months of prepayments. The rent per month is $2,000 (= $24,000/12), so the balance required in the Prepaid Rent account is $16,000 (= 8 x $2,000). Rent Expense for 2006 is $8,000 (= 4 x $2,000 = $24,000 – $16,000).

Prepaid Rent.. 16,000
    Rent Expense.. 16,000

Assets	=	Liabilities	+	Shareholders' Equity	(Class.)
+16,000				+16,000	IncSt → RE

To increase the balance in the Prepaid Rent account, reducing the amount in the Rent Expense account.

b. The Prepaid Rent account on the balance sheet for the end of 2007 should represent eight months of prepayments. The rent per month is $2,500 (= $30,000/12), so the required balance in the Prepaid Rent account is $20,000 (= 8 x $2,500). The balance in that account is already $16,000, so the adjusting entry must increase it by $4,000 (= $20,000 – $16,000).

Prepaid Rent.. 4,000
    Rent Expense.. 4,000

Assets	=	Liabilities	+	Shareholders' Equity	(Class.)
+4,000				+4,000	IncSt → RE

To increase the balance in the Prepaid Rent account, reducing the amount in the Rent Expense account.

The Rent Expense account will have a balance at the end of 2007 before closing entries of $26,000 (= $30,000 – $4,000). This amount comprises $16,000 (= $2,000 x 8) for rent from January through August and $10,000 (= $2,500 x 4) for rent from September through December.

c. The Prepaid Rent account on the balance sheet at the end of 2008 should represent two months of prepayments. The rent per month is $3,000 (= $18,000/6), so the required balance in the Prepaid Rent account is $6,000 (= 2 X $3,000). The balance in that account is $20,000, so the adjusting entry must reduce it by $14,000 (= $20,000 – $6,000).

2.45 c. continued.

Rent Expense	14,000	
Prepaid Rent		14,000

Assets	=Liabilities	+	Shareholders' Equity	(Class.)
−14,000			−14,000	IncSt → RE

To decrease the balance in the Prepaid Rent account, increasing the amount in the Rent Expense account.

The Rent Expense account will have a balance at the end of 2008 before closing entries of $32,000 (= $18,000 + $14,000). This amount comprises $20,000 (= $2,500 X 8) for rent from January through August and $12,000 (= $3,000 X 4) for rent from September through December.

d. The Wages Payable account should have a credit balance of $4,000 at the end of April, but it has a balance of $5,000 carried over from the end of March. The adjusting entry must reduce the balance by $1,000, which requires a debit to the Wages Payable account.

Wages Payable	1,000	
Wage Expense		1,000

Assets	=Liabilities	+	Shareholders' Equity	(Class.)
	−1,000		+1,000	IncSt → RE

To reduce the balance in the Wages Payable account, reducing the amount in the Wage Expense account.

Wage Expense is $29,000 (= $30,000 − $1,000).

e. The Prepaid Insurance account balance of $3,000 represents four months of coverage. Thus, the cost of insurance is $750 (= $3,000/4) per month. The adjusting entry for a single month is as follows:

Insurance Expense	750	
Prepaid Insurance		750

Assets	=Liabilities	+	Shareholders' Equity	(Class.)
−750			−750	IncSt → RE

To recognize cost of one month's insurance cost as expense of the month.

2.45 continued.

f. The Advances from Tenants account has a balance of $25,000 carried over from the start of the year. At the end of 2007, it should have a balance of $30,000. Thus, the adjusting entry must increase the balance by $5,000, which requires a credit to the liability account.

Rent Revenue.. 5,000
    Advance from Tenants..   5,000

Assets	=	Liabilities	+	Shareholders' Equity	(Class.)
		+5,000		–5,000	IncSt → RE

To increase the balance in the Advances from Tenants account, reducing the amount in the Rent Revenue account.

Rent Revenue for 2007 is $245,000 (= $250,000 – $5,000).

g. The Depreciation Expense for the year should be $2,000 (= $10,000/5). The balance in the Accumulated Depreciation account should also be $2,000; thus, the firm must credit Retained Earnings (Depreciation Expense) by $8,000 (= $10,000 – $2,000). The adjusting entry not only reduces recorded depreciation for the period but also sets up the asset account and its accumulated depreciation contra account.

Equipment.. 10,000
    Accumulated Depreciation.......................................   2,000
    Depreciation Expense   8,000

Assets	=	Liabilities	+	Shareholders' Equity	(Class.)
+10,000				+8,000	IncSt → RE
–2,000					

To reduce the recorded amount in Depreciation Expense from $10,000 to $2,000, setting up the asset and its contra account.

This page is intentionally left blank

CHAPTER 3

BALANCE SHEET: PRESENTING AND ANALYZING RESOURCES AND FINANCING

Questions, Exercises, and Problems: Answers and Solutions

3.1 See the text or the glossary at the end of the book.

3.3 One justification relates to the requirement that an asset or liability be measured with sufficient reliability. When there is an exchange between a firm and some other entity, there is market evidence of the economic effects of the transaction. The independent auditor verifies these economic effects by referring to contracts, cancelled checks and other documents underlying the transaction. If accounting recognized events without such a market exchange (for example, the increase in market value of a firm's assets), increased subjectivity would enter into the preparation of the financial statements.

3.5 The justification relates to the uncertainty as to the ultimate economic effects of the contracts. One party or the other may pull out of the contract. The accountant may not know the benefits and costs of the contract at the time of signing. Until one party or the other begins to perform under the contract, accounting usually gives no recognition. Accountants often disclose significant contracts of this nature in the notes to the financial statements.

3.7 a. The contract between the investors and the construction company as well as cancelled checks provide evidence as to the acquisition cost.

b. Adjusted acquisition cost differs from the amount in Part *a.* by the portion of acquisition cost applicable to the services of the asset consumed during the first five years. There are several generally accepted methods of computing this amount (discussed in Chapter 9). A review of the accounting records for the office building should indicate how the firm calculated this amount.

3.7 continued.

c. There are at least two possibilities for ascertaining current replacement cost. One alternative is to consult a construction company to determine the cost of constructing a similar office building (that is, with respect to location, materials, size). The accountant would then adjust the current cost of constructing a new building downward to reflect the used condition of the five-year old office building. The current replacement cost amount could be reduced by 12.5% (= 5/40) if the asset's service potential decreases evenly with age. The actual economic decline in the value of the building during the first five years is likely to differ from 12.5% and, therefore, some other rate is probably appropriate. A second alternative for ascertaining current replacement cost is to consult a real estate dealer to determine the cost of acquiring a used office building providing services similar to the building that the investors own. The accountant might encounter difficulties in locating such a similar building.

d. The accountant might consult a local real estate dealer to ascertain the current market price, net of transactions cost, at which the investors might sell the building. There is always the question as to whether an interested buyer could be found at the quoted price. The accountant might also use any recent offers to purchase the building received by the investors.

e. The accountant might use the amount described in Part *d.* but exclude transactions cost when measuring fair value. The accountant might also measure fair value using the present value of the future net cash flows based on estimated rental receipts and operating expenses (excluding depreciation) for the building's remaining 35-year life. These cash flows are then discounted to the present using an appropriate rate of interest. The inputs to the fair value measurement are those that a market participant would use.

3.9   a. Yes; amount of accrued interest payable.

b. Yes. Because of the indefiniteness of the time of delivery of the goods or services and the amount, the balance sheet reports a liability in the amount of the cash received.

c. No; accounting does not record executory promises.

d. Yes; at the present value, calculated using the yield rate at the time of issue, of the remaining coupon and principal payments.

3.9 continued.

e. Yes; at the expected, undiscounted value of future service costs arising from all sales made prior to the balance sheet date. The income statement includes warranty expense because of a desire to match all expenses of a sale with the sale; presumably, one reason the firm sold the product was the promise of free repairs. When recognizing the expense, the accountant credits a liability account to recognize the need for the future expenditures.

f. No. If the firm expected to lose a reasonably estimable amount in the suit, then it would show an estimated liability.

g. Yes, assuming statutes or contracts require the restoration. The present value of an estimate of the costs is the theoretically correct answer, but many accountants would use the full amount undiscounted.

h. No; viewed as executory.

i. Airlines recognize an expense and a liability for future services as passengers accumulate miles at regular fares, as those passengers reach award levels (for example, 30,000 flown miles). The measurement of the liability might be based on the estimated incremental cost of providing flights in exchange for miles, or on the estimated fair value of the flight services that passengers receive in exchange for accumulated miles.

3.11 a. In the definitions of assets and liabilities, *probable* is used to capture the idea that in commercial operations nothing can be entirely certain. It is used in its ordinary sense to refer to that which can be reasonably expected.

b. In the recognition criteria for liabilities with uncertain amount and/or timing, *probable* is used in U.S. GAAP to refer to a relatively high threshold of likelihood—a rule of thumb used in practice is approximately 80%. In IFRS, *probable* as recognition criterion for liabilities with uncertain amount and/or timing means "more likely than not"—approximately 51%.

3.13   (Delhaize Group; balance sheet formats.)

DELHAIZE GROUP
Balance Sheet
For the Year Ended December 31, 2007
(Amounts in Millions of Euros)

Assets

Current Assets:		
Cash and Cash Equivalents	€	248.9
Receivables		564.6
Inventories		1,262.0
Other Current Assets		121.5
Total Current Assets	€	2,197.0
Noncurrent Assets:		
Property, Plant and Equipment	€	3,383.1
Intangible Assets		552.1
Goodwill		2,445.7
Other Noncurrent Assets		244.0
Total Noncurrent Assets	€	6,624.9
Total Assets	€	8,821.9

Liabilities and Shareholders' Equity

Current Liabilities:		
Accounts Payable	€	1,435.8
Accrued Expenses		375.7
Income Tax Payable		58.7
Short-Term Borrowings		41.5
Long-Term Debt, Current Portion		108.9
Obligations under Finance Lease, Current Portion		39.0
Provisions		41.8
Other Current Liabilities		119.3
Total Current Liabilities	€	2,220.7
Noncurrent Liabilities:		
Long-Term Debt	€	1,911.7
Obligations under Finance Leases		595.9
Provisions		207.2
Other Noncurrent Liabilities		210.4
Total Noncurrent Liabilities	€	2,925.2
Total Liabilities	€	5,145.9
Shareholders' Equity:		
Share Capital	€	50.1
Share Premium		2,698.9
Retained Earnings		2,355.3
Other Reserves and Adjustments		(1,428.3)
Total Shareholders' Equity	€	3,676.0
Total Liabilities and Shareholders' Equity	€	8,821.9

3.15 (Genting Group; balance sheet relations.)

The missing items appear in boldface type below (amounts in millions of ringgit, RM).

	2007	2006	2005	2004
Current Assets..............	RM 10,999.2	RM **9,507.3**	RM **7,202.2**	RM 6,882.6
Noncurrent Assets........	**19,179.7**	18,717.4	11,289.1	9,713.9
Total Assets..............	RM **30,178.9**	RM 28,224.7	RM **18,491.3**	RM **16,596.5**
Current Liabilities........	RM **2,919.9**	RM 4,351.3	RM 1,494.2	RM 1,755.2
Noncurrent Liabilities..	5,721.7	**7,206.5**	**7,995.1**	3,540.7
Shareholders' Equity....	21,537.3	16,666.9	9,002.0	**11,300.6**
Total Liabilities and Shareholders' Equity..................	RM 30,178.9	RM **28,224.7**	RM 18,491.3	RM **16,596.5**

3.17 (Metso; balance sheet relations.)

The missing items appear in boldface type below (amounts in millions of euros).

	2007	2006	2005	2004
Current Assets..................	€ 3,357	€ 2,995	€ **2,477**	€ 2,097
Noncurrent Assets..........	**1,897**	1,973	**1,427**	**1,473**
Total Assets.................	€ **5,254**	€ **4,968**	€ **3,904**	€ **3,570**
Current Liabilities...........	€ **2,706**	€ 2,610	€ **1,802**	€ 1,466
Noncurrent Liabilities.....	957	**908**	**810**	1,109
Total Liabilities............	€ **3,663**	€ **3,518**	€ **2,612**	€ **2,575**
Contributed Capital........	€ **681**	€ 711	€ **739**	€ 634
Retained Earnings..........	910	**739**	553	361
Total Shareholders' Equity........	€ **1,591**	€ **1,450**	€ 1,292	€ **995**
Total Liabilities and Shareholders' Equity.........................	€ 5,254	€ **4,968**	€ **3,904**	€ **3,570**

3.19 (Duke University; asset recognition and measurement.)

The expenditures do not qualify as an asset because: (1) Duke University cannot point to a specific future economic benefit that it controls (employees can choose to work elsewhere even though doing so sacrifices the tuition benefit), and (2) there is not a reasonably reliable measurement attribute for this benefit.

3.21   (Nordstrom; recognition of a loss contingency.)

a. Nordstrom should recognize the contingency as soon as it is probable that it has incurred a loss and it can reasonably estimate the amount of the loss. Whether the store recognizes a loss at the time of the injury on July 5, 2007, depends on the strength of the case the store feels it has against the customer's claims. If the cause of the accident was an escalator malfunction, then Nordstrom may determine it is probable that it has incurred a liability. If, on the other hand, the customer fell while running up the clearly identified down side of the escalator, then Nordstrom may determine that it is probable that it has not incurred a liability. Attorneys, not accountants, must make these probability assessments.

If Nordstrom does not recognize a loss at the time of the injury, the next most likely time is June 15, 2008, when the jury renders its verdict. Unless attorneys for the store conclude that it is probable that the court will reverse the verdict on appeal, Nordstrom should recognize the loss at this time.

If attorneys feel that the grounds for appeal are strong, then the next most likely time to record the loss is on April 20, 2009, when the jury in the lower court reaches the same verdict as previously. This is the latest time in this case, at which the store should recognize the loss. If the store had recognized a loss on June 15, 2008, in the amount of $400,000, it would recognize only the extra damage award of $100,000 on April 20, 2009.

b. Under IFRS, the threshold for recognition is also probable but the meaning differs, such that a lower probability (more than 50%) will result in liability recognition under IFRS than under U.S. GAAP (more than approximately 80%).

3.23   (Ryanair Holdings; asset recognition and measurement.)

a. Under both U.S. GAAP and IFRS, a decision on the part of Ryanair's board of directors does not give rise to an asset.

b. Under both U.S. GAAP and IFRS, Ryanair's placing of an order does not give rise to an asset.

c. Under both U.S. GAAP and IFRS, Ryanair's payment gives rise to an asset on their balance sheet, Deposit on Aircraft (noncurrent asset), €60 million.

d. Under both U.S. GAAP and IFRS, Ryanair's purchase gives rise to an asset, Landing Rights (noncurrent asset), €50 million.

3.23 continued.

    e.   Under both U.S. GAAP and IFRS, Ryanair's purchase gives rise to an asset on their balance sheet, Equipment (noncurrent asset), €77 million. Ryanair would also record a liability, Mortgage Note Payable (noncurrent), HK$65 million.

    f.   Under both U.S. GAAP and IFRS, Ryanair's purchase gives rise to an asset, Equipment (noncurrent asset), €160 million. The carrying, or book, value of the aircraft on the seller's books is not relevant to Ryanair's recording of the purchase.

3.25   (Berlin Philharmonic; liability recognition and measurement.)

    a.   Under both U.S. GAAP and IFRS, the Berlin Philharmonic would record Advances from Customers (current liability), €3,040,000.

    b.   Under both U.S. GAAP and IFRS, the Berlin Philharmonic does not recognize a liability because it has not yet received benefits obligating it to pay.

    c.   Under both U.S. GAAP and IFRS, the Berlin Philharmonic would record Accounts Payable (current liability), €185,000.

    d.   Under both U.S. GAAP and IFRS, the Berlin Philharmonic would not normally recognize a liability for an unsettled lawsuit unless payment is probable and the entity can reliably estimate the loss. Because the suit has not yet come to trial, it is unclear whether any liability exists.

    e.   Under both U.S. GAAP and IFRS, the Berlin Philharmonic would not recognize a liability for this mutually unexecuted contract.

    f.   Under both U.S. GAAP and IFRS, accounting normally does not recognize a liability for mutually unexecuted contracts. Thus, at the time of contract signing, the Berlin Philharmonic would record no liability. In 2012, however, the firm would record a liability for the portion of the yearly compensation earned by Sir Simon Rattle each month, or Salary Payable (current liability), €0.167 million per month.

3.27   (Magyar Telekom; effect of recording errors on balance sheet equation.)
(Amounts in Millions)

Transaction Number	Assets	=	Liabilities	+	Shareholders' Equity
(1)	No		No		No
(2)	O/S HUF 900		O/S HUF 900		No
(3)	U/S HUF 14,500		U/S HUF 14,500		No
(4)	No[a]		No		No
(5)	U/S HUF 6,000		U/S HUF 6,000		No
(6)	U/S HUF 1,200		No		U/S HUF 1,200
(7)	No		No		No

[a]The value of total assets is correctly stated; the problem is that rather than debiting Property for the insurance payment, the firm should have debited Prepaid Insurance.

3.29 (Cathay Pacific; balance sheet format, terminology, and accounting methods.) [Amounts in Millions of HK Dollars (HKD)]

a.

CATHAY PACIFIC AIRWAYS LIMITED
Balance Sheet, U.S. GAAP
(Amounts in Millions of HKD)

	December 31, 2007	December 31, 2006
Assets		
Current Assets:		
Cash and Cash Equivalents[a]	HKD 21,649	HKD 15,624
Trade and Other Receivables	11,376	8,735
Inventory[b]	882	789
Assets Pledged Against Current Liabilities[c]	910	1,352
Total Current Assets	34,817	26,500
Noncurrent Assets:		
Investments in Associates	10,054	8,826
Fixed Assets	62,388	57,602
Other Long-Term Receivables and Investments	3,519	3,406
Intangible Assets	7,782	7,749
Assets Pledged Against Noncurrent Liabilities[d]	7,833	8,164
Total Noncurrent Assets	91,576	85,747
Total Assets	HKD 126,393	HKD 112,247
Liabilities and Shareholders' Equity		
Current Liabilities:		
Trade and Other Payables	HKD 14,787	HKD 10,999
Current Portion of Long-Term Liabilities	4,788	7,503
Unearned Transportation Revenue	6,254	4,671
Income Taxes Payable[e]	2,475	2,902
Total Current Liabilities	28,304	26,075
Noncurrent Liabilities:		
Long-Term Liabilities	40,323	33,956
Retirement Benefit Obligations	268	170
Deferred Tax Liability[f]	6,771	6,508
Total Noncurrent Liabilities	47,362	40,634
Total Liabilities	75,666	66,709
Minority Interests	178	152
Shareholders' Equity:		
Share Capital	788	787
Reserves	49,761	44,599
Total Shareholders' Equity	50,549	45,386
Total Liabilities and Shareholders' Equity[g]	HKD 126,393	HKD 112,247

Footnotes appear on following page.

3.29 a. continued.

Terminology (differences from account names reported by Cathay Pacific).

[a]Liquid Funds.

[b]Stock.

[c]Related Pledged Security Deposits (Current Portion of Long-Term Debt).

[d]Related Pledged Security Deposits (Noncurrent Portion of Long-Term Debt).

[e]Taxation.

[f]Deferred Taxation.

[g]Funds Attributable to Cathay Pacific Shareholders.

b.

CATHAY PACIFIC AIRWAYS LIMITED
Balance Sheet, IFRS
(Amounts in Millions of HKD)

	December 31,	
	2007	2006
Assets		
Noncurrent Assets:		
Intangible Assets...................................	HKD 7,782	HKD 7,749
Fixed Assets...	62,388	57,602
Assets Pledged Against Noncurrent		
Liabilities[d]......................................	7,833	8,164
Investments in Associates..................	10,054	8,826
Other Long-Term Receivables and		
Investments....................................	3,519	3,406
Total Noncurrent Assets	91,576	85,747
Current Assets:		
Inventory[b]	882	789
Assets Pledged Against Current		
Liabilities[c]....................................	910	1,352
Trade and Other Receivables..............	11,376	8,735
Cash and Cash Equivalents[a]..............	21,649	15,624
Total Current Assets......................	34,817	26,500
Total Assets....................................	HKD 126,393	HKD 112,247

3.29 b. continued.

Liabilities and Shareholders' Equity

Noncurrent Liabilities:				
Long-Term Liabilities............................	HKD	40,323	HKD	33,956
Retirement Benefit Obligations..........		268		170
Deferred Tax Liability[f]........................		6,771		6,508
Total Noncurrent Liabilities............		47,362		40,634
Current Liabilities:				
Income Taxes Payable[e].......................		2,475		2,902
Trade and Other Payables...................		14,787		10,999
Current Portion of Long-Term Liabilities...		4,788		7,503
Unearned Transportation Revenue...		6,254		4,671
Total Current Liabilities..................		28,304		26,075
Total Liabilities.................................		75,666		66,709
Shareholders' Equity:				
Minority Interests................................		178		152
Share Capital...		788		787
Reserves..		49,761		44,599
Total Shareholders' Equity..............		50,727		45,538
Total Liabilities and Shareholders' Equity[g]...	HKD	126,393	HKD	112,247

Terminology (differences from account names reported by Cathay Pacific).

[a]Liquid Funds.

[b]Stock.

[c]Related Pledged Security Deposits (Current Portion of Long-Term Debt).

[d]Related Pledged Security Deposits (Noncurrent Portion of Long-Term Debt).

[e]Taxation.

[f]Deferred Taxation.

[g]Funds Attributable to Cathay Pacific Shareholders.

3.31 (Ericsson; balance sheet format, terminology, and accounting methods.)

ERICCSON
U.S. GAAP Balance Sheet
For the Year Ended December 31, 2007
(Amounts in SEK Millions)

Assets

Current Assets:

Cash and Cash Equivalents	SEK	28,310
Short-Term Investments		29,406
Trade Receivables		60,492
Customer Financing, Current		2,362
Other Current Receivables		15,062
Inventories		22,475
Total Current Assets	SEK	158,107

Noncurrent Assets:

Equity in Joint Ventures	SEK	10,903
Other Investments in Shares		738
Customer Financing, Noncurrent		1,012
Other Financial Assets, Noncurrent		2,918
Deferred Tax Assets		11,690
Property, Plant and Equipment		8,404
Intellectual Property Rights, Brands		23,958
Goodwill		22,826
Total Noncurrent Assets	SEK	82,449
Total Assets	SEK	240,556

Liabilities and Shareholders' Equity

Current Liabilities:

Trade Payables	SEK	17,427
Borrowings, Current		5,896
Provisions, Current		8,858
Other Current Liabilities		44,995
Total Current Liabilities	SEK	77,176

Noncurrent Liabilities:

Provisions, Noncurrent	SEK	368
Borrowings, Noncurrent		21,320
Post-Employment Benefits		6,188
Deferred Tax Liabilities		2,799
Other Noncurrent Liabilities		1,714
Total Noncurrent Liabilities	SEK	32,389
Total Liabilities	SEK	109,565
Minority Interest		940
Shareholders' Equity		130,051
Total Liabilities and Equity	SEK	240,556

3.31 continued.

1. U.S. GAAP does not permit the capitalization of development costs. Removal of these costs reduces assets by SEK3,661 million, and reduces shareholders' equity (Retained Earnings) by SEK3,661 million.

2. U.S. GAAP does not permit the upward revaluation of land. In 2007, this upward revaluation led to land being stated at a value SEK900 million higher on Ericsson's balance sheet than would have been permitted under U.S.GAAP. The upward revaluation would also have been included as an unrealized gain, in Ericsson's shareholders' equity. To conform to U.S. GAAP, removal of the upward revaluation of the land would, therefore, reduce assets and shareholders' equity by SEK900 million for 2007.

3. Both U.S. GAAP and IFRS require assessments for impairment of noncurrent assets. Thus, the write down of the equipment in 2007 from SEK2,400 to SEK1,600 would also exist under U.S. GAAP.

4. From the information provided, the probability of loss is 60% for the patent infringement lawsuit. Thus, the lawsuit meets the IFRS threshold for recognition; it does not, however, meet the probable standard under U.S. GAAP (80%). Thus, under U.S. GAAP, Ericsson would not have recognized a liability for this lawsuit. Under IFRS, Ericsson would have recognized the "best" estimate as the amount of the liability. This best estimate was likely SEK500, since this is the amount of expected damages with the largest probability of occurring. Another best estimate that is possible is the expected value of the range of estimates, or SEK994 million. Whatever the best estimate, the amount would need to be removed from current provisions, and added back to shareholders' equity, to derecognize this liability under U.S. GAAP. The balance sheet shown above displays a best estimate of SEK500.

   Summary Calculations for Shareholders' Equity:
Balance per Ericsson Balance Sheet, 2007 (IFRS)	SEK 134,112
Removal of Capitalized Development Costs That Would Be Expensed Under U.S. GAAP.......................	(3,661)
Removal of Upward Revaluation of Land That Would Not Have Been Made under U.S. GAAP	(900)
Removal of Lawsuit Expense That Would Not Have Met the Standard for Recognition Under U.S. GAAP...	500
Balance per Ericsson Balance Sheet, 2007 U.S. GAAP...	SEK 130,051

3.33   (Cemex; common-size balance sheet and interpreting balance sheet changes.)

a.   The common size balance sheet for Cemex for years 2007 and 2006 are shown below.

	2007		2006	
Assets				
Current Assets:				
Cash and Investments...............	$ 8,670	1.6%	$ 18,494	5.3%
Trade Receivables Less Allowance for Doubtful Accounts..	20,719	3.8%	16,525	4.7%
Other Accounts Receivable.......	9,830	1.8%	9,206	2.6%
Inventories, Net...........................	19,631	3.6%	13,974	4.0%
Other Current Assets.................	2,394	0.5%	2,255	0.6%
Total Current Assets.............	$ 61,244	11.3%	$ 60,454	17.2%
Noncurrent Assets:				
Investments in Associates........	$ 10,599	2.0%	$ 8,712	2.5%
Other Investments in Noncurrent Accounts Receivable.....	10,960	2.0%	9,966	2.8%
Property, Machinery and Equipment, Net.......................	262,189	48.3%	201,425	57.4%
Goodwill, Intangible Assets and Deferred Charges............	197,322	36.4%	70,526	20.1%
Total Noncurrent Assets..	$481,070	88.7%	$290,629	82.8%
Total Assets	$542,314	100.0%	$ 351,083	100.0%
Liabilities and Shareholders' Equity:				
Current Liabilities:				
Short-Term Debt Including Current Maturities of Long-Term Debt................................	$ 36,257	6.7%	$ 14,657	4.2%
Trade Payables.........................	23,660	4.4%	20,110	5.7%
Other Accounts Payable and Accrued Expenses	23,471	4.3%	17,203	4.9%
Total Current Liabilities ...	$ 83,388	15.4%	$ 51,970	14.8%

3.33 a. continued.

Noncurrent Liabilities:				
Long-Term Debt	$180,654	33.3%	$ 73,674	21.0%
Pension and Other Retirement Benefits	7,650	1.4%	7,484	2.1%
Deferred Income Tax Liability	50,307	9.3%	30,119	8.6%
Other Noncurrent Liabilities	16,162	3.0%	14,725	4.2%
Total Noncurrent Liabilities	$254,773	47.0%	$126,002	35.9%
Total Liabilities	$338,161	62.4%	$177,972	50.7%
Minority Interest	$ 40,985	7.6%	$ 22,484	6.4%
Shareholders' Equity:				
Common Stock	$ 4,115	0.8%	$ 4,113	1.2%
Additional Paid-in Capital	63,379	11.7%	56,982	16.2%
Less Other Equity Reserves	(104,574)	(19.3%)	(91,244)	(26.0%)
Retained Earnings	200,248	36.9%	180,776	51.5%
Total Shareholders' Equity	$163,168	30.1%	150,627	42.9%
Total Liabilities and Shareholders' Equity	$542,314	100.0%	$351,083	100.0%

b. The largest asset is property, plant, and equipment, which represents the generating and distribution capacity of the construction company. Long-term financing dominates the financing side of the balance sheet, with the largest proportion coming from long-term debt.

c. Between 2006 and 2007, Cemex decreased the percentage of tangible noncurrent assets and increased the percentage of intangible noncurrent assets on its balance sheet. In particular, property, plant and equipment decreased from 57.4% to 48.3% of total assets and intangible assets (including goodwill) increased from 20.1% to 36.4% of total assets. The net increase in noncurrent assets was financed by increased debt, as evidenced by the increase in the common size percentage of long-term borrowings from 21.0% to 33.3% of total assets. These data indicate that Cemex's capital expenditures were largely financed through increases in long term debt.

3.35 (Relating market value to book value of shareholders' equity.)

a. (1) **Pfizer**—Pharmaceutical firms make ongoing expenditures on research and development (R&D) to develop new products. Some of these expenditures result in profitable new products, while other expenditures do not provide any future benefit. The difficulty encountered in trying to identify whether or not a particular R&D expenditure results in a future benefit has led accounting standard setters to require the immediate expensing of R&D costs in the year incurred. Thus, the valuable patents for pharmaceutical products and the value of potential products in the research pipeline do not appear on the balance sheet of Pfizer. The market does place a value on these technologies in deciding on an appropriate market price for the firm's stock.

Students might suggest approaches that technology firms could follow to measure the value of their technology resources. One approach might be to study the past success record of discovering new technologies. For example, if 20% of expenditures in the past resulted in valuable technologies, the firm might report 20% of the expenditures on R&D each period as an asset. If these new technologies provided benefits for, say, seven years on average, then the firm would amortize the amount recognized as an asset over seven years. An alternative approach would be to use the prices paid recently when acquiring firms purchase target firms that have similar technologies. Each of these approaches involves a degree of subjectivity that has led standard setters to require the immediate expensing of R&D expenditures in the year incurred.

(2) **Nestlé**—The products of Nestlé carry a high degree of brand recognition, which leads loyal customers to purchase Nestlé products on a regular basis and new customers to try its products. The value of the Nestlé name and its other brand names is created through advertising, quality control, and new product introductions. Nestlé follows GAAP in expensing these expenditures each year. Thus, the value of the brand name does not appear on the balance sheet as an asset. If the brand name did appear on the balance sheet, assets and shareholders' equity would be larger and the market-to-book value ratio would be closer to 1.0.

One might ask how Nestlé might value its brand names if it were permitted to recognize these valuable resources as assets. One approach might be to determine the profit margin (that is, net income divided by sales) that Nestlé realizes on sales of its products relative to the profit margin of competitors. Nestlé would then multiply the excess profit margin times the number of units expected to be sold in future years to measure its excess profitability. It would then discount the future excess earnings to a present value. An alternative approach is to identify the prices paid recently by firms acquiring other branded consumer products companies to ascertain the approximate price paid for identifiable assets and the portion paid for brand names. Each of these approaches involves a degree of subjectivity and opens the door for firms to cast their balance sheets in the most favorable light possible. Accounting standard setters in most countries recognize this potential source of bias and require firms to expense brand development costs in the year expenditures are made.

3.35 a. continued.

(3) **Promodes**—Promodes is the largest grocery store chain in France and likely has some brand name recognition that does not appear on its balance sheet. In addition, the stores of Promodes are valued at acquisition cost adjusted downward for depreciation to date. The land and perhaps the store buildings probably have market values that exceed their book values. Standard setters in most countries require firms to account for land and buildings using acquisition costs instead of current market values because of the subjectivity in the latter valuations. This real estate is probably easier to value than brand names and technological know how because of active real estate markets. Thus, the market-to-book value ratio probably reflects brand recognition and undervalued fixed assets.

(4) **Deutsche Bank**—Most of the assets of a commercial bank are reported on the balance sheet at current market values. Marketable securities are revalued to market value at each balance sheet date. Loans receivable are stated net of estimated uncollectibles and should therefore reflect cash-equivalent values. Deposits and short-term borrowing on the liability side of the balance sheet appear at current cash-equivalent values. Thus, the market-to-book value ratio should be approximately 1.0. The ratio of 1.7 for Deutsche Bank suggests the presence of intangibles that do not appear on the balance sheet. Possibilities include the size and dominant influence of Deutsche Bank in the German economy, technologically sophisticated information systems, and superior work force. The financial consulting capabilities of its investment banking employees are a valuable resource that does not appear on the balance sheet as an asset.

(5) **British Airways**—The aircraft and ground facilities of British Airways appear at acquisition cost net of depreciation to date. The market values of these fixed assets likely exceed their book values. In addition, British Airways has landing and gateway rights that appear on the balance sheet only to the extent that the firm has paid amounts up front. In most cases, British Airways pays fees periodically as it uses these facilities. Thus, no asset appears on the balance sheet.

Odd-numbered Solutions

3.35 a. continued.

      (6) **New Oji Paper Co.**—The balance sheet of New Oji Paper Co. includes a high proportion of intercorporate investments in securities and property, plant, and equipment. GAAP in Japan reports these assets at acquisition cost, with plant and equipment adjusted downward for depreciation to date. The market value of land probably exceeds its book value. The market values of securities in Japan have decreased significantly in recent years but may still exceed their book values if the investments were made many years ago. Note that the market-to-book value ratio does not exceed 1.0 by as much as the consumer products and pharmaceutical companies with brand recognition.

b. (1) **Pfizer**—One question related to Pfizer is why it would use such a small percentage of long-term debt financing. Pharmaceutical firms face product obsolescence and legal liability risks. They tend not to add financial risk from having a high proportion of long-term debt on the balance sheet. Although this exercise does not provide the needed information, Pfizer is very profitable and generates sufficient cash flow from operations that it does not need much external financing.

      A second question related to Pfizer is the large percentage for other noncurrent liabilities on the balance sheet. This amount includes its healthcare benefit obligation to employees and deferred income taxes. Students generally have not studied these two items sufficiently to generate much discussion.

      A third question related to Pfizer is its high proportion of treasury stock. Economic theory would suggest that if the market fairly values a firm prior to a stock buyback, then the market price of the stock should not change. The economic value of the firm should decrease by the amount of cash paid out. The number of shares of common stock outstanding should decline proportionally and the stock price should remain the same. However, the effect of stock buybacks generally is to increase the market price of the stock. One possible explanation for the market price increase is that the market views the buyback as a positive signal by management about the firm's future prospects. Management knows about the firm's future plans and might feel that the market is underpricing the firm, given these future plans. The buyback signals this positive information and the market price increases.

    (2) **Nestlé**— Nestlé, like Pfizer, has highly predictable cash flows from its brand name products and generates sufficient cash flows in the long term to reduce the need for long-term debt financing. Nestlé, however, extends credit to customers and must carry inventory for some period of time before sale. It uses suppliers and short-term borrowing to finance this working capital.

3.35 b. continued.

(3) **Promodes**—The majority of the assets of Promodes is short-term receivables and inventories. The majority of its financing is likewise short-term. Thus, firms attempt to match the term structure of their financing to the term structure of their assets.

(4) **Deutsche Bank**—Deutsche Bank obtains the vast majority of its funds from depositors and short-term borrowing. Such a high proportion of short-term financing might appear risky. However, a large portion of its assets is in highly liquid cash and short-term investments. A large portion is also in loans to businesses and consumers. Although loans are generally not as liquid as cash and investments, they do have predictable cash flows. The large number of borrowers also diversifies the risk of Deutsche Bank on these loans. The low level of risk on the asset side of the balance sheet and the stability of the deposit base means that banks need only a small proportion of shareholders' equity.

(5) **British Airways**—The majority of the assets of British Airways is in flight and ground support equipment. British Airways matches these long-term assets with long-term financing, either in the form of long-term debt or shareholders' equity. The heavier use of debt financing stems from its lower cost and the availability of the equipment to serve as collateral for the borrowing. Lenders generally prefer that firms have more current assets than current liabilities. The excess current liabilities of British Airways stem from advance sales of airline tickets (appears in Other Current Liabilities). British Airways will satisfy this liability by providing transportation services rather than paying cash. Thus, the net current liability position is not of particular concern.

(6) **New Oji Paper Co.**—The balance sheet of Oji portrays some relationships that are typical of Japanese companies. First, note the high proportion of investments in securities. Many Japanese companies are part of corporate groups (called "Kieretsus"). The investments in firms in the corporate groups tend to represent 20% to 30% of these other companies and appear as intercorporate investments on the balance sheet. Secondly, note the relatively high proportion of short-term bank borrowing. Most corporate groups have a commercial bank as a member. This commercial bank is not likely to force a member of the group into bankruptcy if it is unable to repay a loan at maturity. The bank will more likely simply extend the term of the loan. Short-term borrowing is usually less costly than long-term borrowing and helps explain the high proportion of short-term borrowing on the balance sheet.

This page is intentionally left blank

CHAPTER 4

INCOME STATEMENT: REPORTING THE RESULTS OF OPERATING ACTIVITIES

Questions, Exercises, and Problems: Answers and Solutions

4.1   See the text or the glossary at the end of the book.

4.3   Cost is the economic sacrifice made to acquire goods or services. When the good or service acquired has reliably measurable future benefits to a firm, the cost is an asset. When the firm consumes the good or service, the cost is an expense.

4.5   The assets and income from operations that a firm has decided to discontinue (and dispose of or abandon) will not be part of that firm's future performance. Thus, separating the two income components allows users to form better predictions of future earnings.

4.7   The matching convention assigns expenses to the related revenues. If the firm pays cash to acquire goods in a period before the goods are sold and collects the cash, then under a cash basis system, the expense will appear in a different accounting period than the related revenues.

4.9   The profit margin percentage, because it uses only sales revenues and net income, which are not affected by differences in display and format. Settings where the profit margins of two firms may not be comparable occur when one firm nets certain expenses (such as bad debt expense) directly against revenues, while another shows it as a separate expense.

4.11   (Neiman Marcus; revenue recognition.)

	February	March	April
a.	--	--	$ 800
b.	--	$ 2,160	--
c.	$39,200	--	--
d.	--	$ 59,400	--
e.	--	$ 9,000	$ 9,000
f.	--	$ 9,000	$ 9,000

4.13   (Sun Microsystems; expense recognition.)

	June	July	August
	June	**July**	**August**
a.	--	$ 15,000	$ 15,000
b.	$ 4,560	--	--
c.	--	$ 5,800	$ 6,300
d.	$ 600	$ 600	$ 600
e.	--	--	--
f.	--	--	$ 4,500
g.	$ 6,600	--	--

4.15   (Bombardier Corporation; relating net income to balance sheet changes.)

a.   Net Income = [($1,040 – $765) + $30 – $12] = $293 million.

b.   Net Income = [($20,562 – $18,577) – ($17,444 – $15,844) – ($2,078 – $1,968) + $30 – $12] = $293 million.

4.17   (Lenovo Group Limited; income statement relations.)   (Amounts in Thousands)

The missing items appear in boldface type below:

	2008	2007
Sales	$ 16,351,503	$ 13,978,309
Cost of Goods Sold	(13,901,523)	(12,091,433)
Gross Profit	**$ 2,449,980**	**$ 1,886,876**
Selling and Administrative Expense	(1,103,713)	(1,033,296)
Advertising Expense	(595,902)	(488,150)
Research and Development Expense	(229,759)	(196,225)
Other Income (Expense)	**11,715**	18,130
Profit before Taxes	$ **532,321**	$ **187,335**
Income Tax Expense	(47,613)	(26,197)
Net Income	$ 484,708	$ **161,138**

4.19 (James John Corporation; income and equity relations.) (Amounts in Millions)

The missing items appear in boldface below:

JAMES JOHN CORPORATION
Comparative Balance Sheets
March 31, 2008, 2007, and 2006

	March 31,		
	2008	**2007**	**2006**
Common Stock	$ **1.1**[a]	$ **1.1**[a]	$ 1.1
Accumulated Other Comprehensive Income	**40.5**	(27.2)	0.0
Retained Earnings	1,742.3	**1,379.2**[b]	1,090.3
Treasury Stock	**(321.5)**[c]	(87.1)	(80.0)
Additional Paid-in Capital	872.5	783.6	**664.3**
Total Shareholders' Equity	$ 2,334.9	$ 2,049.6	$ 1,675.7

Calculations:

[a]No new stock issuance implies same balance in common stock for 2007 and 2008 as the balance in this account in 2006.

[b]Retained Earnings, End of 2007 = Retained Earnings, End of 2006 + Net Income, 2007 − Dividend Declared, 2007 = $1,090.3 + $308.5 − $19.6 = $1,379.2.

[c]Treasury Shares, 2008 = Treasury Shares, 2007 + Repurchases, 2008 = $(87.1) + $(234.4) = $(321.5).

4.21 (MosTechi Corporation; accumulated other comprehensive income relations.) (Amounts in Millions of Yen)

The missing items appear in boldface below:

MOSTECHI CORPORATION
Comparative Balance Sheets
March 31, 2008, 2007, and 2006

	March 31,		
	2008	**2007**	**2006**
Common Stock	¥ 626,907	¥ 624,124	¥ 621,709
Accumulated Other Comprehensive Income	**(115,493)**[b]	**(156,437)**[a]	**(385,675)**
Retained Earnings	**1,700,133**[c]	1,602,654	1,506,082
Treasury Stock	**(3,470)**	(3,127)	(6,000)
Additional Paid-in Capital	1,143,423	1,136,638	1,134,222
Total Shareholders' Equity	¥3,351,500	¥3,203,852	¥2,870,338

Calculations:

[a]Accumulated Other Comprehensive Income, End of 2007 = Accumulated Other Comprehensive Income, End of 2006 + Other Comprehensive Income, 2007 = ¥(385,675) + ¥229,238 = ¥(156,437).

[b]Accumulated Other Comprehensive Income, End of 2008 = Accumulated Other Comprehensive Income, End of 2007 + Other Comprehensive Income, 2008 = ¥(156,437) + ¥40,944 = ¥(115,493).

[c]Retained Earnings, End of 2008 = Retained Earnings, End of 2007 + Net Income, 2008 – Dividends Declared, 2008 + Adjustment, 2008 = ¥1,602,654 + ¥126,328 – ¥25,042 – ¥3,807 = ¥1,700,133.

4.23 (Bayer Group; discontinued operations.)

a. In 2007, 51% [= €2,410/(€2,410 + €2,306)] of Bayer's income came from discontinued operations, compared to 9% [= €169/(€169 + €1,526)] in 2006.

b. In 2007, less than 0.2% (= €84/€51,378) of Bayer's total assets were associated with discontinued operations, compared to 5.2% (= €2,925/€55,891) in 2006.

c. The large decline in Bayer's assets held for discontinued operations is due to the fact that Bayer disposed of the assets in 2007. The assets are no longer owned by Bayer and, therefore, no longer a part of Bayer's balance sheet at the end of 2007. The income those assets generated during the year prior to disposal is, however, part of Bayer's income for 2007.

4.25 (Cemex S.A.B.; income statement formats.)

The missing items appear in boldface type below:

CEMEX S.A.B.
IFRS Income Statements
December 31, 2007 and 2006

	December 31,	
	2007	**2006**
Net Sales	$ 236,669	$ 213,767
Cost of Sales	(157,696)	**(136,447)**
Gross Profit	$ **78,973**	$ 77,320
Administrative and Selling Expenses	(33,120)	(28,588)
Distribution Expenses	(13,405)	**(14,227)**
Other Expenses, Net	(3,281)	(580)
Operating Income	$ **29,167**	$ 33,925
Financial Expenses	(8,809)	**(5,785)**
Financial Income	862	536
Income (Expense) from Financial Instruments	2,387	(161)
Other Financial Income (Expense)	6,647	4,905
Equity in Income of Associates	1,487	1,425
Profit before Income Tax	$ **31,741**	$ 34,845
Income Tax	**(4,796)**	**(5,697)**
Consolidated Profit	$ **26,945**	$ **29,148**
Portion of Profit Attributable to Minority Interest	$ 837	$ 1,293
Portion of Profit Attributable to Cemex Shareholders	$ **26,108**	$ 27,855

4.27 (Broyo Corporation; correcting errors in income statement transactions.) (Amounts in Millions of Pounds)

a. Broyo should not have recognized revenue on this transaction because it has yet to perform on the contract. Revenues are overstated by €200 and Cost of Goods Sold is overstated by €160, so income is overstated by €40.

b. Broyo should not have recorded the advance from customer as revenues. It is a liability (Advance from Customer). Revenues are, therefore, overstated by €20.

c. Broyo should have recorded Revenues of €45, and Cost of Goods Sold of €36, for a gross profit of €9.

4.27 continued.

    d.   Because the expenditures do not qualify as capitalized development costs, they should have been expensed not capitalized. Broyo's income in 2008 is, therefore, overstated by €11.

    e.   Broyo had performed all of its obligations with the customer, so on December 1, 2008, it should have recognized Revenues of €266, and Cost of Goods Sold of €250. Because they did not, Revenues are understated by €266, Cost of Goods Sold is understated by €250, and Gross Profit is understated by €16.

    f.   The sale of a plant is not a recurring part of Broyo's business. Therefore, it should not be included as part of Revenues and Cost of Goods Sold, which pertain to recurring transactions. Revenues are, therefore, overstated by €100, and Cost of Goods Sold is overstated by €80. The sale of the plant generated a gain of €20, which should have been included in Other Operating Income.

4.29   (Standard Denim and Blue Label Jeans; interpreting common-size income statements.)

    a.   The decreasing cost of goods sold to sales percentages for both firms suggest a common explanation. One possibility is that the economy was doing well and both firms were able to increase selling prices and thereby their profit margins. Another possibility is that the firms were able to purchase merchandise in larger quantities or pay more quickly to take advantage of discounts. A third possibility is that the firms implemented more effective inventory control systems, thereby reducing obsolescence and the need to reduce selling prices to move their merchandise. Another possibility is that sales grew rapidly and the firms were able to spread their relatively fixed occupancy costs over a larger sales base.

    b.   Blue Label Jeans relies more heavily on in-store promotions, which tend to increase its cost of goods sold to sales percentages, whereas Standard Denim relies more on advertising to stimulate sales, which Standard Denim includes in selling and administrative expenses.

    c.   The increasing selling and administrative expenses to sales percentages for both firms suggest a common explanation. One possibility is that the specialty retailing industry became more competitive over this period (from new entrants and from the Internet) and the firms had to increase marketing expenses to compete. This explanation, however, is inconsistent with a more attractive pricing environment suggested in Part *a.* above. Another possibility is that both firms experienced increased administrative expenses as they introduced new store concepts and opened new stores.

4.29 continued.

d. The explanation in Part *b*. applies here as well. Standard Denim includes its promotion costs in selling and administrative expenses, whereas more of those of Blue Label Jeans appear in cost of goods sold.

e. The interest expense to sales percentage decreased for Standard Denim and increased for Blue Label Jeans. One possible explanation is Standard Denim reduced the amount of debt outstanding or grew it at a slower pace than that of Blue Label Jeans. Another possibility is that the market viewed Standard Denim as increasingly less risky, permitting it to borrow at lower interest rates. On the other hand, the market viewed Blue Label Jeans as more risky and required it to pay a higher interest rate. These two possibilities are not independent. Perhaps Standard Denim was able to borrow at a lower rate because it reduced the amount of debt in its capital structure. The higher interest rate for Blue Label Jeans may reflect increased risk from an increased proportion of debt in its capital structure.

f. Both firms experienced increased net income relative to sales. Both firms should therefore experience increased income tax expense relative to sales. A more meaningful way to interpret income taxes is to relate income tax expense to income before income taxes. The latter is the base on which governments impose income taxes. Consider the following:

	Standard Denim			Blue Label Jeans		
	2008	2007	2006	2008	2007	2006
(1) Income before Income Taxes (Plug)...............	16.3%	14.6%	12.4%	6.9%	6.5%	5.8%
(2) Income Tax Expense...........	(6.6)	(5.5)	(4.2)	(2.4)	(2.3)	(2.0)
(3) Net Income	9.7%	9.1%	8.2%	4.5%	4.2%	3.8%
(2)/(1)......................	40.5%	37.7%	33.9%	34.8%	35.4%	34.5%

The income tax expense to income before income taxes percentages for Standard Denim continually increased while those of Blue Label Jeans remained relatively stable. One possible explanation is that Standard Denim expanded its operations into other countries and perhaps experienced higher income tax rates in those countries than it experiences in the United States.

Odd-numbered Solutions

4.31   (Ericsson; interpreting common-size income statements.)

Ericsson's profit margin declined from 16.0% in 2005, to 14.7% in 2006, to 11.8% in 2007. The decline results primarily from increases in the cost of goods sold to sales percentage and in the selling and administrative expense to sales percentage. One possible explanation for the increase in both cost of sales (as a percentage of sales) and selling and administrative expenses (as a percentage of sales) is that the markets that Ericsson competes in became more competitive over these three years. Competition might force selling prices to not increase at the same rate that costs increase.

4.33   (Identifying industries using common-size income statement percentages.)

Exhibit 4.11 indicates that two firms have relatively low profit margins, two firms have medium profit margins, and two firms have relatively large profit margins. Low barriers to entry, extensive competition, and commodity products characterize firms with low profit margins. The likely candidates for Firms (1) and (2) are Kelly Services and Kroger Stores. The office services offered by Kelly Services are clerical in nature and not particularly unique. Kelly Services serves essentially as an intermediary between the employee and the customer, offering relatively little value added. Grocery products are commodities, with little, if any, differentiation between grocery stores. Firms (1) and (2) differ primarily with respect to depreciation and interest expense. Grocery stores require retail and warehouse space. Kelly Services should require relatively little space, since its employees work on the customers' premises. Thus, Firm (1) is Kroger Stores and Firm (2) is Kelly Services.

Firms with the highest profit margin should operate in industries with high barriers to entry, relatively little competition, and differentiated products. Electric utilities have operated until recently as regulated utilities and require extensive amounts of capital to build capital-intensive plants. Regulation and capital serve as barriers to entry. Tiffany's offers brand name products. The brand names serve as an entry barrier. Customers also perceive its products to be differentiated. Thus, Firm (5) and Firm (6) are likely to be Commonwealth Edison and Tiffany & Co. in some order. Firm (5) has considerably more depreciation and interest expense than Firm (6) and Firm (6) has considerably more selling and administrative expenses than Firm (5). Thus, Firm (5) is Commonwealth Edison and Firm (6) is Tiffany & Co.

This leaves Hewlett-Packard and Delta Airlines with medium profit margins. Hewlett-Packard offers products that are somewhat differentiated and with some brand name appeal. However, competition in the computer industry and rapid technological change drive down profit margins. Delta Airlines offers a commodity product, but the need for capital to acquire airplanes serves as a barrier to entry. Thus, these two firms have some characteristics of firms with relatively low profit margins and some characteristics of firms with relatively high profit margins. Firm (3) appears to have considerably more debt in its capital structure than Firm (4). The short product life cycles in the computer industry tend to drive down their use of debt. The aircraft of Delta Airlines can serve as collateral

4.33 continued.

for borrowing. Thus, one would expect Delta Airlines to have a higher amount of borrowing. This clue suggests that Firm (3) is Delta Airlines and Firm (4) is Hewlett-Packard.

4.35   (Dyreng Plc.; classification and interpretation of income statements.)

a. Dyreng should not have recognized any revenues (nor any costs) of this project in 2008 because it had performed no work. 2008 Revenues are overstated by €240, causing both Gross Profit and Pre-tax Profit from Continuing Operations to be overstated by this amount.

b. 2008 Revenues are overstated by €700. The revenues and associated costs should have been recorded in 2007 when the work was performed. The receipt of cash is irrelevant to the timing of the revenue recognition. 2008 Gross Profits and Pre-tax Profit from Continuing Operations are overstated by €40 (= €700 – €660).

c. The sale of the office building was not a normal part of Dyreng's operations. It should not, therefore, have been included in Sales or Cost of Sales. The net effect of the sale, a loss of €40, should have been included in Other Operating Income. Gross Profit is understated by €40, but Pre-tax Profit from Continuing Operations is correctly stated.

d. Other Operating Income is overstated by €45. Gross Profit is correctly stated, but Pre-tax Profit from Continuing Operations is overstated by €45.

e. Dyreng performed all work in 2008, and so should have recognized Revenues of €450 and Cost of Sales of €230. 2008 Gross Profits and Pre-tax Profit from Continuing Operations are both understated by €220 (= €450 – €230).

f. The sale of the advertising space is not a normal part of Dyreng's business model. It should, therefore, have been included as a Source of Other Operating Income, not as a Reduction to Cost of Sales. In addition, only half of the amount should have been recognized because Dyreng has not performed completely on this obligation. Gross Profit is, therefore, overstated by €960, whereas Pre-tax Profit from Continuing Operations is over-stated by €480.

4.35 continued.

A summary of the effects of reclassifying the items on gross profit and net income is provided below:

	Gross Profit	Pre-tax Profit
Original Amount	€ 4,795.3	€ 604.5
Effect of (a)	(240.0)	(240.0)
Effect of (b)	(700.0)	(700.0)
Effect of (c)	40.0	No effect
Effect of (d)	No effect	(45.0)
Effect of (e)	220.0	220.0
Effect of (f)	(960.0)	(480.0)
Revised Amount	€ 3,155.3	€ (640.5)

CHAPTER 5

STATEMENT OF CASH FLOWS: REPORTING THE EFFECTS OF OPERATING, INVESTING, AND FINANCING ACTIVITIES ON CASH FLOWS

Questions, Exercises, and Problems: Answers and Solutions

5.1   See the text or the glossary at the end of the book.

5.3   Accrual accounting attempts to provide a measure of operating performance that relates inputs to output without regard to when a firm receives or disburses cash. Accrual accounting also attempts to portray the resources of a firm and the claims on those resources without regard to whether the firm holds the resource in the form of cash. Although accrual accounting may satisfy user's needs for information about operating performance and financial position, it does not provide sufficient information about the cash flow effects of a firm's operating, investing, and financing activities. The latter is the objective of the statement of cash flows.

5.5   The indirect method reconciles net income, the primary measure of a firm's profitability, with cash flow from operations. Some argue that the relation between net income and cash flow from operations is less evident when a firm reports using the direct method. More likely, the frequent use of the indirect method prior to the issuance of FASB *Statement No. 95* probably explains its continuing popularity. Why might accountants have preferred the indirect method before FASB *Statement No. 95*? We have heard the following, but cannot vouch for this from first-hand experience: The direct method's format resembles the income statement. Where the income statement has a line for revenues, the direct method has a line for cash collections from customers. Where the income statement has a line for cost of goods sold, the direct method might have a line for payments to suppliers of income. Where the income statement has a line for income tax expense, the direct method has a line for income tax payments. The old-timers thought the resemblance of the two statements, the income statement and the direct method presentation in the statement of cash flows, would cause confusion. They were likely right, but we think its confusion is less than the confusion resulting from the indirect method. Some argue that preparing the direct method costs more. But you can see

Odd-numbered Solutions

5.5 continued.

> how easy preparing the direct method's version is; you learn how in this chapter. We have told those who say it's costly that they can hire any one of our students to do this for under $100. Are yours available?

5.7 The classification in the statement of cash flows parallels that in the income statement, where interest on debt is an expense but dividends are a distribution of earnings, not an expense. This is, in our opinion, a feeble explanation. The overarching rule seems to be that 'if it's in the income statement, it's operating.' We think that dividends on shares and interest on borrowings are both financing transactions, but we are in the minority.

5.9 This is an investing and financing transaction whose disclosure helps the statement user understand why property, plant and equipment and long-term debt changed during the period. Because the transaction does not affect cash directly, however, firms must distinguish it from investing and financing transactions that do affect cash flow. The rules used to allow the firm to report this single transaction as though it were two—the issue of debt for cash and the use of cash to acquire the property—and the appearance of both of these two in the so-called funds statement, the predecessor sometimes called the Statement of Changes in Financial Position.

5.11 The firm must have increased substantially its investment in accounts receivable or inventories or decreased substantially its current liabilities.

5.13 Direct Method: The accountant classifies the entire cash proceeds from the equipment sale as an investing activity. Indirect Method: As above, the entire cash proceeds appear as an investing activity. Because the calculation of cash flow from operations starts with net income (which includes the gain on sale of equipment), the accountant must subtract the gain to avoid counting cash flow equal to the gain twice, once as an operating activity and once as an investing activity.

5.15 (General Electric; derive cost of goods sold from data in the statement of cash flows.) (Amounts in Millions)

Cash Payments for Inventories for the Year	$ 64,713
Subtract: Increase in Inventories for the Year	(1,753)
Cost of Goods Sold for the Year	$ 62,960

5.17 (AMR; derive wages and salaries expense from data in the statement of cash flows.) (Amounts in Millions)

Cash Payments for Wages and Salaries for the Year	$ 8,853
Subtract: Decrease in Wages and Salaries Payable during the Year	(21)
Wages and Salaries Expense for the Year	$ 8,832

5.19 (Gillette; effect of borrowing and interest on statement of cash flows.) (Amounts in Millions)

Cash.. 250.00
    Bonds Payable..   250.00

Change in Cash	=	Change in Liabilities	+	Change in Shareholders' Equity	−	Change in Non-cash Assets
+250.0 Finan		+250.0				

October 1 bond issue. Refer to Exhibit 5.16. Line (11) increases by $250. Line (8) increases by $250.

Interest Expense... 3.75
    Interest Payable [(.06/12) x $250.00 x 3 Months].......   3.75

Change in Cash	=	Change in Liabilities	+	Change in Shareholders' Equity	−	Change in Non-cash Assets
		+3.75		−3.75		

Refer to Exhibit 5.16. Line (3) decreases by $3.75. Line (4) increases by $3.75.

5.21 (Effect of rent transactions on statement of cash flows.)

Rent Expense.. 1,200
    Prepaid Rent..   1,200

Change in Cash	=	Change in Liabilities	+	Change in Shareholders' Equity	−	Change in Non-cash Assets
				−1,200		−1,200

January rent expense.

Prepaid Rent.. 18,000
    Cash...   18,000

Change in Cash	=	Change in Liabilities	+	Change in Shareholders' Equity	−	Change in Non-cash Assets
−18,000 Opns						+18,000

Payment on February 1.

5.21 continued.

Rent Expense.. 16,500

Prepaid Rent.. 16,500

Change in Cash	=	Change in Liabilities	+	Change in Shareholders' Equity	–	Change in Non-cash Assets
				–16,500		–16,500

Rent expense for February through December; $18,000/12 per month = $1,500. 11 x $1,500 = $16,500.

All of these combine as:

Rent Expense.. 17,700

Prepaid Rent.. 300

Cash.. 18,000

Change in Cash	=	Change in Liabilities	+	Change in Shareholders' Equity	–	Change in Non-cash Assets
–18,000 Opns				–17,700		+300

All transactions of the year. Refer to Exhibit 5.16. Line (2) increases by $18,000. Line (3) decreases by $17,700. Line (5) increases by $300. Line (11) decreases by $18,000.

5.23   (Information Technologies; calculating components of cash outflow from operations.) (Amounts in Thousands)

a. Cost of Goods Sold for the Year... $ 11,596

Subtract: Increase in Accounts Payable for Inventories ..... (90)

Subtract: Decrease in Inventories for the Year.................... (66)

Cash Payments for Inventories for the Year......................... $ 11,440

b. Other Expenses, Total... $ 2,276

Subtract: Decrease in Prepayments for Other Costs .... (102)

Add: Decrease in Wages and Salaries Payable during the
    Year... 240

Cash Payments to Employees and Suppliers of Other Services for the Year .... $ 2,414

5.25 (American Airlines; working backwards from changes in buildings and equipment account.) (Amounts in Millions)

Buildings and Equipment (Original Cost)		Accumulated Depreciation	
Balance, 1/1	$16,825	Balance, 1/1	$ 4,914
Outlays during Year	1,314	Depreciation during Year..	1,253
	$18,139		$ 6,167
Balance, 12/31	17,369	Balance, 12/31	5,465
Retirements during Year	$ 770	Retirements during Year...	$ 702

Proceeds = Book Value at Retirement
= $770 – $702
= $68.

5.27 (Bamberger Enterprises; calculating and interpreting cash flow from operations.)

a.

Net Income	$ 290
Additions:	
Depreciation Expense	210
Decrease in Accounts Receivable	780
Decrease In Inventories	80
Decrease in Prepayments	100
Increase in Accounts Payable	90
Subtraction:	
Decrease in Other Current Liabilities	(240)
Cash Flow from Operations	$ 1,310

b. Bamberger Enterprises decreased its noncash current assets, particularly accounts receivable, generating positive cash flows. Although it repaid other current liabilities, the reduction in accounts receivable dominated and caused cash flow from operations to exceed net income.

5.29   (Marketing Communications; calculating and interpreting cash flows.)

a.   **MARKETING COMMUNICATIONS**
                 Comparative Statement of Cash Flows
                        (Amounts in Millions)

	2008	2007	2006
Operations			
Net Income	$ 499	$ 363	$ 279
Depreciation and Amortization	226	196	164
(Inc.) Dec. in Accounts Receivable	(514)	(648)	(238)
(Inc.) Dec. in Inventories	(98)	(13)	(35)
(Inc.) Dec. in Prepayments	(125)	10	(64)
Inc. (Dec.) in Accounts Payable	277	786	330
Inc. (Dec.) in Other Current Liabilities	420	278	70
Cash Flow from Operations	$ 685	$ 972	$ 506
Investing			
Acquisition of Property, Plant and Equipment	$ (150)	$ (130)	$ (115)
Acquisition of Investments in Securities	(885)	(643)	(469)
Cash Flow from Investing	$ (1,035)	$ (773)	$ (584)
Financing			
Long-term Debt Issued	$ 599	$ 83	$ 208
Common Stock Issued (Reacquired)	(187)	(252)	42
Dividends Paid	(122)	(104)	(88)
Cash Flow from Financing	$ 290	$ (273)	$ 162
Change in Cash	$ (60)	$ (74)	$ 84

b. Interpreting cash flow from operations for a marketing services firm requires a comparison of the change in accounts receivable from clients and accounts payable to various media. Marketing services firms act as agents between these two constituents. In Year 2006 and Year 2007, the increase in accounts payable slightly exceeded the increase in accounts receivable, indicating that Marketing Communications used the media to finance its accounts receivable. In Year 2008, however, accounts payable did not increase nearly as much as accounts receivable. It is unclear whether the media demanded earlier payment, whether the media offered incentives to pay more quickly, or some other reason. As a consequence, cash flow from operations decreased in Year 2008. Cash flow from operations continually exceeds expenditures on property, plant, and equipment. This relation is not surprising, given that marketing services firms are not capital intensive. Marketing Communications invested signif-

5.29 b. continued.

icantly in other entities during the three years. The classification of these investments as noncurrent suggests that they were not made with temporarily excess cash but as a more permanent investment. Cash flow from operations was not sufficient to finance both capital expenditures and these investments, except in Year 2007. The firm relied on long-term debt to finance the difference. Given the marketing services firms are labor-intensive, one might question the use of debt instead of equity financing for these investments. In fact, Marketing Communications repurchased shares of its common stock in Year 2007 and Year 2008. Thus, the capital structure of the firm became more risky during the three years.

5.31 (Effect of various transactions on statement of cash flows.)

Note to instructors: If you use transparencies in class, it is effective to flash onto the screen the answer transparency for some problem showing a comprehensive statement of cash flows. Then you can point to the lines affected as the students attempt to answer the question. It helps them by letting them see the possibilities. We use this question for in-class discussion. We seldom assign it for actual homework. A favorite form of question for examinations is to present a schematic statement of cash flows and to ask which lines certain transactions affect and how much. When we use this problem in class, we invariably tell students that it makes a good examination question; this serves to strengthen their interest in the discussion.

a. Amortization Expense 600
     Patent 600

Change in Cash	=	Change in Liabilities	+	Change in Shareholders' Equity	–	Change in Non-cash Assets
				–600		–600

(3) Decreases by $600; reduces net income through amortization expense.

(4) Increases by $600; amount of expense is added back to net income in deriving cash flow from operations.

No effect on net cash flow from operations or cash.

5.31 continued.

b. Factory Site... 50,000
    Common Stock.. 50,000

Change in Cash	=	Change in Liabilities	+	Change in Shareholders' Equity	–	Change in Non-cash Assets
				+50,000		+50,000

The transaction does not appear in the statement of cash flows because it does not affect cash. The firm must disclose information about the transaction in a supplemental schedule or note.

c. Inventory... 7,500
    Accounts Payable.. 7,500

Change in Cash	=	Change in Liabilities	+	Change in Shareholders' Equity	–	Change in Non-cash Assets
		+7,500				+7,500

(4) Increases by $7,500; operating increase in cash from increase in Accounts Payable.

(5) Increases by $7,500; operating decrease in cash for increase in inventory.

The net effect of these two transactions is to leave cash from operations unchanged, because the amounts added and subtracted change in such a way as to cancel out each other.

d. Inventory... 6,000
    Cash.. 6,000

Change in Cash	=	Change in Liabilities	+	Change in Shareholders' Equity	–	Change in Non-cash Assets
–6,000 Opns						+6,000

(2) Increases by $6,000; use of cash in operations.

(5) Increase the subtraction by $6,000; increase in Inventory account, subtracted.

5.31 d. continued.

(11) Decreases by $6,000.

The net effect is to reduce cash from operations and cash by $6,000 the cash expenditure for an operating asset, inventory.

e. Fire Loss 1,500
   Inventory 1,500

Change in Cash	=	Change in Liabilities	+	Change in Shareholders' Equity	–	Change in Non-cash Assets
				−1,500		−1,500

(3) Decreases by $1,500; net income goes down.

(4) Increases by $1,500; additions go up because inventory, not cash, was destroyed. OK to show as a reduction to a subtraction for Line (5).

No net effect on cash flow including cash flow from operations or cash.

f. Cash 1,450
   Accounts Receivable 1,450

Change in Cash	=	Change in Liabilities	+	Change in Shareholders' Equity	–	Change in Non-cash Assets
+1,450 Opns						−1,450

(1) Increases by $1,450 for collection of cash from customers.

(4) Increases by $1,450; operating increase in cash reflected by decrease in the amount of Accounts Receivable. OK to show as a reduction in the subtraction on Line (5).

(11) Increases by $1,450.

Cash flow from operations increases by $1,450, which causes cash to increase by $1,450.

5.31 continued.

g. Cash.. 10,000

      Bonds Payable... 10,000

Change in Cash	=	Change in Liabilities	+	Change in Shareholders' Equity	−	Change in Non-cash Assets
+10,000 Finan		+10,000				

(8) Increases by $10,000; increase in cash from security issue.

(11) Increases by $10,000.

h. Cash.. 4,500

      Equipment (Net)... 4,500

Change in Cash	=	Change in Liabilities	+	Change in Shareholders' Equity	−	Change in Non-cash Assets
+4,500 Invst						−4,500

(6) Increases by $4,500; increase in cash from sale of noncurrent asset.

(11) Increases by $4,500.

5.33   (Digit Retail Enterprises, Inc.; inferring cash flows from balance sheet and income statement data.)

a. Sales Revenue .... $ 270,000

    Less Increase in Accounts Receivable ($38,000 −
      $23,000)... (15,000)

    Less Decrease in Advances from Customers ($6,100 −
      $8,500)... (2,400)

    Cash Received from Customers during the Year.................... $ 252,600

b. Cost of Goods Sold... $ (145,000)

    Less Increase in Merchandise Inventory ($65,000 −
      $48,000)... (17,000)

    Acquisition Cost of Merchandise Purchased during the
      Year... $ (162,000)

5.33 continued.

c. Acquisition Cost of Merchandise Purchased during the Year (from Part *b*.).. $ (162,000)
    Plus Increase in Accounts Payable—Merchandise Suppliers ($20,000 – $18,000)... 2,000
    Cash Paid for Acquisitions of Merchandise during the Year.. $ (160,000)

d. Salaries Expense .... $ (68,000)
    Plus Increase in Salaries Payable ($2,800 – $2,100)............. 700
    Cash Paid to Salaried Employees during the Year .... $ (67,300)

e. Insurance Expense.. $ (5,000)
    Less Increase in Prepaid Insurance ($12,000 – $9,000)....... (3,000)
    Cash Paid to Insurance Companies during the Year............ $ (8,000)

f. Rent Expense... $ (12,000)
    Plus Decrease in Prepaid Rent ($0 – $2,000)......................... 2,000
    Plus Increase in Rent Payable ($3,000 – $0)........................... 3,000
    Cash Paid to Landlords for Rental of Space during the Year.. $ (7,000)

g. Increase in Retained Earnings ($11,800 – $11,500).............. $ 300
    Less Net Income... (9,600)
    Dividend Declared.. $ (9,300)
    Less Decrease in Dividend Payable ($2,600 – $4,200).......... (1,600)
    Cash Paid for Dividends during the Year............................... $ (10,900)

h. Depreciation Expense.. $ (20,000)
    Plus Increase in Accumulated Depreciation ($35,000 – $20,000)... 15,000
    Accumulated Depreciation of Property, Plant and Equipment Sold... $ (5,000)
    Cost of Property, Plant and Equipment Sold ($100,000 – $90,000)... 10,000
    Book Value of Property, Plant and Equipment Sold............. $ 5,000
    Plus Gain on Sale of Property, Plant and Equipment.......... 3,200
    Cash Received from Sale of Property, Plant and Equipment.. $ 8,200

5.35 (Dickerson Manufacturing Company; preparing and interpreting a statement of cash flows using a T-account work sheet.)

a. **DICKERSON MANUFACTURING COMPANY**
Statement of Cash Flows
For the Year

Operations:		
Net Income	$ 568,000	
Additions:		
Depreciation	510,000	
Loss on Sale of Machinery	5,000	
Increase in Accounts Payable	146,000	
Increase in Taxes Payable	16,000	
Increase in Short-Term Payables	138,000	
Subtractions:		
Increase in Accounts Receivable	(106,000)	
Increase in Inventory	(204,000)	
Cash Flow from Operations		$ 1,073,000
Investing:		
Sale of Machinery	$ 25,000	
Acquisition of Land	(36,000)	
Acquisition of Buildings and Machinery	(1,018,000)	
Cash Flow from Investing		(1,029,000)
Financing:		
Issue of Common Stock	$ 32,000	
Dividends Paid	(60,000)	
Bonds Retired	(50,000)	
Cash Flow from Financing		(78,000)
Net Change in Cash		$ (34,000)
Cash, January 1		358,000
Cash, December 31		$ 324,000

5.35 a. continued.

The amounts in the T-account work sheet below are in thousands.

Cash

√	358	

Operations

Net Income	(1)	568	106	(5)	Increase in Accounts Receivable
Depreciation Expense	(3)	510			
Loss on Sale of Equipment	(4)	5	204	(6)	Increase in Inventory
Increase in Accounts Payable	(9)	146			
Increase in Taxes Payable	(10)	16			
Increase in Other Short-Term Payables	(11)	138			

Investing

Sale of Machinery	(4)	25	1,018	(7)	Acquisition of Buildings and Machinery
			36	(8)	Acquisition of Land

Financing

Issue of Common Stock	(13)	32	60	(2)	Dividends
			50	(12)	Retirement of Bonds
	√	324			

Accounts Receivable

√	946	
(5)	106	
√	1,052	

Inventory

√	1,004	
(6)	204	
√	1,208	

Buildings and Machinery

√	8,678			
(7)	1,018	150	(4)	
√	9,546			

Accumulated Depreciation— Buildings and Machinery

		3,974	√	
(4)	120	510	(3)	
		4,364	√	

5.35 a. continued.

Land			Accounts Payable		
√	594			412	√
(8)	36			146	(9)
√	630			558	√

Taxes Payable			Other Short-Term Payables		
		274 √			588 √
		16 (10)			138 (11)
		290 √			726 √

Bonds Payable			Common Stock		
		1,984 √			1,672 √
(12)	50			32	(13)
		1,934 √			1,704 √

Retained Earnings		
		2,676 √
(2)	60	568 (1)
		3,184 √

b. Dickerson Manufacturing Company is heavily capital intensive. Its cash flow from operations exceeds net income because of the depreciation expense addback. Cash flow from operations appears substantial, but so are its expenditures for building and equipment. The firm's relatively low dividend payout rate suggests that it expects large capital expenditures to continue.

5.37 (CVS Caremark Corporation; interpreting a statement of cash flows based on the direct method for presenting cash flow from operations.)

a.

	2007
Net Revenues	$ 76,329.5
Less Cash Receipts from Revenues	(61,986.3)
Increase in Accounts Receivable	$ 14,343.2

b.

Cash Paid for Inventory	$ 45,772.6
Increase in Accounts Payable for Inventory	181.4
Purchases for Inventory	$ 45,954.0
Less Cost of Revenues	(60,221.8)
Change (Decrease) in Inventories for the Year	$(14,267.8)

Beginning Inventory + Purchases – COGS = Ending Inventory
Purchases – COGS = Ending Inventory – Beginning Inventory
Change in Inventory = Purchases – COGS

5.37 continued.

    c.   Amount Paid for Interest.. $ 468.2

           Interest Expense...   (434.6)

           Payment Exceeded Expenses by .... $ 33.6

    d.   The company acquired another large company. In fact, CVS acquired Caremark.

5.39 (Nordstrom Inc.; Derive cash flow from operations presented with the direct method from annual report presentation that uses the indirect method.)

Deriving Direct Method Cash Flow from Operations Using Data from T-Account Work Sheet (All Dollar Amounts in Millions)

Fiscal Year 2006 Operations	(a)	Indirect Method (b)	Changes in Related Balance Sheet Accounts from T-Account Work Sheet (c)	Direct Method (d)	
Net Sales............	$ 8,560.7	$ 17.1	= Provision for Bad Debt Expense	$ 8,577.8	
		(61.3)	= Accounts Receivable Increase	(61.3)	$ 8,515.5 Receipts from Customers
Cost of Goods Sold...	(5,353.9)	(38.6)	= Merchandise Inventories Increase	$ (5,392.5)	
		84.3	= Accounts Payable Increase	84.3	(5,308.2) Payments to Suppliers of Merchandise
Selling General and Administrative Expenses............	(2,296.9)	248.2	= Depreciation and Amortization, Net not Using Cash this Period	$ 248.2	
		37.4	= Stock-Based Compensation Expense	(2,259.5)	
		(4.7)	= Prepaid Expenses Increase	(4.7)	
		48.7	= Accrued Salaries, Wages and Related Benefits Increase	48.7	(1,967.3) Payments for S, G & A
Interest Expense	(42.8)	(42.8)		$ (42.8)	(42.8) Payments for Interest
Other Income, Net....	238.5	128.0	= Asset Backed Securities Decrease (Increase)	$ 366.5	
		(7.7)	= Other Assets Increase	(7.7)	
		23.5	= Other Current Liabilities Increase	23.5	
		30.7	= Deferred Property Incentives Increase	30.7	
		17.3	= Other Liabilities Increase	17.3	430.3 New Receipts for Other Items
Income Tax Expense	(427.6)	(58.3)	= Deferred Income Tax Benefits	$ (485.9)	
		43.6	= Tax Benefits from Stock-Based Payments	43.6	
		(38.3)	= Excess Stock Benefits from Stock-Based Payments	(38.3)	
		(5.5)	= Income Taxes Payable Decrease	(5.5)	(486.1) Payments for Income Taxes
Net Income	$ 678.0	$ 678.0			
		$ 1,142.4	= Cash Flow from Operations Derived via Indirect Method	$ 1,142.4	$ 1,142.4 Cash Flow from Operations Derived via the Direct Method

5.41 (Quinta Company; working backwards through the statement of cash flows.)

QUINTA COMPANY
Condensed Balance Sheet
January 1, 2008
($ in 000's)

Assets

Current Assets:

Cash...	$ 20	
Accounts Receivable....................................	190	
Merchandise Inventories.............................	280	
Total Current Assets............................		$ 490
Land..		50
Buildings and Equipment..............................	$ 405	
Less Accumulated Depreciation....................	(160)	245
Investments...		140
Total Assets...		$ 925

Liabilities and Shareholders' Equity

Current Liabilities:

Accounts Payable...	$ 255	
Other Current Liabilities..............................	130	
Total Current Liabilities.......................		$ 385
Bonds Payable		60
Common Stock...		140
Retained Earnings..		340
Total Liabilities and Shareholders' Equity...		$ 925

Shown below are T-accounts for deriving the solution. Entries (1)—(13) are reconstructed from the statement of cash flows. Changes for the year are appropriately debited or credited to end-of-year balances to get beginning-of-year balances. T-account amounts are shown in thousands.

	Cash			Accounts Receivable			Merchandise Inventories	
	20			190			280	
(1)	200	30 (4)	(4)	30		(5)	40	
(2)	60	40 (5)						
(3)	25	45 (6)						
(7)	40	130(10)						
(8)	15	200(13)						
(9)	10							
(11)	60							
(12)	40							
√	25		√	220		√	320	

5.41 continued.

Land		Buildings and Equipment		Accumulated Depreciation	
50		405			160
	10 (9)	(10) 130	35 (8)	(8) 20	60 (2)
√ 40		√ 500			200 √

Investments		Accounts Payable		Other Current Liabilities	
140			255		130
	40 (7)		25 (3)	(6) 45	
√ 100			280 √		85 √

Bonds Payable		Common Stock		Retained Earnings	
	60		140		340
	40 (12)		60 (11)	(13) 200	200 (1)
	100 √		200 √		340 √

Shown on the following page is the Transactions Spreadsheet. Entries (1)–(13) are reconstructed from the statement of cash flows. Changes for the year are appropriately debited or credited to end-of-year balances to get beginning-of-year balances. Amounts are shown in thousands.

5.41 continued.

Following, we show the Transaction Spreadsheet for those who prefer to work problems with it, not with T-accounts.

Transactions spreadsheet.

Transactions, By Number and Description

Balance Sheet Accounts	Balance: Beginning of Period (Derived)	1 Net Income for Year	2 Depreciation Expense	3 Increase in Accounts Payable	4 Increase in Accounts Receivable	5 Increase in Merchandise Inventories	6 Decrease in Other Current Liabilities	7 Sale of Investments	8 Sale of Buildings and Equipment	9 Sale of Land	10 Acquire New Buildings and Equipment	11 Issue Common Stock	12 Issue Bonds Payable	13 Dividends Paid in Cash	Balance: End of Period (Given)
ASSETS															
Current Assets:															
Cash	20	200	60	25	−30	−40	−45	40	15	10	−130	60	40	−200	25
Accounts Receivable	190				30										220
Merchandise Inventories	280					40									320
Total Current Assets	490														565
Noncurrent Assets:															
Land	50									−10					40
Building and Equipment	405								−35		130				500
Accumulated Depreciation	−160		−60						20						(200)
Investments	140							−40							100
Total Noncurrent Assets	435														440
Total Assets	925														1,005
LIABILITIES AND SHARE-HOLDERS' EQUITY															
Current Liabilities:															
Accounts Payable	255			25											280
Other Current Liabilities	130						−45								85
Total Current Liabilities	385														365
Noncurrent Liabilities:															
Bonds Payable	60												40		100
Total Noncurrent Liabilities	60														100
Total Liabilities	445														465
Shareholders' Equity:															
Common Stock	140											60			200
Retained Earnings	340	200												−200	340
Total Shareholders' Equity	480														540
Total Liabilities and Shareholders' Equity	925														1,005
Imbalance, if Any	-	-	-	-	-	-	-	-	-	-	-	-	-	-	-
Income Statement Accounts															
Income Summary															

5.43   (Spokane Corporation; interpreting the statement of cash flows.) (We have based this problem on the actual financial statements of the former Boise Cascade Corporation.)

a. Forest products companies are capital intensive. Depreciation is therefore a substantial non-cash expense each year. The addback for depreciation converts a net loss each year into positive cash flow from operations. Note that cash flow from operations increased each year as the net loss decreased.

b. Spokane Corporation had substantial changes in its property, plant and equipment during the three years. It likely built new, more efficient production facilities and sold off older, less efficient facilities.

c. For the three years combined, Spokane Corporation reduced its long-term debt and replaced it with preferred stock. The sales of forest products are cyclical. When the economy is in a recession, as apparently occurred during the three years, the high fixed cost of capital-intensive manufacturing facilities can result in net losses. If Spokane Corporation is unable to repay debt on schedule during such years, it causes expensive financial distress or even bankruptcy. Firms have more latitude with respect to dividends on preferred stock than interest on debt. Thus, a shift toward preferred stock and away from long-term debt reduces the bankruptcy risk of Spokane Corporation. Note that Spokane Corporation continued to pay, and even increase, dividends despite operating at a net loss. Most shareholders prefer less rather than more fluctuation in their dividends over the business cycle.

5.45   (Fierce Fighters Corporation; interpreting direct and indirect methods.)

(We have taken these data from the statements of cash flows of Northrop Grumman Corporation, which was for many years the only large company to use the direct method for present cash flows from operations. As we write this, they are still one of few. We use the particular years here, which were 1999, 2000, and 2001, because of the steady progression downwards, about ten percent per year, in cash flow from operations.)

a. We think this is hopeless. We cannot write a coherent explanation of the decline from these data alone, at least not without further analysis.

5.45 continued.

b. Some academics think that even the question is nonsense—that is, trying to explain changes in the data which themselves explain changes in cash. The statement of cash flows explains the change in the cash account from year to year. Consider that the statement of income and retained earnings explains the change in Retained Earnings from year to year. Most analysts think it sensible comparing income statements from one year to the next, to understand the causes of the change in income (which itself explains the causes of part of the changes in Retained Earnings). We think it sensible comparing statements of cash flows from one year to the next to explain the causes of the changes in cash flow from operations (which itself explains the causes of part of the changes in Cash).

In this case, the decline in cash flow from operations appears to result from a decreased margin of collections from customers for sales. The focus must be on what is going on with long-term and other sales contracts. From 2007 to 2008, we see increased payments to supplie4rs and employees that the analysis should investigate. We cannot be sure what is happening, but we can see where to inquire. Focus on those contracts, not on the changes in balance sheet operating accounts.

c. A reader can more easily interpret the direct method. The fundamental problem with the indirect method is that not a single number is itself a cash flow. So, changes in those numbers from year to year do not illuminate.

Odd-numbered Solutions

This page is intentionally left blank

CHAPTER 6

INTRODUCTION TO FINANCIAL STATEMENT ANALYSIS

Questions, Exercises, and Problems: Answers and Solutions

6.1   See the text or the glossary at the end of the book.

6.3   The adjustment in the numerator of rate of return on assets is for the *incremental* effect on *net* income of having versus not having interest expense. Because interest expense reduces taxable income and, therefore, income taxes otherwise payable, the tax savings from interest expense incrementally affect net income. The computation of the numerator must, therefore, incorporate this tax effect.

6.5   The profit margin for ROA ignores how a firm has financed its assets (that is, the extent of debt versus equity financing), whereas the profit margin for ROCE takes the mix of financing into account. A firm with increased pricing power in its markets, more efficient inventory controls, or benefits of economies of scale for administrative costs might experience increases in its profit margin for ROA. However, if interest rates increased or the firm engaged in substantial new borrowing, its profit margin for ROCE could decline because of increased financing costs.

6.7   Management strives to keep its inventories at a level that is neither too low so that it loses sales nor too high so that it incurs high storage costs. Thus, there is an optimal level of inventory for a particular firm in a particular period and an optimal inventory turnover ratio.

6.9   This statement suggests that the difference between the rate of return on assets and the after-tax cost of debt is positive but small. Increasing the amount of debt will require a higher interest rate that will eliminate this positive difference and financial leverage will work to the disadvantage of the common shareholders.

6.11   (CBRL Group and McDonald's; calculating and disaggregating rate of return on assets.) (Amounts in Millions)

   a. **CBRL Group:** $$\frac{\$76+(1-.35)(\$59)}{\$1,473} = 7.8\%.$$

      McDonald's: $$\frac{\$2,335+(1-.35)(\$417)}{\$29,183} = 8.9\%.$$

Odd-numbered Solutions

6.11 continued,

b.

	Rate of Return on Assets	=	Profit Margin for ROA	x	Total Assets Turnover Ratio

CBRL Group:

$$\frac{\$76+(1-.35)(\$59)}{\$1,473} = \frac{\$76+(1-.35)(\$59)}{\$2,352} \times \frac{\$2,352}{\$1,473}$$

$$7.8\% = 4.9\% \times 1.6$$

McDonald's:

$$\frac{\$2,335+(1-.35)(\$417)}{\$29,183} = \frac{\$2,335+(1-.35)(\$417)}{\$22,787} \times \frac{\$22,787}{\$29,183}$$

$$8.9\% = 11.4\% \times .8$$

c. McDonald's has a higher ROA, the result of a higher profit margin for ROA offset by a lower total assets turnover. McDonald's higher profit margin for ROA might result from its larger size, permitting it to benefit from spreading fixed costs over a larger sales base. McDonald's also generates revenues from franchise fees, which increase net income but not sales revenue. McDonald's lower total assets turnover might result from having the land and buildings of some of its franchisees on its balance sheet but not including the sales of these franchisees in its sales.

6.13 (Exxon Mobil; calculating and disaggregating rate of return on common shareholders' equity.) (Amounts in Millions)

a.

Year	Numerator	Denominator	Rate of Return on Common Shareholders' Equity
2005	$ 36,130	$ 106,471	33.9%
2006	39,500	112,515	35.1%
2007	40,610	117,803	34.5%

b. **Profit Margin for ROCE**

Year	Numerator	Denominator	Profit Margin for ROCE
2005	$ 36,130	$ 370,680	9.7%
2006	39,500	377,635	10.5%
2007	40,610	404,552	10.0%

6.13 b. continued.

Total Assets Turnover

Year	Numerator	Denominator	Total Assets Turnover
2005	$ 370,680	$ 201,796	1.84
2006	377,635	213,675	1.77
2007	404,552	230,549	1.75

Capital Structure Leverage Ratio

Year	Numerator	Denominator	Capital Structure Leverage Ratio
2005	$ 201,796	$ 106,471	1.90
2006	213,675	112,515	1.90
2007	230,549	117,803	1.96

c. The rate of return on common shareholders' equity was relatively steady during the three years. The profit margin for ROCE and the capital leverage ratio increased but the total assets turnover decreased. Sales increased at a higher rate in 2007 than in 2006 but the profit margin for ROCE declined. Part of the explanation for the decreased profit margin for ROCE might relate to higher interest expense from the higher capital structure leverage ratio. Exxon Mobil might have increased expenditures on exploration or development of petroleum resources in 2007, which lowered net income. The higher sales level should have provided Exxon Mobil with benefits of economies of scale, but any such benefits were offset by higher other expenses.

6.15 (Intel and Verizon Communications; profitability analysis for two companies.) (Amounts in Millions)

a.

	Rate of Return on Assets	=	Profit Margin for ROA	X	Total Assets Turnover
Company A:	$\dfrac{\$6,986}{\$52,010}$	=	$\dfrac{\$6,986}{\$38,334}$	X	$\dfrac{\$38,334}{\$52,010}$
	13.4%	=	18.2%	X	.74
Company B:	$\dfrac{\$6,999}{\$187,882}$	=	$\dfrac{\$6,999}{\$93,469}$	X	$\dfrac{\$93,469}{\$187,882}$
	3.7%	=	7.5%	X	.50

6.15 continued.

b.

	Rate of Return on Common Shareholders' Equity		Profit Margin for ROCE	x	Total Assets Turnover	x	Capital Structure Leverage Ratio
Company A:	$\dfrac{\$6,976}{\$39,757}$	=	$\dfrac{\$6,976}{\$38,334}$	x	$\dfrac{\$38,334}{\$52,010}$	x	$\dfrac{\$52,010}{\$39,757}$
	17.5%	=	18.2%	x	.7	x	1.3
Company B:	$\dfrac{\$5,510}{\$49,558}$	=	$\dfrac{\$5,510}{\$93,469}$	x	$\dfrac{\$93,469}{\$187,882}$	x	$\dfrac{\$187,882}{\$49,558}$
	11.1%	=	5.9%	x	.5	x	3.8

c. Company A is Intel and Company B is Verizon Communications. Both of these firms are fixed-asset intensive, so their total assets turnovers are small. Their ROAs and ROCEs differ with respect to profit margin and capital structure leverage. Semiconductors are technology-intensive products and can command high profit margins if the products are on the technology edge. Telecommunication services, on the other hand, are commodity products and are difficult to differentiate from competitors. The technological intensity of semiconductors leads to short product life cycles. Firms in this industry tend not to take on substantial debt because of the short product life cycles. Telecommunication services are somewhat less technology intensive, at least with respect to the need to create the technologies. Firms in the telecommunications industry have capital-intensive fixed assets that can serve as collateral for borrowing and a somewhat more stable revenue stream, relative to semiconductors.

6.17 (Mattel; analyzing inventories over three years.) (Amounts in Millions)

a.

Year	Numerator	Denominator	Inventory Turnover
2005	$ 2,806	$ 415	6.76
2006	3,038	380	7.99
2007	3,193	406	7.86

6.17 continued.

b.

Year	Numerator	Denominator	Days Inventory Held
2005	365	6.76	54.0
2006	365	7.99	45.7
2007	365	7.86	46.4

c.

Year	Numerator	Denominator	Cost of Goods Sold Percentage
2005	$ 2,806	$ 5,179	54.2%
2006	3,038	5,650	53.8%
2007	3,193	5,970	53.5%

d. Mattel experienced an increasing inventory turnover and a decreasing cost of goods sold to sales percentage between 2005 and 2006. Toys are trendy products. Mattel's products might have received rapid market acceptance, so that it was both able to move products more quickly and to achieve a higher gross margin on products sold. The faster turnover for trendy products means that Mattel would not need to mark down products in order to sell them or to incur additional storage costs. Mattel's cost of goods sold to sales percentage declined further in 2007 but its inventory turnover declined. Sales increased 9.1% [= ($5,650/$5,179) − 1] between 2005 and 2006 but only 5.7% [= ($5,970/$5,650) − 1] between 2006 and 2007. Perhaps Mattel increased inventory levels in 2007 expecting a larger sales increase than actually occurred. The unsold inventory resulted in a decrease in the inventory turnover rate.

6.19   (Relating profitability to financial leverage.)

a.

Case	Net Income Plus After-Tax Interest Expense[a]	After-Tax Interest Expense[b]	Net Income[c]	Rate of Return on Common Shareholders' Equity		
A	$12	$6.0	$ 6	$ 6/$100	=	6%
B	$16	$6.0	$ 10	$ 10/$100	=	10%
C	$16	$7.2	$ 8.8	$ 8.8/$80	=	11%
D	$ 8	$6.0	$ 2	$ 2/$100	=	2%
E	$12	$3.0	$ 9	$ 9/$100	=	9%
F	$10	$3.0	$ 7	$ 7/$100	=	7%

[a]Numerator of the rate of return on assets. In Case A, $12 = .06 x $200.

[b]After-tax cost of borrowing times interest-bearing debt. In Case A, $6.0 = .06 x $100.

[c]Net income plus after-tax interest expense minus after-tax interest expense. In Case A, $6 = $12 – $6.

b.   Leverage works successfully in Cases B, C, E, and F with respect to total debt. With respect to interest-bearing debt, leverage works successfully in Cases B and C.

6.21   (NIKE; calculating and interpreting short-term liquidity ratios.) (Amounts in Millions)

a.   **Current Ratio**

Year End	Numerator	Denominator	Current Ratio
2004	$ 5,528	$ 2,031	2.72
2005	6,351	1,999	3.18
2006	7,346	2,613	2.81
2007	8,077	2,584	3.13

Quick Ratio

Year End	Numerator	Denominator	Quick Ratio
2004	$ 3,349	$ 2,031	1.65
2005	4,087	1,999	2.04
2006	4,686	2,613	1.79
2007	5,342	2,584	2.07

6.21 continued.

b. **Cash Flow from Operations to Current Liabilities Ratio**

Year	Numerator	Denominator	Cash Flow from Operations to Current Liabilities Ratio
2005	$ 1,571	$ 2,015.0[a]	78.0%
2006	1,668	2,306.0[b]	72.3%
2007	1,879	2,598.5[c]	72.3%

[a].5($2,031 + $1,999) = $2,015.0.
[b].5($1,999 + $2,613) = $2,306.0.
[c].5($2,613 + $2,584) = $2,598.5.

Accounts Receivable Turnover Ratio

Year	Numerator	Denominator	Accounts Receivable Turnover Ratio
2005	$13,740	$ 2,191.0[a]	6.27
2006	14,955	2,322.5[b]	6.44
2007	16,326	2,439.0[c]	6.69

[a].5($2,120 + $2,262) = $2,191.0.
[b].5($2,262 + $2,383) = $2,322.5.
[c].5($2,383 + $2,495) = $2,439.0.

Inventory Turnover Ratio

Year	Numerator	Denominator	Inventory Turnover Ratio
2005	$ 7,624	$ 1,730.5[a]	4.41
2006	8,368	1,944.0[b]	4.30
2007	9,165	2,099.5[c]	4.37

[a].5($1,650 + $1,811) = $1,730.5.
[b].5($1,811 + $2,077) = $1,944.0.
[c].5($2,077 + $2,122) = $2,099.5.

6.21 b. continued.

Accounts Payable Turnover Ratio

Year	Numerator	Denominator	Accounts Payable Turnover Ratio
2005	$ 7,785[a]	$ 777.5[d]	10.01
2006	8,634[b]	863.5[e]	10.00
2007	9,210[c]	996.0[f]	9.25

[a]$7,624 + $1,811 − $1,650 = $7,785.   [d].5($780 + $775) = $777.5.

[b]$8,368 + $2,077 − $1,811 = $8,634.   [e].5($775 + $952) = $863.5.

[c]$9,165 + $2,122 − $2,077 = $9,210.   [f].5($952 + $1,040) = $996.0.

c. The short-term liquidity risk of Nike did not change significantly during the three-year period. The current and quick ratios fluctuated but are well above 1.0. Its cash flow from operations to current liabilities ratio declined slightly but is well above the 40% benchmark for a healthy company. Nike increased its accounts receivable turnover each year, providing operating cash flows. Its inventory turnover was relatively stable. Although the accounts payable turnover decreased between 2006 and 2007, providing operating cash flows, it does not appear that the slower rate of paying suppliers is due to a shortage of liquid assets. Another factor affecting the assessment of short-term liquidity risk is the increased profit margin, net income divided by revenues, between 2005 and 2006. The increasing profit margin ultimately provides more cash than if the profit margin had remained stable.

6.23 (Tokyo Electric; calculating and interpreting long-term liquidity ratios.) (Amounts in Billions of Japanese Yen)

a. **Long-Term Debt Ratio**

Year End	Numerator	Denominator	Long-Term Debt Ratio
2004	¥7,391	¥11,540 + ¥2,360	53.2%
2005	7,150	11,247 + 2,502	52.0%
2006	6,278	10,814 + 2,780	46.2%
2007	5,871	10,488 + 3,034	43.4%

Debt-Equity Ratio

Year End	Numerator	Denominator	Debt-Equity Ratio
2004	¥7,391	¥ 2,360	313.2%
2005	7,150	2,502	285.8%
2006	6,278	2,780	225.8%
2007	5,871	3,034	193.5%

6.23 continued.

b. **Cash Flow from Operations to Total Liabilities Ratio**

Year	Numerator	Denominator	Cash Flow from Operations to Total Liabilities Ratio
2005	¥ 1,411	.5(¥ 11,540 + ¥ 11,247)	12.4%
2006	936	.5(¥ 11,247 + ¥ 10,814)	8.5%
2007	1,074	.5(¥ 10,814 + ¥ 10,488)	10.1%

Interest Coverage Ratio

Year	Numerator	Denominator	Interest Coverage Ratio Earned
2005	¥ 538	¥ 165	3.3
2006	635	161	3.9
2007	651	155	4.2

c. The proportion of long-term debt in the capital structure declined during the three-year period, but still appears to be at a high level. The cash flow from operations to average total liabilities ratio is low, relative to the 20% level commonly found for healthy firms. The interest coverage ratio was low in 2005 but improved by 2007. If this firm were a manufacturer, we would probably conclude that its long-term liquidity risk level is high. However, Tokyo Electric has a monopoly position in its service area. Regulators would not likely allow the firm to experience bankruptcy. Its protected status allows it to carry heavier levels of debt than a nonregulated manufacturing firm.

6.25   (Effect of various transactions on financial statement ratios.)

Transaction	Rate of Return on Common Shareholders' Equity	Current Ratio	Liabilities to Assets Ratio
a.	No Effect	(1)	Increase
b.	Increase	Increase	Decrease
c.	No Effect	No Effect	No Effect
d.	No Effect	(2)	Decrease
e.	No Effect	Increase	No Effect
f.	Increase	Decrease	Increase
g.	Decrease	Increase	Decrease
h.	No Effect	Decrease	Increase

6.25 continued.

(1) The current ratio remains the same if it was one to one prior to the transaction, decreases if it was greater than one, and increases if it was less than one.

(2) The current ratio remains the same if it was equal to one prior to the transaction, increases if it was greater than one, and decreases if it was less than one.

6.27 (Target Corporation; calculating and interpreting profitability and risk ratios in a time series setting.) (Amounts in Millions)

a. 1. Rate of Return on Assets $= \dfrac{\$2,849 + (1 - .35)(\$669)}{.5(\$38,599 + \$46,373)} = 7.7\%.$

2. Profit Margin for Rate of Return on Assets $= \dfrac{\$2,849 + (1 - .35)(\$669)}{\$61,471} = 5.3\%.$

3. Total Assets Turnover $= \dfrac{\$61,471}{.5(\$38,599 + \$46,373)} = 1.4 \text{ times}.$

4. Other Revenues/Sales $= \dfrac{\$1,918}{\$61,471} = 3.1\%.$

5. Cost of Goods Sold/Sales $= \dfrac{\$41,895}{\$61,471} = 68.2\%.$

6. Selling and Administrative Expense/Sales $= \dfrac{\$16,200}{\$61,471} = 26.4\%.$

7. Interest Expense/Sales $= \dfrac{\$669}{\$61,471} = 1.1\%.$

8. Income Tax Expense/Sales $= \dfrac{\$1,776}{\$61,471} = 2.9\%.$

9. Accounts Receivable Turnover Ratio $= \dfrac{\$61,471}{.5(\$6,194 + \$8,054)} = 8.6 \text{ times}.$

10. Inventory Turnover Ratio $= \dfrac{\$41,895}{.5(\$6,254 + \$6,780)} = 6.4 \text{ times}.$

6.27 a. continued.

11. Fixed Asset Turnover $= \dfrac{\$61,471}{.5(\$22,681 + \$25,908)} = 2.5$ times.

12. Rate of Return on Common Shareholders' Equity $= \dfrac{\$2,849}{.5(\$15,633 + \$15,307)} = 18.4\%$.

13. Profit Margin for Return on Common Shareholders' Equity $= \dfrac{\$2,849}{\$61,471} = 4.6\%$.

14. Capital Structure Leverage Ratio $= \dfrac{.5(\$38,599 + \$46,373)}{.5(\$15,633 + \$15,307)} = 2.7$.

15. Current Ratio $= \dfrac{\$18,906}{\$11,782} = 1.6$.

16. Quick Ratio $= \dfrac{\$2,450 + \$8,054}{\$11,782} = .9$.

17. Accounts Payable Turnover Ratio $= \dfrac{(\$41,895 + \$6,780 - \$6,254)}{.5(\$6,575 + \$6,721)} = 6.4$ times.

18. Cash Flow from Operations to Current Liabilities Ratio $= \dfrac{\$4,125}{.5(\$11,117 + \$11,782)} = 36.0\%$.

19. Liabilities to Assets Ratio $= \dfrac{\$31,066}{\$46,373} = 67.0\%$.

20. Long-Term Debt Ratio $= \dfrac{\$16,939}{\$46,373} = 36.5\%$.

21. Debt-Equity Ratio $= \dfrac{\$16,939}{\$15,307} = 110.7\%$.

6.27 a. continued.

22. Cash Flow from Operations to Total Liabilities Ratio $= \dfrac{\$4,125}{.5(\$22,966 + \$31,066)} = 15.3\%.$

23. Interest Coverage Ratio $= \dfrac{(\$2,849 + \$1,776 + \$669)}{\$669} = 7.9$ times.

b. **Rate of Return on Assets (ROA)**
The ROA of Target Corporation increased between the fiscal years ended January 31, 2006 and 2007 and then decreased between fiscal years ended January 31, 2007 and 2008. The improved ROA between 2006 and 2007 results from an increased profit margin for ROA. The decreased ROA between 2007 and 2008 results from both a decreased profit margin for ROA and a decreased total assets turnover.

Profit Margin for ROA The changes in the profit margin for ROA result primarily from changes in the selling and administrative expense to sales percentage. Sales increased 12.9% between 2006 and 2007 but only 6.2% between 2007 and 2008. Most administrative expenses and some selling expenses are relatively fixed in amount. Variations in sales growth cause this expense percentage to vary as well.

Total Assets Turnover The total assets turnover declined between 2007 and 2008. Target Corporation experienced declines in all three individual asset turnovers. These declines are also likely due to the significant decline in the growth rate in sales in 2008. Customers perhaps purchased more on credit and did not pay as quickly. Target Corporation geared its inventory levels expecting a higher growth rate in sales than actually occurred, slowing the inventory turnover. The firm opened new stores expecting a larger growth in sales than occurred, slowing the fixed asset turnover.

c. **Rate of Return on Common Shareholders' Equity**
ROCE follows the same path as ROA, increasing between 2006 and 2007 and then decreasing between 2007 and 2008. The profit margin for ROCE increased between 2006 and 2007 and decreased between 2007 and 2008, primarily for the same reasons as the variations in the profit margin for ROA. The total assets turnover declined between 2007 and 2008 for the reasons discussed in Part b. above. The capital structure leverage ratio declined between 2006 and 2007 and increased between 2007 and 2008. The decreased capital structure leverage ratio between 2006 and 2007 resulted primarily from the retention of earnings. Total liabilities changed only slightly between the end of 2006

and 2007, but shareholders' equity increased because of the retention of earnings. The capital structure leverage ratio increased between 2007 and 2008 for two principal reasons: an increase in long-term debt and the repurchase of common stock. The increased capital structure leverage ratio in 2008 moderated the decline in ROA and resulted in a smaller decline in ROCE than would have otherwise been the case.

d. **Short-Term Liquidity Risk**

The current and quick ratios of Target Corporation vary inversely with changes in the accounts receivable and inventory turnovers. Increased turnovers for these assets between 2006 and 2007 resulted in declines in the current and quick ratios, whereas decreased turnovers for these assets between 2007 and 2008 resulted in increases in the current and quick ratios. When turnovers increase, the firm turns accounts receivable and inventories into cash more quickly, which the firm can use to pay current liabilities, invest in new stores, or pay dividends. When turnovers decrease, the opposite occurs. The levels of the current and quick ratios are not at troublesome levels in any year. The cash flow from operations to current liabilities ratio declined between 2006 and 2008 and was less than the 40% benchmark in 2008. The decline below 40% in 2008 occurred because of decreases in the accounts receivable and inventory turnovers and an increase in the accounts payable turnover. Either the sales growth rate will return to more normal levels in 2009 or Target Corporation will adjust its accounts receivable and inventory policies for a lower level of sales growth. Thus, Target Corporation does not exhibit high short-term liquidity risk.

e. **Long-Term Solvency Risk**

The debt ratios declined between 2006 and 2007 and increased between 2007 and 2008, as Part b. discusses. The cash flow from operations to total liabilities declined between 2007 and 2008 for the reasons discussed in Part d. Although this ratio is below the 20% benchmark in 2008, it is likely the result of the slower rate of sales growth experienced in that year. The interest coverage ratio declined in all three years but is not at a level in any year that would suggest high long-term liquidity risk. Thus, Target Corporation does not exhibit high long-term liquidity risk.

6.29   (The Gap and Limited Brands; calculating and interpreting profitability and risk ratios.)

The financial statement ratios on pages 6-16, 6-17, and 6-18 form the basis for the responses to the questions raised.

a. Limited Brands has a higher ROA in the fiscal year ended January 31, 2008, the result of a higher profit margin for ROA, offset by a lower total assets turnover. The higher profit margin for ROA results from a higher other revenues to sales percentage and a lower selling and administrative expenses to sales percentage. The higher other revenues results primarily from gains on the divestment of stores. The analyst would need to examine previous years to see if Limited Brands regularly sells stores or if the gains in fiscal year 2008 are unusual. The lower selling and administrative expense to sales percentage for Limited Brands is unexpected, given its smaller size and need to emphasize its more fashion-oriented product line. The lower cost of goods sold to sales percentage for The Gap occurs because its clothes are more standardized than those of Limited Brands, perhaps permitting lower manufacturing costs (for example, from quantity discounts on materials, fewer machine setups, less training of employees). The Gap probably also incurs fewer inventory writedowns from obsolescence because its clothing line is less fashion oriented.

The slower total asset turnover of Limited Brands is not due to either inventories or fixed assets, because Limited Brands has faster turnover ratios for these assets. Accounts receivable comprises such a small proportion of the total assets of Limited Brands that the differences in the accounts receivable turnover ratios exert very little influence on the total assets turnover. The difference in total assets turnover relates to the proportion of Other Noncurrent Assets on the balance sheet of each company. Other Noncurrent Assets averages 4.9% of total assets for The Gap for the two years, whereas it averages 35.2% of total assets for Limited Brands. Other Noncurrent Assets likely relates to goodwill and other intangibles from corporate acquisitions. These items increase total assets and reduce the total assets turnover.

The larger rate of return on assets of Limited Brands carries over to the rate of return on common shareholders' equity. In addition to larger operating profitability, Limited Brands carries substantially more financial leverage, enhancing its profitability advantage over The Gap.

6.29 continued.

b. The current and quick ratios vary considerably between fiscal 2007 and fiscal 2008, but neither company appears risky by these measures. Limited Brands pays its suppliers more quickly than The Gap. The cash flow from operations to average current liabilities ratios for The Gap and Limited Brands both exceed the 40% benchmark, particularly for The Gap. Although neither company appears to have much short-term liquidity risk, the ratios for Limited Brands are not as strong as those of The Gap.

c. Limited Brands has higher levels of debt than The Gap. Its cash flow from operations to total liabilities ratio is less than the 20% benchmark. Its interest coverage ratio is less than that of The Gap but not at a troublesome level. Thus, Limited Brands has higher long-term liquidity risk.

6.29 continued.

		The Gap	Limited Brands
1.	Rate of Return on Assets	$= \dfrac{\$867+(1-.35)(\$26)}{.5(\$7,838+\$8,544)} = 10.8\%$	$= \dfrac{\$718+(1-.35)(\$149)}{.5(\$7,437+\$7,093)} = 11.2\%$
2.	Profit Margin for Return on Assets	$= \dfrac{\$867+(1-.35)(\$26)}{\$15,763} = 5.6\%$	$= \dfrac{\$718+(1-.35)(\$149)}{\$10,134} = 8.0\%$
3.	Total Assets Turnover	$= \dfrac{\$15,763}{.5(\$7,838+\$8,544)} = 1.9$ times per year.	$= \dfrac{\$10,134}{.5(\$7,437+\$7,093)} = 1.4$ times per year.
4.	Other Revenues/Sales	$= \dfrac{\$117}{\$15,763} = .7\%.$	$= \dfrac{(\$146+230)}{\$10,134} = 3.7\%.$
5.	Cost of Goods Sold to Sales	$= \dfrac{\$10,071}{\$15,763} = 63.9\%.$	$= \dfrac{\$6,592}{\$10,134} = 65.0\%.$
6.	Selling and Administration Expenses to Sales	$= \dfrac{\$4,377}{\$15,763} = 27.8\%.$	$= \dfrac{\$2,640}{\$10,134} = 26.1\%.$
7.	Interest Expenses to Sales	$= \dfrac{\$26}{\$15,763} = .2\%.$	$= \dfrac{\$149}{\$10,134} = 1.5\%.$
8.	Income Tax Expenses to Sales	$= \dfrac{\$539}{\$15,763} = 3.4\%.$	$= \dfrac{\$411}{\$10,134} = 4.1\%.$
9.	Accounts Receivable Turnover	$= \dfrac{\$15,763}{.5(\$0+\$0)} = $ N/A.	$= \dfrac{\$10,134}{.5(\$355+\$176)} = 38.2$ times per year.
10.	Inventory Turnover	$= \dfrac{\$10,071}{.5(\$1,575+\$1,796)} = 6.0$ times per year.	$= \dfrac{\$6,592}{.5(\$1,251+\$1,770)} = 4.4$ times per year.

6.29 continued.

11. Fixed Asset Turnover

$$= \frac{\$15,763}{.5(\$3,267 + \$3,197)} = 4.9 \text{ times per year.}$$

$$\frac{\$10,134}{.5(\$1,862 + \$1,862)} = 5.4 \text{ times per year.}$$

12. Rate of Return on Common Shareholders' Equity

$$= \frac{\$867}{.5(\$4,274 + \$5,174)} = 18.4\%.$$

$$\frac{\$718}{.5(\$2,219 + \$2,955)} = 27.8\%.$$

13. Profit Margin for Return on Common Shareholders' Equity

$$= \frac{\$867}{\$15,763} = 5.5\%.$$

$$\frac{\$718}{\$10,134} = 7.1\%.$$

14. Capital Structure Leverage Ratio

$$= \frac{.5(\$7,838 + \$8,544)}{.5(\$4,274 + \$5,174)} = 1.7.$$

$$\frac{.5(\$7,437 + \$7,093)}{.5(\$2,219 + \$2,955)} = 2.8.$$

15. Current Ratio:

January 31, 2007:
$$= \frac{\$5,029}{\$2,272} = 2.2.$$

$$\frac{\$2,771}{\$1,709} = 1.6.$$

January 31, 2008:
$$= \frac{\$4,086}{\$2,433} = 1.7.$$

$$\frac{\$2,919}{\$1,374} = 2.1.$$

16. Quick Ratio:

January 31, 2007:
$$= \frac{\$2,644}{\$2,272} = 1.2.$$

$$\frac{(\$500 + \$176)}{\$1,709} = .4.$$

January 31, 2008:
$$= \frac{\$1,939}{\$2,433} = .8.$$

$$\frac{(\$1,018 + \$355)}{\$1,374} = 1.0.$$

17. Days Accounts Receivable

$$= \frac{365}{0} = \text{N/A.}$$

$$\frac{365}{38.2} = 9.6.$$

18. Days Inventory

$$= \frac{365}{4.1} = 89.0.$$

$$\frac{365}{4.4} = 83.0.$$

19. Accounts Payable Turnover

$$= \frac{(\$10,071 + \$1,796 - \$1,575)}{.5(\$1,006 + \$772)} = 11.6.$$

$$\frac{(\$6,592 + \$1,770 - \$1,251)}{.5(\$517 + \$593)} = 12.8.$$

6.29 continued.

20. Days Accounts Payable

$$= \frac{365}{11.6} = 31.5. \qquad \frac{365}{12.8} = 28.5.$$

21. Cash Flow from Operations to Current Liabilities

$$= \frac{\$2,081}{.5(\$2,433+\$2,272)} = 88.5\%. \qquad \frac{\$765}{.5(\$1,374+\$1,709)} = 49.6\%.$$

22. Liabilities to Assets Ratio:

January 31, 2007

$$= \frac{\$3,370}{\$8,544} = 39.4\%. \qquad \frac{\$4,138}{\$7,093} = 58.3\%.$$

January 31, 2008

$$= \frac{\$3,564}{\$7,838} = 45.5\%. \qquad \frac{\$5,218}{\$7,437} = 70.2\%.$$

23. Long-Term Debt Ratio:

January 31, 2007

$$= \frac{\$188}{\$8,544} = 2.2\%. \qquad \frac{\$1,665}{\$7,093} = 23.5\%.$$

January 31, 2008

$$= \frac{\$50}{\$7,838} = .6\%. \qquad \frac{\$2,905}{\$7,437} = 39.1\%.$$

24. Debt-Equity Ratio:

January 31, 2007

$$= \frac{\$188}{\$5,174} = 3.6\%. \qquad \frac{\$1,665}{\$2,955} = 56.3\%.$$

January 31, 2008

$$= \frac{\$50}{\$4,274} = 1.2\%. \qquad \frac{\$2,905}{\$2,219} = 130.9\%.$$

25. Cash Flow from Operations to Total Liabilities

$$= \frac{\$2,081}{.5(\$3,564+\$3,370)} = 60.0\%. \qquad \frac{\$765}{.5(\$5,218+\$4,138)} = 16.4\%.$$

26. Interest Coverage Ratio

$$= \frac{(\$867+\$539+\$26)}{\$26} = 55.1 \text{ times.} \qquad \frac{(\$718+\$411+\$149)}{\$149} = 8.6 \text{ times.}$$

6.31   (Scania; interpreting profitability and risk ratios.)

a. The increase in the profit margin for ROA results from decreases in the cost of goods sold to sales percentage and the selling and administrative expense to sales percentage. Both of these expenses include depreciation and other fixed costs. Scania experienced rapid sales growth in all three years and likely benefited from economies of scale as it spread these fixed costs over a larger sales base. Investment and net financing income as a percentage of revenues both declined and would not account for the increased profit margin for ROA.

b. Economies of scale (see the discussion in Part a. above) explains the decreased cost of goods sold to sales percentage but not the increasing inventory turnover. Any benefits from economies of scale affect both the numerator and denominator of the inventory turnover ratio. One possibility is that the firm instituted just-in-time manufacturing, which reduced raw materials and finished goods inventories and lowered inventory-carrying costs. Another possibility is that the sales mix shifted to higher margin, made-to-order vehicles. The high growth rates in sales also suggest that Scania enjoyed pricing advantages for its products and experienced little difficulty in selling its products quickly.

c. The growth rate in sales in 2007 was higher than in 2005 and 2006. Perhaps Scania had geared its productive capacity for 2007 for sales growth of approximately 12%. With a 19.4% sales growth in 2007, Scania had to utilize its plant capacity more intensely, driving up the fixed asset turnover. Another possibility is that Scania enjoyed pricing advantages in its markets and was able to increase sales revenue without having to raise production levels.

d. Scania must have experienced increases in cash, investments, or other assets besides accounts receivable, inventories, or fixed assets. The firm's annual report indicates that other noncurrent assets increased during these years.

e. Cash flow from operations likely increased as a result of the increase in the accounts receivable and inventory turnovers and the decrease in the days accounts payable. The explanation does not appear to be in the denominator of these cash flow ratios because total liabilities to assets did not change significantly and the long-term debt ratio declined.

f. The increase in the accounts receivable and inventory turnovers moderated the increase in current assets for these two items, thereby affecting the numerator of these ratios. The firm might have sold marketable securities and used the cash proceeds to acquire property, plant and equipment, pay dividends, or other purposes. Current liabilities likely increased as a percentage of total assets, given that the

6.31 f. continued.

liabilities to assets ratio increased 2.6 percentage points (= 72.9% – 70.3%) whereas the long-term debt ratio increased only 1.4 percentage points (= 21.7% – 20.3%).

g. Financial leverage works to the advantage of the common shareholders whenever the rate of return on assets exceeds the after-tax cost of borrowing. Given that ROCE exceeds ROA each year, the after-tax cost of borrowing must be less than ROA. The capital structure leverage ratio increased over the three year period, so Scania made increasing use of financial leverage to enhance ROCE.

6.33 (Target Corporation; preparing pro forma financial statements requires Appendix 6.1.)

a. See attached pro forma financial statements and related financial ratios.

b. Target Corporation needs to increase borrowing. Cash flow from operations is positive in each year. Thus, the financing need does not appear to be short term. Although Target Corporation increases long-term debt at the growth rate in property, plant and equipment, the amount invested in property, plant and equipment at the end of fiscal 2008 of $25,908 million is larger than long-term debt at the end of fiscal 2008 of $16,939. Growing long-term debt at the same growth rate as property, plant and equipment does not adequately finance the fixed assets. If we assume that long-term debt increases at 2 times the growth rate in property, plant and equipment, long-term debt (after reclassifications to current liabilities), grows 20% (= 2 times 10%) annually and provides adequate cash.

c. The pro forma financial statement ratios indicate a decreasing ROCE. The projected profit margin for ROCE and total assets turnover ratios are stable. The declining ROCE results from a declining capital structure leverage ratio. Even if we grow long-term debt at 2 times the growth rate in property, plant and equipment (see Part b. above), the capital structure leverage ratio and ROCE decline. The reason for the declining capital structure leverage ratio is that retained earnings grows faster than borrowing. Still further increases in borrowing to stabilize the capital structure leverage ratio results in too much cash on the balance sheet. Target Corporation would then need to increase its dividends or repurchase common stock with the excess cash. To stabilize the capital structure leverage ratio, Target Corporation needs to increase borrowing, increase the growth rate in dividends, or repurchase common stock.

6.33 a. continued.

The following pro forma financial statements were generated by a spreadsheet program that rounds to many decimal places. Rounding causes some of the sub-totals and totals to differ from the sum of the amounts that comprise them.

TARGET CORPORATION
PRO FORMA INCOME STATEMENT
YEAR ENDED JANUARY 31
(Amounts in Millions)

	2008	2009	2010	2011	2012	2013
Sales Revenue........	$ 61,471	$ 67,003	$ 73,034	$ 79,607	$ 86,771	$ 94,581
Other Revenues	1,918	2,010	2,191	2,388	2,603	2,837
Total Revenues..	$ 63,389	$ 69,013	$ 75,225	$ 81,995	$ 89,374	$ 97,418
Expenses:						
Cost of Goods Sold.................	$ 41,895	$ 45,629	$ 49,736	$ 54,212	$ 59,091	$ 64,409
Selling and Administration..	16,200	17,421	18,989	20,698	22,561	24,591
Interest................	669	934	911	906	894	913
Income Taxes.....	1,776	1,911	2,124	2,348	2,595	2,852
Total Expenses.........	$ 60,540	$ 65,895	$ 71,760	$ 78,164	$ 85,141	$ 92,766
Net Income	$ 2,849	$ 3,118	$ 3,465	$ 3,831	$ 4,233	$ 4,652
Less Dividends........	442	513	595	690	800	928
Increase in Retained Earnings..	$ 2,407	$ 2,606	$ 2,870	$ 3,141	$ 3,433	$ 3,724

Assumptions:

Growth Rate of Sales....	9.0%	
Other Revenues.............	3.0%	of sales
Cost of Goods Sold.........	68.1%	of sales
Selling and Administration Expense...............	26.0%	of sales
Interest Expense...........	5.0%	on average amount of interest bearing debt
Income Tax Rate...........	38.0%	of income before income taxes
Dividends........................	16.0%	growth rate

6.33 a. continued.

TARGET CORPORATION
PRO FORMA BALANCE SHEET
JANUARY 31
(Amounts in Millions)

	2008	2009	2010	2011	2012	2013
Cash	$ 2,450	$ 1,778	$ 768	$ 680	$ (668)	$ 292
Accounts Receivable	8,054	8,779	9,569	10,430	11,369	12,392
Inventories	6,780	7,390	8,055	8,780	9,571	10,432
Prepayments	1,622	1,768	1,927	2,101	2,290	2,496
Total Current Assets	$ 18,906	$ 19,715	$ 20,319	$ 21,991	$ 22,561	$ 25,612
Property, Plant and Equipment	25,908	28,499	31,349	34,484	37,932	41,725
Other Assets	1,559	1,559	1,559	1,559	1,559	1,559
Total Assets	$ 46,373	$ 49,773	$ 53,227	$ 58,033	$ 62,052	$ 68,896
Accounts Payable	$ 6,721	$ 7,507	$ 8,001	$ 8,902	$ 9,523	$ 10,561
Notes Payable	0	0	0	0	0	0
Current Portion— Long-Term Debt	1,964	1,951	1,251	2,236	107	2,251
Other Current Liabilities	3,097	3,376	3,680	4,011	4,372	4,765
Total Current Liabilities	$ 11,782	$ 12,833	$ 12,932	$ 15,149	$ 14,001	$ 17,577
Long-Term Debt	16,939	16,487	16,759	15,976	17,456	16,725
Other Noncurrent Liabilities	2,345	2,556	2,786	3,037	3,310	3,608
Total Liabilities	$ 31,066	$ 31,876	$ 32,477	$ 34,162	$ 34,767	$ 37,910
Common Stock	$ 68	$ 68	$ 68	$ 68	$ 68	$ 68
Additional Paid-in Capital	2,656	2,656	2,656	2,656	2,656	2,656
Retained Earnings	12,761	15,367	18,237	21,378	24,812	28,536
Accumulated Other Comprehensive Income	(178)	(194)	(211)	(231)	(251)	(274)
Total Shareholders' Equity	$ 15,307	$ 17,897	$ 20,750	$ 23,872	$ 27,284	$ 30,986
Total Liabilities and Shareholders' Equity	$ 46,373	$ 49,773	$ 53,227	$ 58,033	$ 62,052	$ 68,896

(See Following Page for Assumptions)

6.33 a. continued.

(Assumptions for Pro Forma Balance Sheet)

Assumptions:

Cash................................	PLUG					
Accounts Receivable	Sales Growth Rate					
Inventory	Sales Growth Rate					
Prepayments..................	Sales Growth Rate					
Property, Plant and Equipment..................	10.0% Growth Rate					
Other Assets	0.0% Growth Rate					
Accounts Payable Turnover	6.4	6.5	6.5	6.5	6.5	6.5
Merchandise Pur- chases...........................		46,240	50,401	54,937	59,882	65,271
Average Payables		7,114	7,754	8,452	9,213	10,042
Notes Payable................	No change					
Other Current Liabilities	Sales Growth Rate					
Long-Term Debt	Property, Plant and Equipment Growth Rate					
Other Noncurrent Liabilities	Sales Growth Rate					
Common Stock, APIC.............................	0.0% Growth Rate					
Accumulated Other Comprehensive Income.........................	Sales Growth Rate					

6.33 a. continued.

TARGET CORPORATION
PRO FORMA STATEMENT OF CASH FLOWS
FOR THE YEAR ENDED JANUARY 31
(Amounts in Millions)

Cash Flow Statement	2008	2009	2010	2011	2012	2013
Operations:						
Net Income	$ 2,849	$ 3,118	$ 3,465	$ 3,831	$ 4,233	$ 4,653
Depreciation	1,659	1,825	2,007	2,208	2,429	2,672
Other	485	195	213	232	253	275
(Inc.)/Dec. in Accounts Receivable	(602)	(725)	(790)	(861)	(939)	(1,023)
(Inc.)/Dec. in Inventory	(525)	(610)	(665)	(725)	(790)	(861)
(Inc.)/Dec. in Prepayments	(38)	(146)	(159)	(173)	(189)	(206)
Inc./(Dec.) in Accounts Payable	111	786	495	901	621	1,038
Inc./(Dec.) in Other Current Liabilities	186	279	304	331	361	393
Cash Flow from Operations	$ 4,125	$ 4,722	$ 4,869	$ 5,743	$ 5,979	$ 6,940
Investing:						
Acquisition of Property, Plant, and Equipment	$ (4,369)	$ (4,416)	$ (4,857)	$ (5,343)	$ (5,877)	$ (6,465)
Other Investing	0	0	0	0	0	0
Cash Flow from Investing	$ (4,369)	$ (4,416)	$ (4,857)	$ (5,343)	$ (5,877)	$ (6,465)
Financing:						
Inc./(Dec.) in Short-Term Borrowing	$ 500	$ 0	$ 0	$ 0	$ 0	$ 0
Inc./(Dec.) in Long-Term Borrowing	6,291	(465)	(427)	201	(649)	1,413
Inc./(Dec.) in Common Stock	(2,598)	0	0	0	0	0
Dividends	(442)	(513)	(595)	(690)	(800)	(928)
Other Financing	(44)	0	0	0	0	0
Cash Flow from Financing	$ 3,707	$ (978)	$ (1,022)	$ (489)	$ (1,449)	$ 485
Change in Cash	$ 1,637	$ (672)	$ (1,010)	$ (88)	$ (1,348)	$ 960
Cash, Beginning of Year	813	2,450	1,778	768	680	(668)
Cash, End of Year	$ 2,450	$ 1,778	$ 768	$ 680	$ (668)	$ 292
Cash Balance from Balance Sheet	2,450	1,778	768	680	(668)	292
Difference	$ 0	$ 0	$ 0	$ 0	$ 0	$ 0

(See Following Page for Assumptions)

6.33 a. continued.

(Assumptions for Pro Forma Statement of Cash Flows)

Assumptions:

Depreciation Growth Rate	Same as Property, Plant, and Equipment
Other Operating Add-backs	Change in Other Noncurrent Liabilities and Change in Accumulated Other Comprehensive Income
Other Investing Cash Flows............................	Change in Other Noncurrent Assets
Other Financing Cash Flows............................	Zero

TARGET CORPORATION
PRO FORMA FINANCIAL RATIOS

	2008	2009	2010	2011	2012	2013
Rate of Return on Assets......	7.7%	7.7%	7.8%	7.9%	8.0%	8.0%
Profit Margin for ROA............	5.3%	5.5%	5.5%	5.5%	5.5%	5.5%
Total Assets Turnover..........	1.4	1.4	1.4	1.4	1.4	1.4
Cost of Goods Sold/Sales	68.2%	68.1%	68.1%	68.1%	68.1%	68.1%
Selling and Administrative Expenses/Sales	26.4	26.0	26.0	26.0	26.0	26.0
Interest Expense/Sales	1.1%	1.4%	1.2%	1.1%	1.0%	1.0%
Income Tax Expense/Sales...	2.9%	2.9%	2.9%	2.9%	3.0%	3.0%
Accounts Receivable Turnover Ratio	8.6	8.0	8.0	8.0	8.0	8.0
Inventory Turnover Ratio.....	6.4	6.4	6.4	6.4	6.4	6.4
Fixed Assets Turnover Ratio.................................	2.5	2.5	2.4	2.4	2.4	2.4
Rate of Return on Common Equity.................................	18.4%	18.8%	17.9%	17.2%	16.6%	16.0%
Profit Margin for ROCE.........	4.6%	4.7%	4.7%	4.8%	4.9%	4.9%
Capital Structure Leverage Ratio.................................	2.7	2.9	2.7	2.5	2.3	2.2
Current Ratio	1.60	1.54	1.57	1.45	1.61	1.46
Quick Ratio	0.89	0.82	0.80	0.73	0.76	0.72
Cash Flow from Operations/ Current Liabilities	36.0%	38.4%	37.8%	40.9%	41.0%	44.0%
Accounts Payable Turnover Ratio.................................	6.4	6.5	6.5	6.5	6.5	6.5
Liabilities to Assets Ratio.....	67.0%	64.0%	61.0%	58.9%	56.0%	55.0%
Long-Term Debt Ratio...........	36.5%	33.1%	31.5%	27.5%	28.1%	24.3%
Debt-Equity Ratio	110.7%	92.1%	80.8%	66.9%	64.0%	54.0%
Cash Flow from Operations/ Total Liabilities	15.3%	15.0%	15.1%	17.2%	17.3%	19.1%
Interest Coverage Ratio........	7.9	6.4	7.1	7.8	8.6	9.2

This page is intentionally left blank

CHAPTER 7

REVENUE RECOGNITION, RECEIVABLES, AND ADVANCES FROM CUSTOMERS

Questions, Exercises, and Problems: Answers and Solutions

7.1 See the text or the glossary at the end of the book.

7.3 Both approaches apply accounting criteria to determine the amount and timing of revenue recognition when an arrangement with a customer (a contract) is not yet complete. The percentage-of-completion method uses the cost of work performed to date as the criterion. The accounting for a multiple element arrangement first determines the number of separable components (or deliverables) in the contract; the criterion for revenue recognition timing is the performance of a deliverable and the amount is based on the relative fair value of the deliverable, compared to the contract price as a whole.

7.5 a. This statement is valid. Most businesses ought not to set credit policies so stringent that they have no uncollectible accounts. To do so would require extremely careful screening of customers, which is costly, and the probable loss of many customers who will take their business elsewhere. So long as the revenues collected from credit sales exceed the sum of both selling costs and the cost of goods sold on credit, then the firm should not be concerned if some percentage of its accounts receivable are uncollectible.

b. When the larger uncollectible accounts result from a credit granting policy that increases income overall. A business might liberalize its credit policy by granting to a group of customers, who were not previously granted this privilege, the right to buy on account, with the intent of generating net revenues from the new credit customers that exceed the cost of goods sold to them and the selling expenses of executing the sales. The extension of credit to new customers can increase net income even though it results in more uncollectible accounts.

c. When the net present value of the receipts from selling to new customers is larger than the net present value of the costs of putting goods into their hands.

7.7   Manufacturing firms typically do not identify a customer or establish a firm selling price until they sell products. Thus, these firms do not satisfy the criteria for revenue recognition while production is taking place. In contrast, construction companies usually identify a customer and establish a contract price before construction begins. In addition, the production process for a manufacturing firm is usually much shorter than for a construction firm. The recognition of revenue at the time of production or at the time of sale does not result in a significantly different pattern of income for a manufacturing firm. For a construction company, the pattern of income could differ significantly.

7.9   Application of the installment method requires a reasonably accurate estimate of the total amount of cash the firm expects to receive from customers, but a firm cannot use this method unless cash collections are uncertain. The cost-recovery-first method does not require such an estimate.

7.11   Both customer returns and bad debts ultimately affect the net cash collected from customers. In accounting for estimated sales returns, the firm debits a contra revenue account (thus reducing net revenues) and in accounting for bad debt expense, the firm typically debits an expense account, which does not affect net revenues. The accounting is similar in that income is reduced in the period in which sales occur, not in the period in which the customer returns an item or a when a customer's account is determined to be uncollectible.

7.13   (Revenue recognition for various types of businesses.)

We have found this question to be an excellent one for class discussion because it forces the student to think about both revenue *and* expense timing and measurement questions. It also generates active student interest. Some of the items are relatively obvious while others require more discussion.

a. Time of sale.

b. Probably as work progresses using the percentage-of-completion method. Students normally assume the sale is to the United States Government. We ask them if it would make any difference if the sale was to a relatively weak government in Africa or South America. This question gets at the issue of whether the amount of cash the firm will receive is subject to reasonably accurate estimation.

c. Probably as the firm collects cash using the installment method.

d. At the time of sale.

e. At the time the firm picks citrus products and delivers them to customers. We ask students if their response would change if the citrus firm had a five-year contract at a set price to supply a particular quantity of citrus products to a citrus processor. The issue here is whether, given uncertainties about future weather conditions, the citrus grower will be able to make delivery on the contract.

f. AICPA *Statement of Position 79-4* stipulates that the firm should not recognize revenue until it meets all of the following conditions:

1. The firm knows the sales price.

2. The firm knows the cost of the film or can reasonably estimate the loss.

3. The firm is reasonably assured as to the collectibility of the selling price.

4. A licensee has accepted the film in accordance with the license agreement.

5. The film is available (that is, the licensee can exercise the right to use the film and all conflicting licenses have expired).

Revenue recognition from the sale of rights to the television network is appropriate as soon as the firm meets these conditions even though the license period is three years. The firm cannot recognize revenues from the sale of subsequent rights to others until the three-year licensing period has expired. An important question in this example is when to recognize the production costs as an expense. Should the firm recognize all of the costs as an expense on the initial sale to the television network? Or, should it treat some portion of the costs as an asset, matched against future sales of license rights? Most accountants would probably match all of the costs against revenue from the television network license agreement, unless the firm has signed other license agreements for periods beginning after the initial three-year period at the same time as the television license agreement.

g. At the time of sale of each house to a specific buyer.

h. At the time of sale to a specific buyer at a set price. This will vary, depending on who owns the whiskey during the aging process. We pose the following situation: Suppose a particular whiskey producer has an on-going supplier relationship with a whiskey distributor. The quantity purchased by the distributor and the price set depend on supply and demand conditions at the time aged whiskey is brought to the market. The supplier always purchases some minimum quantity. When should the firm recognize revenue? This question gets at the issue of measuring revenue in a reasonably reliable manner. You may also want to discuss the following other wrinkle. Suppose the whiskey producer doubles capacity. The firm cannot sell any of the whiskey produced from this new capacity for six years. What should the firm do with the costs of this new capacity?

i. As time passes and the firm lets borrowers use funds.

j. The alternatives here are (1) as customers make reservations, (2) as customers make some formal commitments to confirm their reservations, or (3) as the agency receives cash from commissions. The second alternative is probably best. However, past experience may provide sufficient evidence as to the proportion of reservations that customers ultimately confirm to justify earlier recognition.

k. At the completion of the printing activity.

l. The issue here is whether to recognize revenue when the firm sells stamps to food stores or when customers turn in the stamps for redemption. One might argue for revenue recognition at the time of sale of the stamps, since the seller must have some estimate of the redemption rate in setting the price for the sale of the stamps.

m. At the time, the wholesaler delivers food products to stores.

n. The issue here is whether to recognize revenue while the livestock is growing. A grower of timber faces a similar issue. For the reasons Part *h*. above discusses, it is probably best to await the time of delivery to a specific customer at an agreed upon price.

o. Probably during each period in a manner similar to the percentage-of-completion method. In practice firms use several methods.

7.15   (Meaning of allowance for uncollectible accounts.)

a. This characterization of the allowance account is incorrect. The allowance account normally has a credit balance and assets have debit balances. Firms do not set aside assets in an amount equal to the credit balance in the allowance account.

b. This characterization of the allowance account is incorrect for the same reasons as in Part *a*. above. Firms do not set aside cash in an amount equal to the balance in the allowance account.

c. This characterization of the allowance account is incorrect. The balance in the allowance accounts is an estimate of the amount from sales on account in all periods, not just the current period, that firms have not yet collected nor expect to collect.

d. This characterization of the allowance account is incorrect.

e. This characterization of the allowance account is correct.

f. This characterization of the allowance account is incorrect. The issue with uncollectible accounts is nonpayment of amounts owed not obligations to accept returns of goods from customers.

g. Although the allowance account normally has a credit balance, like liabilities, firms do not owe amounts to anyone if customers fail to pay.

h. This characterization of the allowance account for the same reasons as in Part *f*. above.

i. This characterization is incorrect. The balance in the allowance account is an estimate of the amount of sales in all periods, not just the current period, that firms have not yet collected and never expect to collect. A portion of the balance in the allowance account does likely result from recognizing bad debt expense during the current period. However, the balance also includes portions of bad debt expense of earlier periods as well. There is no way to know how much of the balance in the allowance account relates to provisions made during the current period versus earlier periods.

j. This characterization is incorrect. Deferred revenues, commonly called advances from customers, have credit balances and are liabilities. The firm owes cash to those making advances if the firm does not deliver the goods and services as promised. The firm does not receive cash when it credits the allowance for uncollectibles account, nor does it owe cash to customers.

7.15 continued

    k. This characterization is incorrect. When firms credit the allowance account, they debit bad debt expense, a part of the retained earnings account. Thus, the allowance account indirectly links with retained earnings but is not an accurate characterization of its nature.

7.17   (Bed, Bath & Beyond; revenue recognition at and after time of sale.)

Cash..	556.5
Sales Revenue..	280.0
Advances from Customer (Gift Certificate)............	250.0
Sales Taxes Payable...	26.5

Assets	=	Liabilities	+	Shareholders' Equity	(Class.)
		+250.0			
+556.5		+26.5		+280.0	IncSt → RE

7.19   (Lentiva, revenue recognition at time of sale.)

Fair Value of Laptop Component (= $1,500 x 50,000 Laptops)...	$ 75,000,000
Fair Value of Training Component (= $100 x 50,000 Laptops)...	5,000,000
Total	$ 80,000,000

Journal Entries on January 1, 2008

Cash 15,000,000	
Accounts Receivable.. 60,000,000	
Sales Revenue..	70,312,500
Advances from Customer..	4,687,500

Assets	=	Liabilities	+	Shareholders' Equity	(Class.)
+15,000,000		+4,687,500		+70,312,500	IncSt → RE

To record the sale of the laptops and training services.

The laptop sales meet the criteria for recognizing revenue equaling $70,312,500 [= ($75,000,000/$80,000,000) x $75,000,000]. The training revenue equaling $4,687,500 [= ($5,000,000/$80,000,000) x $75,000,000] is deferred and will be earned as training services are delivered.

Cost of Goods Sold.. 60,000,000

    Inventory.. 60,000,000

Assets	=	Liabilities	+	Shareholders' Equity	(Class.)
–60,000,000				–60,000,000	IncSt → RE

To record the cost of the laptop sales.

Journal Entries on December 31, 2008

Advances from Customer.. 2,343,750

Cost of Training Services... 1,250,000

    Sales Revenue.. 2,343,750

    Salaries Payable.. 1,250,000

Assets	=	Liabilities	+	Shareholders' Equity	(Class.)
		–2,343,750		+2,343,750	IncSt → RE
		+1,250,000		–1,250,000	IncSt → RE

To record the revenues and expenses for training services provided during 2008. Revenues equal $2,343,750 (= $4,687,500/2 years); Expenses equal $1,250,000 [= ($50 per laptop x 50,000 laptops)/2 years].

Journal Entries on December 31, 2009

Advances from Customer.. 2,343,750

Cost of Training Services... 1,250,000

    Sales Revenue.. 2,343,750

    Salaries Payable.. 1,250,000

Assets	=	Liabilities	+	Shareholders' Equity	(Class.)
		–2,343,750		+2,343,750	IncSt → RE
		+1,250,000		–1,250,000	IncSt → RE

To record the revenues and expenses for training services provided during 2009. Revenues equal $2,343,750 (= $4,687,500/2 years); Expenses equal $1,250,000 [= ($50 per laptop x 50,000 laptops)/2 years].

7.21   (Abson Corporation; journal entries for service contracts.)

a. **1/31/08–3/31/08**
Cash.. 180,000
    Service Contract Fees Received in Advance   180,000

Assets	=	Liabilities	+	Shareholders' Equity	(Class.)
+180,000		−180,000			

To record sale of 300 annual contracts.

3/31/08
Service Contract Fees Received in Advance............. 22,500
    Contract Revenues   22,500

Assets	=	Liabilities	+	Shareholders' Equity	(Class.)
		−22,500		+22,500	IncSt → RE

To recognize revenue on 200 contracts sold during
the first quarter; 1.5/12 x $180,000.

1/01/08–3/31/08
Service Expenses... 32,000
    Cash (and Other Assets and Liabilities)................   32,000

Assets	=	Liabilities	+	Shareholders' Equity	(Class.)
−32,000				−32,000	IncSt → RE

4/01/08–6/30/08
Cash.. 300,000
    Service Contract Fees Received in Advance   300,000

Assets	=	Liabilities	+	Shareholders' Equity	(Class.)
+300,000		−300,000			

To record the sale of 500 annual contracts.

7.21 a. continued

6/30/08

Service Contract Fees Received in Advance............. 82,500

    Contract Revenues..   82,500

Assets	=	Liabilities	+	Shareholders' Equity	(Class.)
		−82,500		+82,500	IncSt → RE

To recognize revenue on 500 contracts sold during the
second quarter and 300 contracts outstanding from
the first quarter:

    First Quarter:

        3/12   x $180,000 = $ 45,000

    Second Quarter:

        1.5/12 x $300,000 =   37,500

                                      $ 82,500

4/01/08–6/30/08

Service Expenses 71,000

    Cash (and Other Assets and Liabilities)................   71,000

Assets	=	Liabilities	+	Shareholders' Equity	(Class.)
−71,000				−71,000	IncSt → RE

7/01/08–9/30/08

Cash... 240,000

    Service Contract Fees Received in Advance   240,000

Assets	=	Liabilities	+	Shareholders' Equity	(Class.)
+240,000		−240,000			

To record the sale of 400 annual contracts.

7.21 a. continued

9/30/08

Service Contract Fees Received in Advance.............. 150,000
    Contract Revenues 150,000

Assets	=	Liabilities	+	Shareholders' Equity	(Class.)
		−150,000		+150,000	IncSt → RE

To recognize revenue on 400 contracts sold during the
third quarter and 800 contracts outstanding from sales
in prior quarters:

    First Quarter Sales:
        3/12   x $180,000   = $ 45,000
    Second Quarter Sales:
        3/12   x $300,000   =   75,000
    Third Quarter Sales:
        1.5/12 x $240,000   =   30,000
                              = $ 150,000

7/01/08–9/30/08

Service Expenses 105,000
    Cash (and Other Assets and Liabilities)............... 105,000

Assets	=	Liabilities	+	Shareholders' Equity	(Class.)
−105,000				−105,000	IncSt → RE

b. Balances in Service Contract Fees Received in Advance Account:

January 1, 2008	--
Less First Quarter Expirations....................................	$ (22,500)
Plus First Quarter Sales...	180,000
March 31, 2008...	$ 157,500
Less Second Quarter Expirations	(82,500)
Plus Second Quarter Sales..	300,000
June 30, 2008..	$ 375,000
Less Third Quarter Expirations	(150,000)
Plus Third Quarter Sales	240,000
September 30, 2008	$ 465,000
Less Fourth Quarter Expirations	(195,000)
Plus Fourth Quarter Sales	120,000
December 31, 2008..	$ 390,000

7.21 b. continued

OR

Contracts	x	Balance Remaining	x	$600	=	Amount
300	x	1.5/12	x	$600	=	$ 22,500
500	x	4.5/12	x	$600	=	112,500
400	x	7.5/12	x	$600	=	150,000
200	x	10.5/12	x	$600	=	105,000
						$ 390,000

7.23   (York Company; aging accounts receivable.)

Bad Debt Expense 9,050
    Allowance for Uncollectible Accounts 9,050

Assets	=	Liabilities	+	Shareholders' Equity	(Class.)
−9,050				−9,050	IncSt → RE

The Allowance account requires a balance of $25,050 [= (.005 x $1,200,000) + (.01 x $255,000) + (.10 x $75,000) + (.30 x $30,000)]. The adjusting entry *increases* the Allowance account by $9,050 (= $25,050 − $16,000) and recognizes Bad Debt Expense for the period by the same amount.

7.25   (Hamilia S.A.; aging accounts receivable.)

Allowance for Uncollectible Accounts 21,500
    Bad Debt Expense 21,500

Assets	=	Liabilities	+	Shareholders' Equity	(Class.)
+21,500				+21,500	IncSt → RE

The Allowance account requires a balance of €75,100 [= (.005 x €980,000) + (.03 x €130,000) + (.15 x €102,000) + (.75 x €68,000)]. The adjusting entry *decreases* the Allowance account by €21,500 (= €96,600 − €75,100) and recognizes a credit to Bad Debt Expense by the same amount.

7.27 (Pandora Company; allowance method: reconstructing journal entry from events.)

Bad Debt Expense... 3,700
   Allowance for Uncollectible Accounts...........................   3,700

Assets	=	Liabilities	+	Shareholders' Equity	(Class.)
–3,700				–3,700	IncSt → RE

Writeoff of $2,200 + Ending Balance of Allowance of $5,000 – Beginning Balance of $3,500 = $3,700.

7.29 (Reconstructing events from journal entries.)

a. Estimated bad debt expense for the period is $2,300 using the allowance method.

b. A firm writes off specific customers' accounts totaling $450 as uncollectible under the allowance method.

c. A firm realizes that its expected uncollectibles in the future are less than the amount already reserved in the allowance for uncollectibles. It records an adjustment to Bad Debt Expense for $200 to reduce the balance in the Allowance for Uncollectibles to the necessary (lower) amount.

7.31 (Schneider Corporation; journal entries for the allowance method.)

a. **2006**
Bad Debt Expense (.02 x $750,000) 15,000
   Allowance for Uncollectible Accounts   15,000

Assets	=	Liabilities	+	Shareholders' Equity	(Class.)
–15,000				–15,000	IncSt → RE

Allowance for Uncollectible Accounts......................... 1,300
   Accounts Receivable..   1,300

Assets	=	Liabilities	+	Shareholders' Equity	(Class.)
+1.300					
–1,300					

7.31 a. continued.

2007

Bad Debt Expense (.02 x $1,200,000)........................ 24,000
    Allowance for Uncollectible Accounts 24,000

Assets	=	Liabilities	+	Shareholders' Equity	(Class.)
−24,000				−24,000	IncSt → RE

Allowance for Uncollectible Accounts........................ 11,200
    Accounts Receivable....................................... 11,200

Assets	=	Liabilities	+	Shareholders' Equity	(Class.)
+11.200					
−11,200					

2008

Bad Debt Expense (.02 x $2,400,000)........................ 48,000
    Allowance for Uncollectible Accounts 48,000

Assets	=	Liabilities	+	Shareholders' Equity	(Class.)
−48,000				−48,000	IncSt → RE

Allowance for Uncollectible Accounts........................ 23,600
    Accounts Receivable....................................... 23,600

Assets	=	Liabilities	+	Shareholders' Equity	(Class.)
+23.600					
−23,600					

b. Yes. The actual loss experience is 1.9% (= $82,500/$4,350,000) of sales on account for sales during 2006 through 2008.

7.33 (WollyMartin; effects of transactions involving suppliers and customers on cash flows.)

a. €127,450 = €130,000 − (€8,600 − €8,000) + (€750 − €700) − €2,000
         = €130,000 − €600 + €50 − €2,000.

b. €84,700 = €85,000 − (€7,500 − €7,000) + (€11,200 − €11,000)
         = €85,000 − €500 + $200.

7.35 (Raytheon; percentage-of-completion and completed contract methods of income recognition.)

Percentage-of-Completion Method

Year	Degree of Completion	Revenue	Expense	Income
2006	$200/$700 = 28.6%	$ 257.4	$ 200	$ 57.4
2007	$200/$700 = 28.6%	257.4	200	57.4
2008	$300/$700 = 42.8%	385.2	300	85.2
		$ 900.0	$ 700	$ 200.0

Completed Contract Method

Year	Revenue	Expense	Income
2006	--	--	--
2007	--	--	--
2008	$ 900	$ 700	$ 200
	$ 900	$ 700	$ 200

7.37 (Boeing; installment and cost recovery methods of income recognition.) (Amounts in Millions)

Installment Method

Year	Revenue	(PLUG) Expense[b]	Income[a]
2007	$ 24	$ 19	$ 5
2008	24	19	5
2009	24	19	5
	$ 72	$ 57	$ 15

[a]Income = Gross Margin Percentage $\times$ Cash Received, or ($15/$72) $\times$ $24 = $5 million.

[b]Expense = Revenue – Income = $24 – $5 = $19 million.

Cost-Recovery-First Method

Year	Revenue	Expense	Income
2007	$ 24	$ 24	$ -0-
2008	24	24	-0-
2009	24	9	15
	$ 72	$ 57	$ 15

7.39   (Hilton Hotels; revenue recognition at or after time of sale.)

a. **February 2, 2008:** Journal entry to record internet special reservation for four nights at $150 per night.

Cash.. 600
   Advances from Customer.. 600

Assets	=	Liabilities	+	Shareholders' Equity	(Class.)
+600		+600			

February 20, 2008: Journal entry to record revenue after services supplied.

Advances from Customer.. 600
   Sales Revenue... 600

Assets	=	Liabilities	+	Shareholders' Equity	(Class.)
		−600		+600	IncSt → RE

b. **February 2, 2008:** Journal entry to record internet special reservation for four nights at $150 per night.

Cash.. 600
   Advances from Customer.. 600

Assets	=	Liabilities	+	Shareholders' Equity	(Class.)
+600		+600			

February 14, 2008: Journal entry to record revenue after customer cancels the reservation.

Advances from Customers.. 600
   Sales Revenue... 600

Assets	=	Liabilities	+	Shareholders' Equity	(Class.)
		−600		+600	IncSt → RE

7.39 continued.

c. **February 2, 2008:** Journal entry to record refundable room reservation for four nights at $220 per night.

Cash.. 880
    Advances from Customer... 880

Assets	=	Liabilities	+	Shareholders' Equity	(Class.)
+880		+880			

February 20, 2008: Journal entry to record revenue after services supplied.

Advances from Customer... 880
    Sales Revenue... 880

Assets	=	Liabilities	+	Shareholders' Equity	(Class.)
		−880		+880	IncSt → RE

d. **February 2, 2008:** Journal entry to record refundable room reservation for four nights at $220 per night.

Cash.. 880
    Advances from Customer... 880

Assets	=	Liabilities	+	Shareholders' Equity	(Class.)
+880		+880			

February 14, 2008: Journal entry to record cancellation of refundable room reservation.

Advances from Customer... 880
    Cash 880

Assets	=	Liabilities	+	Shareholders' Equity	(Class.)
−880		−880			

7.39 continued.

e. **February 2, 2008:** Journal entry to record refundable room reservation for four nights at $220 per night.

Cash... 880
    Advances from Customer.. 880

Assets	=	Liabilities	+	Shareholders' Equity	(Class.)
+880		+880			

February 16, 2008: Journal entry to record revenue (for one night) after customer cancels the reservation after 3 p.m., and to refund the remaining three nights.

Advances from Customer... 880
    Sales Revenue.. 220
    Cash 660

Assets	=	Liabilities	+	Shareholders' Equity	(Class.)
−660		−880		+220	IncSt → RE

7.41 (Kajima Corporation; analyzing changes in accounts receivable.) (Amounts in Millions)

a.

	2007	2006	2005
(1) Sales on Account			
Accounts Receivable ...	1,891,466	1,775,274	1,687,380
Sales Revenue	1,891,466	1,775,274	1,687,380

Assets	=	Liabilities	+	Shareholders' Equity	(Class.)
+1,891,466				+1,891,466	IncSt → RE
+1,775,274				+1,775,274	IncSt → RE
+1,687,380				+1,687,380	IncSt → RE

7-17

7.41 a. continued.

		2007	2006	2005

(2) Provision for Estimated Uncollectible Accounts

Bad Debt Expense........ 1,084   3,152   2,999

Allowance for Uncollectible Accounts 1,084   3,152   2,999

Assets	=	Liabilities	+	Shareholders' Equity	(Class.)
−1,084				−1,084	IncSt → RE
−3,152				−3,152	IncSt → RE
−2,999				−2,999	IncSt → RE

(3) Write Off of Actual Bad Debts

Allowance for Uncollectible Accounts .... 6,471[a]   820[b]   8,099[c]

Accounts Receivable......................... 6,471   820   8,099

[a] ¥10,673 + ¥1,084 − ¥5,286 = ¥6,471.

[b] ¥8,341 + ¥3,152 − ¥10,673 = ¥820.

[c] ¥13,441 + ¥2,999 − ¥8,341 = ¥8,099.

Assets	=	Liabilities	+	Shareholders' Equity	(Class.)
+6,471/−6,471					
+820/−820					
+8,099/−8,099					

7.41 a. continued.

	2007	2006	2005
(4) Collection of Cash from Customers			
Cash	1,723,338[d]	1,761,584[e]	1,606,456[f]
Accounts Receivable	1,723,338	1,761,584	1,606,456

[d]¥468,387 + ¥1,891,466 − ¥6,471 − ¥630,044 = ¥1,723,338.

[e]¥455,517 + ¥1,775,274 − ¥820 − ¥468,387 = ¥1,761,584.

[f]¥382,692 + ¥1,687,380 − ¥8,099 − ¥455,517 = ¥1,606,456.

Assets	=	Liabilities	+	Shareholders' Equity	(Class.)
+1,723,338/ −1,723,338					
+1,761,584/ −1,761,584					
+1,606,456/ −1,606,456					

b.

	2007	2006	2005

(1) Accounts Receivable Turnover
2007: ¥1,891,466/.5(¥624,758 + ¥457,714)...3.49
2006: ¥1,775,274/.5(¥457,714 + ¥447,176)...   3.92
2005: ¥1,687,380/.5(¥447,176 + ¥369,251)...   4.13

(2) Bad Debt Expense/Revenues
2007: ¥1,084/¥1,891,466...0.06%
2006: ¥3,152/¥1,775,274...   0.18%
2005: ¥2,999/¥1,687,380...   0.18%

(3) Allowance for Uncollectible Accounts/ Gross Accounts Receivable at End of Year
2007: ¥5,286/¥630,044...0.84%
2006: ¥10,673/¥468,387...   2.28%
2005: ¥8,341/¥455,517...   1.83%

(4) Accounts Written Off/Average Gross Accounts Receivable
2007: ¥6,471/.5(¥630,044 + ¥468,387)...1.18%
2006: ¥820/.5(¥468,387 + ¥455,517)...   0.18%
2005: ¥8,099/.5(¥455,517 + ¥382,692)...   1.93%

7.41 continued.

    c.   The accounts receivable turnover ratio decreased during the three-year period from 4.13 (in 2005) to 3.92 (in 2006) to 3.49 (in 2007). The firm decreased the amount of accounts written off between 2005 and 2006, from 1.54% to 0.18%, leading to a decrease in the allowance account relative to the gross accounts receivable. The firm decreased its provision for estimated uncollectible accounts in 2007 (the percentage of bad debt expense to sales declined from 0.18% in 2005 and 2006 to 0.06% in 2007), consistent with the build up in the allowance account. The accounts written off as a percentage of gross accounts receivable increased in 2007, from 0.18% in 2006 to 1.47% in 2007, perhaps because credit conditions worsened in that year. The latter is consistent with the decrease in the accounts receivable turnover ratio, from 3.92 in 2006 to 3.49 in 2007.

7.43   (Aracruz Celulose; analyzing changes in accounts receivable.) (Amounts in Thousands)

    a.   Carrying Value = Accounts Receivable, Net.
       For 2007: $361,603 (= $365,921 – $4,318).
       For 2006: $285,795 (= $290,429 – $4,634).

    b.   Total Amount Customers Owe = Accounts Receivable, Gross.
       For 2007: $365,921.
       For 2006: $290,429.

    c.   Journal Entries for Bad Debt Expense:

2007
Bad Debt Expense.. 117
    Allowance for Uncollectible Accounts   117

Assets	=	Liabilities	+	Shareholders' Equity	(Class.)
–117				–117	IncSt → RE

Bad Debt Expense equals $117 (= $4,318 + $433 – $4,634).

7.43 c. continued.

2006
Bad Debt Expense... 592
    Allowance for Uncollectible Accounts   592

Assets	=	Liabilities	+	Shareholders' Equity	(Class.)
−592				−592	IncSt → RE

Bad Debt Expense equals $592 (= $4,634 + $25 − $4,067).

7.45   (Pins Company; reconstructing transactions affecting accounts receivable and uncollectible accounts.)

    a. $192,000 Dr. = $700,000 − $500,000 − $8,000.

    b. $6,000 Cr. = (.02 × $700,000) − $8,000.

    c. $21,000 = $10,000 + $11,000.

    d. $16,000 = $6,000 + $10,000.

    e. $676,000 = $192,000 + $800,000 − $16,000 − $300,000.

    f. $289,000 = $300,000 − $11,000.

7.47   (Areva Group: income recognition for uranium enrichment plant.) (Amounts in Millions)

    a.1. **Percentage-of-Completion Method**

Year	Incremental Percentage Complete	Revenue Recognized	Expenses Recognized	Income
2008	340/1,700 (.20)	$ 400	$ 340	$ 60
2009	238/1,700 (.14)	280	238	42
2010	238/1,700 (.14)	280	238	42
2011	238/1,700 (.14)	280	238	42
2012	238/1,700 (.14)	280	238	42
2013	238/1,700 (.14)	280	238	42
2014	170/1,700 (.10)	200	170	30
Total.....	120/120 (1.00)	$ 2,000	$ 1,700	$ 300

7.47 a. continued.

2. Completed Contract Method

Year	Revenue Recognized	Expenses Recognized	Income
2008	-0-	-0-	-0-
2009	-0-	-0-	-0-
2010	-0-	-0-	-0-
2011	-0-	-0-	-0-
2012	-0-	-0-	-0-
2013	-0-	-0-	-0-
2014	$2,000	$1,700	$300
Total....	$2,000	$1,700	$300

b. **Journal Entries:**

1. Percentage-of-Completion Method

2007
December 20, 2007: At time of contract signing.

Cash...	20	
Advances from Customer...		20

Assets	=	Liabilities	+	Shareholders' Equity	(Class.)
+20		+20			

2008

Construction in Process..	340	
Cash		340

Assets	=	Liabilities	+	Shareholders' Equity	(Class.)
+340					
−340					

Cash...	100	
Advances from Customer...	20	
Receivable from Customer...	280	
Sales Revenue..		400

Assets	=	Liabilities	+	Shareholders' Equity	(Class.)
+100		−20		+400	IncSt → RE
+280					

7.47 b. continued.

Cost of Sales... 340
    Construction in Process 340

Assets	=	Liabilities	+	Shareholders' Equity	(Class.)
−340				−340	IncSt → RE

2009–2013
Construction in Process.. 238
    Cash 238

Assets	=	Liabilities	+	Shareholders' Equity	(Class.)
+238					
−238					

Cash... 100
Receivable from Customer.. 180
    Sales Revenue 280

Assets	=	Liabilities	+	Shareholders' Equity	(Class.)
+100				+280	IncSt → RE
+180					

Cost of Sales... 238
    Construction in Process 238

Assets	=	Liabilities	+	Shareholders' Equity	(Class.)
−238				−238	IncSt → RE

2014
Construction in Process.. 170
    Cash 170

Assets	=	Liabilities	+	Shareholders' Equity	(Class.)
+170					
−170					

7.47 b. continued.

Cash.. 1,380
    Receivable from Customer... 1,180
    Sales Revenue.. 200

Assets	=	Liabilities	+	Shareholders' Equity	(Class.)
+1,380				+200	IncSt → RE
−1,180					

Cost of Sales... 170
    Construction in Process... 170

Assets	=	Liabilities	+	Shareholders' Equity	(Class.)
−170				−170	IncSt → RE

2. Completed Contract Method

2007
December 20, 2007: At time of contract signing.
Cash.. 20
    Advances from Customer... 20

Assets	=	Liabilities	+	Shareholders' Equity	(Class.)
+20		+20			

2008
Construction in Process.. 340
    Cash.. 340

Assets	=	Liabilities	+	Shareholders' Equity	(Class.)
+340					
−340					

Cash.. 100
    Advances from Customer... 100

Assets	=	Liabilities	+	Shareholders' Equity	(Class.)
+100		+100			

7.47 b. continued.

2009–2013

Construction in Process..	238	
Cash..		238

Assets	= Liabilities	+	Shareholders' Equity	(Class.)
+238				
−238				

Cash..	100	
Advances form Customer..		100

Assets	= Liabilities	+	Shareholders' Equity	(Class.)
+100	+100			

2014

Construction in Process..	170	
Cash..		170

Assets	= Liabilities	+	Shareholders' Equity	(Class.)
+170				
−170				

Cash..	1,380	
Advances from Customer..	620	
Sales Revenue..		2,000

Assets	= Liabilities	+	Shareholders' Equity	(Class.)
+1,380	−620		+2,000	IncSt → RE

Cost of Sales..	1,700	
Construction in Process		1,700

Assets	= Liabilities	+	Shareholders' Equity	(Class.)
−1,700			−1,700	IncSt → RE

7.49   (Furniture Retailers; revenue recognition when payment is uncertain.)

a. **Installment Method**

   (1) **January 2008**

   Accounts Receivable 8,400
      Inventory.. 6,800
      Deferred Gross Margin... 1,600

Assets	=	Liabilities	+	Shareholders' Equity	(Class.)
+8,400					
−6,800		+1,600			

   (2) **When Furniture Retailer Receives Each Payment**

   The customer will make 21 payments of $400 each. The gross margin percentage is 19% (= $1,600/$8,400). When each monthly payment is received, Furniture Retailers will recognize $400 of revenues and $76 (= 0.19 x $400) of Deferred Gross Margin.

   Cash... 400
   Deferred Gross Margin 76
   Cost of Goods Sold (Plug)... 324
      Sales Revenue.. 400
      Accounts Receivable.. 400

Assets	=	Liabilities	+	Shareholders' Equity	(Class.)
+400		−76		−324	IncSt → RE
−400				+400	IncSt → RE

b. **Cost Recovery Method**

   (1) **January 2008**

   Accounts Receivable 8,400
      Inventory.. 6,800
      Deferred Gross Margin... 1,600

Assets	=	Liabilities	+	Shareholders' Equity	(Class.)
+8,400		+1,600			
−6,800					

7.49 b. continued.

(2) When Each Payment is Received

The customer will make 21 payments of $400 each. Furniture Retailers will recover the $6,800 cost of furniture after the customer has made seventeen payments (= $6,800/$400). To record the first seventeen payments, Furniture Retailers makes the following journal entry:

Cash.. 400
Cost of Goods Sold.. 400
    Sales Revenue... 400
    Accounts Receivable....................................... 400

Assets	=	Liabilities	+	Shareholders' Equity	(Class.)
+400				+400	IncSt → RE
−400				−400	IncSt → RE

To record the last four payments, Furniture Retailers makes the following journal entry:

Cash.. 400
Deferred Gross Margin... 400
    Sales Revenue... 400
    Accounts Receivable....................................... 400

Assets	=	Liabilities	+	Shareholders' Equity	(Class.)
+400		−400		+400	IncSt → RE
−400					

7.51   (J. C. Spangle; point-of-sales versus installment method of income recognition.)

a.	2008	2007
Sales	$300,000	$ 200,000
Expenses:		
Cost of Goods Sold*	$186,000	$ 120,000
All Other Expenses	44,000	32,000
Total Expenses	$230,000	$ 152,000
Net Income	$ 70,000	$ 48,000
*Beginning Inventory	$ 60,000	$ 0
Purchases	240,000	180,000
Goods Available	$300,000	$ 180,000
Ending Inventory	(114,000)	(60,000)
Cost of Goods Sold	$186,000	$ 120,000

Cost of Goods Sold/Sales:
   2007—$120,000/$200,000 = 60%.
   2008—$186,000/$300,000 = 62%.

b.	2008	2007
Collections from Customers	$230,000	$ 90,000
Expenses:		
Merchandise Cost of Collections*	$140,400	$ 54,000
All Other Expenses	44,000	32,000
Total Expenses	$184,400	$ 86,000
Net Income	$ 45,600	$ 4,000

*Calculation	2008	2007
Merchandise Cost of Collections:		
Of Goods Sold:		
In 2007, 60% of $90,000		$ 54,000
In 2008, 60% of $110,000	$ 66,000	
Of Goods Sold in 2008:		
62% of $120,000	74,400	
	$140,400	$ 54,000

An Alternative Presentation Would Be:	2008	2007
Realized Gross Margin	$ 89,600	$ 36,000
All Other Expenses	44,000	32,000
Net Income	$ 45,600	$ 4,000

7.53   (Income recognition for various types of businesses.)

a. **Amgen**—The principal income recognition issue for Amgen is the significant lag between the incurrence of research and development expenditures and the realization of sales from any resulting products. Biotechnology firms are a relatively new industry and, therefore, have few commercially feasible products. Thus, research and development expenditures will likely represent a significant percentage of revenues, as is the case for Amgen. More established technology firms, such as pharmaceuticals, have established products as well as products in the pipeline and, therefore, research and development expenditures represent both a smaller and a more stable percentage of revenues. GAAP requires biotechnology firms to expense research and development expenditures in the year incurred.

Brown Forman—The principal revenue recognition issue for Brown Forman is whether it should recognize the increase in value of hard liquors while they are aging (that is, revalue the liquors to market value each year) or wait until the liquors are sold at the end of the aging process. Most accountants would argue that the market values of aging liquors are too uncertain prior to sale to justify periodic revaluations and revenue recognition. Brown Forman should include in the cost of the liquor inventory not only the initial production costs but also the cost incurred during the aging process. In this way, the firm can match total incurred costs with revenues generated at the time of sale.

Deere—Deere faces issues of revenue recognition with respect to both the sale of farm equipment to dealers and the provision of financing services. The concern with respect to the sale of farm equipment to dealers is the right of dealers to return any unsold equipment. If dealers have no right of return, then recognition of revenue at the time of sale is appropriate. If dealers can return any equipment discovered to be faulty prior to sale and the amount of such returns is reasonably predictable, then Deere can reduce the amount of revenue recognized each year for estimated returns. If dealers can return any unsold equipment, then delaying recognition of revenue until the dealer sells the equipment is appropriate. Deere should match the cost of manufacturing the equipment against the sales revenue. Deere reports research and development expense in its income statement. Given the farm equipment industry, one wonders about what proportions of these expenditures Deere makes to enhance existing products versus to develop new products. Although contrary to GAAP, one can make the case that Deere should capitalize and amortize expenditures on new products.

Deere should accrue revenue from financing (interest) and insurance (premiums) services over time. To achieve matching, Deere should capitalize and amortize any initial administrative costs to check customer credit quality and prepare legal documents.

Odd-numbered Solutions

7.53 a. continued.

Fluor—The appropriate timing of revenue recognition for Fluor depends on the basis for pricing its services. If the fee is fixed for any particular construction project, then Fluor should recognize the fee in relation to the degree of completion of the construction project. If the fee is a percentage of total construction costs incurred on the project, then Fluor should recognize revenue in relation to costs incurred. If the fee is a percentage of the costs incurred by Fluor (salaries of their employees working on the project), then it should recognize revenue in relation to the incurrence of these costs. It seems clear that the percentage-of-completion method of revenue recognition is more appropriate than the completed contract method.

Golden West—Golden West should recognize interest revenue from home mortgage loans as time passes. It should provide for estimated uncollectible accounts each year. The uncollectible amount should reflect the resale value of homes repossessed. The more difficult question relates to recognition of revenue from points. One possibility is to recognize the full amount in the initial year of the loan. The rationale for such a procedure is that the points cover administrative costs of setting up the loan. Both the points and the administrative costs would be recognized in full in the initial year of the loan. An alternative view is that the points effectively reduce the amount lent by the savings and loan company and increase its yield beyond the stated interest rate. This view suggests that Golden West amortize the points over the term of the loan and match against this revenue amortization of the initial administrative costs to set up the loan. Golden West should recognize interest expense on deposits as time passes. There is no direct relation between interest expense on deposits and interest revenue from loans so Golden West matches interest expense to the period it is incurred.

Merrill Lynch—The principal income recognition issue for Merrill Lynch is whether it should report financial instruments held as assets and liabilities at their acquisition cost or their current fair value. These assets and liabilities generally have easily measured fair values. They are typically held for short periods of time (days or weeks). Thus, one can argue that use of current fair values is appropriate. However, we are still left with the question as to whether the unrealized gain or loss should flow through to the income statement immediately or wait until realization at the time of sale. The argument for immediate recognition is that Merrill Lynch takes short-term financing and investing positions for short-term returns. Its income statement should reflect its operating performance during this period. The case for not recognizing the unrealized gains and losses is that they could reverse prior to realization and, in any case, will be realized very soon. Merrill Lynch should recognize revenue from fee-based services as it provides the services.

7.53 a. continued.

Rockwell—The absence of research and development expense from the income statement suggests that Rockwell charges all such costs to specific contracts. These costs become expenses as Rockwell recognizes revenue from the contracts. The multi-year nature of its contracts and the credit quality of the U.S. government suggest use of the percentage-of-completion method of income recognition. One difficulty encountered in applying the percentage-of-completion method is that Rockwell's contracts for projects such as the space shuttle get continually renewed. This procedure makes it difficult to identify a single contract price and accumulate costs for a single contract, which the percentage-of-completion method envisions.

b. **Amgen**—Amgen realized the highest profit margin of the seven companies. Its biotechnology products are protected by patents. It therefore maintains a monopoly position. Note that the cost of manufacturing its products is a small percent of revenues. Amgen's major cost is for research and development. Sales of its existing products are not only sufficient to cover its high, on-going research work but to provide a substantial profit margin as well. Its relatively low revenue to assets percentage is somewhat unexpected, given that its major "assets" are patents and research scientists. The reason for this low percentage (reason not provided in the case) is that cash and marketable securities comprise approximately 25% of its assets. These assets generated a return of approximately 3% during the year. This rate of return decreased the overall ratio of revenues to assets for Amgen.

Brown Forman—Brown Forman realized the third highest profit margin among the seven companies. If one views the excise taxes as a reduction in revenues rather than as an expense, its profit margin is 10.4% [= 8.8%/(100.0% − 15.4%)]. Concerns about excess alcoholic drinking in recent years have resulted in some exodus of companies from the industry, leaving the remaining companies with a larger share of a smaller market. The products of Brown Forman carry brand name recognition, permitting the firm to obtain attractive prices.

Deere—Deere's relatively low profit margin reflects (1) weaknesses in the farming industry in recent years, which puts downward pressure on margins, and (2) decreased interest rates, which lowers profit margins. The revenue-to-assets percentage of Deere reflects its capital-intensive manufacturing operations and the low interest rate on outstanding loans to dealers and customers.

Fluor—The low profit margin of Fluor reflects the relatively low value added of construction services. It may also reflect recessionary conditions when construction activity is weak and profit margins are thin.

7.53 b. continued.

Golden West—The 12% profit margin (ignoring an addback for interest expense, which is common for financial services firms) seems high, relative to interest rates in recent years. Recall though that Golden West pays short-term interest rates on its deposits but obtains long-term interest rates on its loans. An upward-sloping yield curve provides a positive differential. Also, the existence of shareholders' equity funds in the capital structure means that Golden West has assets earning returns for which it recognizes no expense in its income statement (that is, firms do not recognize an expense for the implicit cost of shareholders' funds). Note also that the ratio of revenue to assets is only .1. Thus, the assets of Golden West earned a return of only 1.2% (= 12.0% X .1) during the year.

Merrill Lynch—The lower profit margin for Merrill Lynch relative to Golden West reflects in part the fact that both the investments and financing of Merrill Lynch are short term. Merrill Lynch, however, realizes revenue from fee-based services. Firms like Merrill Lynch can differentiate these services somewhat and realize attractive profit margins. However, such services have been quickly copied by competitors in recent years, reducing the profit margins accordingly.

Rockwell—Rockwell's profit margin is in the middle of the seven companies. Factors arguing for a high profit margin include Rockwell's technological know-how and its role in long-term contracts with the U.S. government. Factors arguing for a lower profit margin include cutbacks in defense expenditures and excess capacity in the aerospace industry.

CHAPTER 8

WORKING CAPITAL

Questions, Exercises, and Problems: Answers and Solutions

8.1   See the text or the glossary at the end of the book.

8.3   The underlying principle is that acquisition cost includes all costs required to prepare an asset for its intended use. Assets provide future services. Costs that a firm must incur to obtain those expected services are, therefore, included in the acquisition cost valuation of the asset. In the case of merchandise inventory, this includes the costs associated with obtaining the goods (purchase price, transportation costs, insurance costs). For inventory, which the firm manufactures, acquisition costs include labor, overhead, and materials.

8.5   Both the Merchandise Inventory and Finished Goods Inventory accounts include the cost of completed units ready for sale. A merchandising firm acquires the units in finished form and debits Merchandise Inventory for their acquisition cost. A manufacturing firm incurs direct material, direct labor, and manufacturing overhead costs in transforming the units to a finished, salable condition. The Raw Materials Inventory and Work-in-Process Inventory accounts include such costs until the completion of manufacturing operations. Thus, the accountant debits the Finished Goods Inventory account for the cost of producing completed units. The accountant credits both the Merchandise Inventory and Finished Goods Inventory accounts for the cost of units sold and reports the inventory accounts as current assets on the balance sheet.

8.7   **Rising Purchase Prices**
Higher Inventory Amount: FIFO
Lower Inventory Amount: LIFO
Higher Cost of Goods
    Sold Amount: LIFO.
Lower Cost of Goods
    Sold Amount: FIFO

8.9   The Parker School should accrue the salary in ten monthly installments of $360,000 each at the end of each month, September through June. It will have paid $300,000 at the end of each of these months, so that by the end of the reporting year, it reports a current liability of $600,000 [= $3,600,000 − (10 x $300,000)].

8.11   **Similarities:** The accountant makes estimates of future events in both cases. The accountant charges the cost of estimated uncollectibles or warranties to income in the period of sale, not in the later period when specific items become uncollectible or break down. The income statement reports the charge against income as an expense in both cases, although some accountants report the charge for estimated uncollectibles as a revenue contra.

Differences: The balance sheet account showing the expected costs of future uncollectibles reduces an asset account, whereas that for estimated warranties appears as a liability.

8.13   (Delhaize Group; accounting for prepayments.)

a. Journal entry to record insurance premium payments in 2007, 2006, and 2005:

Prepayments..	50.0
Cash	50.0

Assets	=	Liabilities	+	Shareholders' Equity	(Class.)
+50.0					
−50.0					

b. Adjusting journal entries required each year.

2006:

Insurance Expense	66.3
Prepayments..	66.3

Assets	=	Liabilities	+	Shareholders' Equity	(Class.)
−66.3				−66.3	IncSt → RE

To adjust Prepayments for the amount consumed during 2006, of €66.3 million (= €42.1 + €50.0 − €25.8).

2007:

Insurance Expense	45.1
Prepayments..	45.1

Assets	=	Liabilities	+	Shareholders' Equity	(Class.)
−45.1				−45.1	IncSt → RE

To adjust Prepayments for the amount consumed during 2007, of €45.1 million (= €25.8 + €50.0 − €30.7).

8.15   (Harnet Winery; identifying inventory cost inclusions.)

Harnet should include the costs to acquire the grapes, process them into wine, and mature the wine, but not the expenditures on advertising or research and development. Thus, the cost of the wine inventory (prior to its sale) is $3,673,000 (= $2,200,000 + $50,000 + $145,000 + $100,000 + $250,000 + $600,000 + $120,000 + $180,000 + $28,000).

8.17   (ResellFast; effect of inventory valuation on the balance sheet and net income.) (Amounts in Millions)

	Carrying Value	Effect on Income
Q1	$ 20.0	$ 0.0
Q2	16.5	(3.5)
Q3	16.5	0.0
Q4	0.0	11.0

8.19   (Tesco Plc.; inventory and accounts payable journal entries.)

a. Trade Payables... 43,558
       Cash 43,558

Assets	=	Liabilities	+	Shareholders' Equity	(Class.)
–43,558		–43,558			

b. Beginning Balance in Trade Payables + Purchases of Merchandise Inventory = Payments to Venders + Ending Balance in Trade Payables.

€3,317 + Purchases of Merchandise Inventory = €43,558 (from Part a.) + €3,936.

Purchases of Merchandise Inventory = €44,177.

Merchandise Inventory... 44,177
       Accounts Payable... 44,177

Assets	=	Liabilities	+	Shareholders' Equity	(Class.)
+44,177		+44,177			IncSt → RE

c. Beginning Balance in Merchandise Inventory + Purchases of Inventory = Amount Sold (Cost of Goods Sold) + Ending Balance in Merchandise Inventory.

€1,911 + €44,177 (from Part b.) = Cost of Goods Sold + €2,420.
Cost of Goods Sold = €43,668.

Odd-numbered Solutions

8.19 c. continued.

Cost of Goods Sold... 43,668
    Merchandise Inventory   43,668

Assets	=	Liabilities	+	Shareholders' Equity	(Class.)
–43,668				–43,668	IncSt → RE

8.21   (GenMet; income computation for a manufacturing firm.)

Sales..	$ 6,700.2
Less Cost of Goods Sold...	(2,697.6)
Less Selling and Administrative Expenses	(2,903.7)
Less Interest Expense..	(151.9)
Income before Income Taxes	$ 947.0
Income Tax Expense at 35%..	(331.5)
Net Income	$ 615.5

Work-in-Process Inventory, October 31, 2007.............................	$ 100.8
Plus Manufacturing Costs Incurred during Fiscal Year 2008......	2,752.0
Less Work-in-Process Inventory, October 31, 2008......................	(119.1)
Cost of Goods Completed during Fiscal Year 2008.......................	$ 2,733.7
Plus Finished Goods Inventory, October 31, 2007.........................	286.2
Less Finished Goods Inventory, October 31, 2008........................	(322.3)
Cost of Goods Sold	$ 2,697.6

8.23   (Warren Company; effect of inventory errors.)

a. None.
b. None.
c. Understatement by $1,000.
d. Overstatement by $1,000.
e. Overstatement by $1,000.

f. Understatement by $1,000.
g. Understatement by $1,000.
h. None.
i. None.

8.25   (Ericsson; lower of cost or market for inventory.)

a. SEK22,475 million (= SEK25,227 – SEK2,752).

b. Journal entry to record impairment charge for inventory during 2007:

Impairment Loss on Inventory................................... 1,276
    Allowance for Impairment..   1,276

8.25 b. continued.

Assets	=	Liabilities	+	Shareholders' Equity	(Class.)
–1,276				–1,276	IncSt → RE

The carrying value of the inventory is now SEK2,224
(= SEK3,500 – SEK1,276).

c. January 2008: Journal entry to record a reversal of a portion of the impairment charge for inventory taken in 2007:

Allowance for Impairment.. 576
    Reversal of Impairment Loss on Inventory..........   576

Assets	=	Liabilities	+	Shareholders' Equity	(Class.)
+576				+576	IncSt → RE

To reverse a portion of the impairment loss; SEK576
= SEK2,800 – SEK2,224.

d. U.S. GAAP would not permit Ericsson to reverse a previous impairment of inventory.

8.27   (Arnold Company; computations involving different cost flow assumptions.)

	a.	b.	c.
	Pounds	FIFO	Weighted Average	LIFO
Raw Materials Available for Use................................	10,700	$24,384	$24,384	$ 24,384
Less Ending Inventory	(3,500)	(8,110)[a]	(7,976)[c]	(7,818)[e]
Raw Materials Issued to Production......................................	7,200	$16,274[b]	$16,408[d]	$ 16,566[f]

[a](3,000 X \$2.32) + (500 X \$2.30) = \$8,110.

[b](1,200 X \$2.20) + (2,200 X \$2.25) + (2,800 X \$2.28) + (1,000 X \$2.30) = \$16,274.

[c](\$24,384/10,700) X 3,500 = \$7,976.

[d](\$24,384/10,700) X 7,200 = \$16,408.

[e](1,200 X \$2.20) + (2,200 X \$2.25) + (100 X \$2.28) = \$7,818.

[f](3,000 X \$2.32) + (1,500 X \$2.30) + (2,700 X \$2.28) = \$16,566.

8.29   (EKG Company; LIFO provides opportunity for income manipulation.)

a. Largest cost of goods sold results from producing 70,000 (or more) additional units at a cost of $22 each, giving cost of goods sold of $1,540,000.

b. Smallest cost of goods sold results from producing no additional units, giving cost of goods sold of $980,000 [= ($8 x 10,000) + ($15 x 60,000)].

c.

	Income Reported	
	Minimum	**Maximum**
Revenues ($30 x 70,000)	$2,100,000	$2,100,000
Less Cost of Goods Sold	(1,540,000)	(980,000)
Gross Margin	$ 560,000	$1,120,000

8.31   (Ford Motor Company; analysis of LIFO and FIFO disclosures.)

a. Ford Motor Company uses LIFO, so the carrying value of its inventories would be $10,121 million as of December 31, 2007 and $10,017 as of December 31, 2006.

b.

	LIFO	Difference	FIFO
Beginning Inventory	$ 10,017	$ 1,015	$ 11,032
Production Costs (Plug)	142,691	--	142,691
Goods Available for Sale (Plug)	$152,708	$ 1,015	$153,723
Less Ending Inventory	(10,121)	(1,100)	(11,221)
Cost of Goods Sold	$142,587	$ (85)	$142,502

8.33   (Hurley Corporation; accounting for uncollectible accounts and warranties.)

a. **Allowance for Uncollectible Accounts**

Balance, December 31, 2008	$ 355
Plus Bad Debt Expense for 2009: .02 x $18,000	360
Less Accounts Written Off (Plug)	(310)
Balance, December 31, 2009	$ 405
Plus Bad Debt Expense for 2010: .02 x $16,000	320
Less Accounts Written Off (Plug)	(480)
Balance, December 31, 2010	$ 245

b. **Estimated Warranty Liability**

Balance, December 31, 2008	$ 1,325
Plus Warranty Expense for 2009: .06 x $18,000	1,080
Less Actual Warranty Costs (Plug)	(870)
Balance, December 31, 2009	$ 1,535
Plus Warranty Expense for 2010: .06 x $16,000	960
Less Actual Warranty Costs (Plug)	(775)
Balance, December 31, 2010	$ 1,720

8.35   (Kingspeed Bikes; journal entries for estimated warranty liabilities and subsequent expenditures.)

a. **2008**

Cash.. 800,000

    Sales Revenue.. 800,000

Assets	=	Liabilities	+	Shareholders' Equity	(Class.)
+800,000				+800,000	IncSt → RE

Warranty Liability... 22,000

    Cash 13,200

    Parts Inventory 8,800

Assets	=	Liabilities	+	Shareholders' Equity	(Class.)
−13,200		−22,000			
−8,800					

Warranty Expense.. 48,000

    Warranty Liability... 48,000

Assets	=	Liabilities	+	Shareholders' Equity	(Class.)
		+48,000		−48,000	IncSt → RE

.06 x $800,000 = $48,000.

2009

Cash.. 1,200,000

    Sales Revenue.. 1,200,000

Assets	=	Liabilities	+	Shareholders' Equity	(Class.)
+1,200,000				+1,200,000	IncSt → RE

Warranty Liability... 55,000

    Cash 33,000

    Parts Inventory 22,000

Assets	=	Liabilities	+	Shareholders' Equity	(Class.)
−33,000		−55,000			
−22,000					

8.35 a. continued.

Warranty Expense.. 72,000
    Warranty Liability 72,000

Assets	=	Liabilities	+	Shareholders' Equity	(Class.)
		+72,000		−72,000	IncSt → RE

.06 x $1,200,000 = $72,000.

2010
Cash.. 900,000
    Sales Revenue.. 900,000

Assets	=	Liabilities	+	Shareholders' Equity	(Class.)
+900,000				+900,000	IncSt → RE

Warranty Liability... 52,000
    Cash 31,200
    Parts Inventory 20,800

Assets	=	Liabilities	+	Shareholders' Equity	(Class.)
−31,200		−52,000			
−20,800					

Warranty Expense.. 54,000
    Warranty Liability 54,000

Assets	=	Liabilities	+	Shareholders' Equity	(Class.)
		+54,000		−54,000	IncSt → RE

.06 x $900,000 = $54,000.

b. $48,000 − $22,000 + $72,000 − $55,000 + $54,000 − $52,000 = $45,000.

8.37   (Delhaize Group; journal entries for restructuring liabilities and subsequent expenditures.)

a. **Journal entries for 2007**
Restructuring Expense...................................... 14.2
    Restructuring Provision 14.2

8.37 a. continued.

Assets	=	Liabilities	+	Shareholders' Equity	(Class.)
		+14.2		−14.2	IncSt → RE

To record new restructuring charges made during 2007.

Restructuring Provision.. 7.3

    Restructuring Expense... 7.3

Assets	=	Liabilities	+	Shareholders' Equity	(Class.)
		−7.3		+7.3	IncSt → RE

To record the reversal of prior period restructuring charges.

Restructuring Provision.. 40.0

    Cash 40.0

Assets	=	Liabilities	+	Shareholders' Equity	(Class.)
−40.0		−40.0			

To record cash expenditures to settle restructuring Provisions; 40.0 = [(84.0 + 14.2) − (7.3 + 50.9)].

b. Delhaize will report a total restructuring provision of €50.9, classified as follows on its balance sheet:

Current Portion of Restructuring Provision........................ € 12.5 million

Noncurrent Portion of Restructuring Provision................. € 38.4 million

c. Delhaize's income in 2007 is lower by €6.9 million (= €14.2 million − €7.3 million). The net change in income of €6.9 million is added to income as a noncash expense to calculate cash flow from operations in the statement of cash flows:

8.39   (Lord Cromptom Plc.; flow of manufacturing costs through the accounts.)

a. Beginning Raw Materials Inventory .... € 46,900
    Raw Materials Purchased 429,000
    Raw Materials Available for Use .... € 475,900
    Subtract Ending Raw Materials Inventory .... (43,600)·
    Cost of Raw Materials Used .... € 432,300

    Beginning Factory Supplies Inventory .... € 7,600
    Factory Supplies Purchased 22,300
    Factory Supplies Available for Use .... € 29,900
    Subtract Ending Factory Supplies Inventory .... (7,700)
    Cost of Factory Supplies Used .... € 22,200

b. Beginning Work-in-Process Inventory .... € 110,900
    Cost of Raw Materials Used (from Part *a*.) 432,300
    Cost of Factory Supplies Used (from Part *a*.) 22,200
    Direct Labor Costs Incurred 362,100
    Heat, Light, and Power Costs 10,300
    Insurance 4,200
    Depreciation of Factory Equipment 36,900
    Prepaid Rent Expired 3,600
    Total Beginning Work-in-Process and Manufacturing Costs
      Incurred .... € 982,500
    Subtract Ending Work-in-Process Inventory .... (115,200)
    Cost of Units Completed and Transferred to Finished Goods
      Storeroom .... € 867,300

c. Beginning Finished Goods Inventory .... € 76,700
    Cost of Units Completed and Transferred to Finished Goods
      Storeroom (from Part *b*.) 867,300
    Subtract Ending Finished Goods Inventory .... (71,400)
    Cost of Goods Sold .... € 872,600

d. Net Income is €110,040 [= (1 − .40)(€1,350,000 − €872,600 − €246,900 − €47,100)].

8.41   (Sandvik Group; flow of manufacturing costs.)

a. Ending Balance of Total Inventory = Ending Balance of Raw Materials Inventory + Ending Balance of Work-in-Process Inventory + Ending Balance of Finished Goods Inventory.

    Ending Balance of Total Inventory = SEK6,964 + SEK5,157 + SEK13,180 = SEK25,301 million.

8.41 continued.

b. Loss on Impairment of Inventory................................. 281
      Finished Goods Inventory 281

Assets	=	Liabilities	+	Shareholders' Equity	(Class.)
−281				−281	IncSt → RE

c. Cost of Sales, after Writedown = Cost of Sales, before Writedown + Writedown.

SEK57,222 = (Cost of Sales, before Writedown) + SEK281.
Cost of Sales, before Writedown = SEK56,941 million.

d. Beginning Finished Goods Inventory + Cost of Units Completed = Cost of Sales + Writedowns + Ending Finished Goods Inventory.

SEK8,955 + Cost of Units Completed = SEK56,941 + SEK281 + SEK13,180.

Cost of Units Completed = SEK61,447 million.

e. Beginning Balance in Work-in-Process Inventory + Direct Materials + Direct Labor + Overhead = Cost of Units Completed + Ending Balance in Work-in-Process Inventory.

SEK4,093 + Direct Material Costs + 3 × Direct Material Costs = SEK61,447 (from Part d.) + SEK5,157.

Direct Material Costs = SEK62,511/4 = SEK15,628 million.

Work-in-Process Inventory.. 15,628
      Raw Materials Inventory.. 15,628

Assets	=	Liabilities	+	Shareholders' Equity	(Class.)
+15,628					
−15,628					

f. Beginning Balance in Raw Materials Inventory + Raw Materials Purchases = Raw Materials Used in Production + Ending Balance of Raw Materials Inventory.

SEK5,690 + Raw Material Purchases = SEK15,628 (from Part e.) + SEK6,964.

Raw Materials Purchases = SEK16,902 million.

      Odd-numbered Solutions

8.43   (Burton Corporation; detailed comparison of various choices for inventory accounting.)

	FIFO	LIFO	Weighted Average
Inventory, 1/1/2007.........................	$ 0	$ 0	$ 0
Purchases during 2007....................	14,400	14,400	14,400
Goods Available for Sale during 2007	$14,400	$14,400	$ 14,400
Less Inventory, 12/31/2007	(3,000)[1]	(2,000)[2]	(2,400)[3]
Cost of Goods Sold for 2007...........	$11,400	$12,400	$ 12,000
Inventory, 1/1/2008.........................	$ 3,000 [1]	$ 2,000 [2]	$ 2,400 [3]
Purchases during 2008....................	21,000	21,000	21,000
Goods Available for Sale during 2008	$24,000	$23,000	$ 23,400
Less Inventory, 12/31/2008	(5,000)[4]	(6,200)[5]	(5,850)[6]
Cost of Goods Sold for 2008...........	$19,000	$16,800	$ 17,550

[1]$200 \times \$15 = \$3,000$.

[2]$200 \times \$10 = \$2,000$.

[3]$(\$14,400/1,200) \times 200 = \$2,400$.

[4]$500 \times \$10 = \$5,000$.

[5]$(200 \times \$10) + (300 \times \$14) = \$6,200$.

[6]$(\$23,400/2,000) \times 500 = \$5,850$.

a. $11,400.   d. $19,000.
b. $12,400.   e. $16,800.
c. $12,000.   f. $17,550.

g. FIFO results in higher net income for 2007. Purchase prices for inventory items increased during 2007. FIFO uses older, lower purchase prices to measure cost of goods sold, whereas LIFO uses more recent, higher prices.

h. LIFO results in higher net income for 2008. Purchase prices for inventory items decreased during 2008. LIFO uses more recent, lower prices to measure cost of goods sold, whereas FIFO uses older, higher prices.

8.45   (Burch Corporation; reconstructing underlying events from ending inventory amounts [adapted from CPA examination].)

a. Down. Notice that lower of cost or market is lower than acquisition cost (FIFO); current market price is less than cost.

8.45 continued.

b. Up. FIFO means last-in, still-here. The last purchases (FIFO = LISH) cost $44,000 and the earlier purchases (LIFO = FISH) cost $41,800. Also, lower-of-cost-or-market basis shows acquisition costs which are greater than or equal to current cost.

c. LIFO Cost. Other things being equal, the largest income results from the method that shows the largest *increase* in inventory during the year.

   Margin = Revenues − Cost of Goods Sold
   = Revenues − Beginning Inventory − Purchases + Ending Inventory
   = Revenues − Purchases + Increase in Inventory.

   Because the beginning inventory in 2006 is zero, the method with the largest closing inventory amount implies the largest increase and hence the largest income.

d. Lower of Cost or Market. The method with the "largest increase in inventory" during the year in this case is the method with the smallest decrease, because all methods show declines in inventory during 2007. Lower of cost or market shows a decrease in inventory of only $3,000 during 2007—the other methods show larger decreases ($3,800; $4,000).

e. Lower of Cost or Market. The method with the largest increase in inventory: $10,000. LIFO shows a $5,400 increase while FIFO shows $8,000.

f. LIFO Cost. The lower income for all three years results from the method that shows the smallest increase in inventory over the three years. Because all beginning inventories were zero under all methods, we need merely find the method with the smallest ending inventory at 2008 year-end.

g. FIFO lower by $2,000. Under FIFO, inventories increased $8,000 during 2008. Under lower of cost or market, inventories increased $10,000 during 2008. Lower of cost or market has a bigger increase—$2,000—and therefore lower of cost or market shows a $2,000 larger income than FIFO for 2008.

8.47 (Toyota; interpreting inventory disclosures.)

a. **March 31, 2008:**

   If Toyota had used FIFO, inventory values would have been ¥13,780 less than LIFO amounts.

   Ending Balance of Total Inventory (FIFO) = (¥374,210 + ¥239,937 + ¥1,211,569) − ¥13,780 = ¥1,825,716 − ¥13,780 = ¥1,811,936 million.

8.47 a. continued.

March 31, 2007:

If Toyota had used FIFO, inventory values would have been ¥30,360 less than LIFO amounts.

Ending Balance of Total Inventory (FIFO) = (¥362,686 + ¥236,749 + ¥1,204,521) – ¥30,360 = ¥1,803,956 – ¥30,360 = ¥1,773,596 million.

b. Beginning Balance in Finished Goods (FIFO) + Cost of Units Completed = Cost of Products Sold (FIFO) + Ending Balance in Finished Goods (FIFO).

Beginning Balance of Finished Goods Inventory (FIFO) = ¥1,204,521 – ¥30,360 = ¥1,174,161 million.

Ending Balance of Finished Goods Inventory (FIFO) = ¥1,211,569 – ¥13,780 = ¥1,197,789 million.

¥1,174,161 + ¥20,459,386 (from Problem 8.40, Part b.) = Cost of Products Sold (FIFO) + ¥1,197,789.

Cost of Goods Sold (FIFO) = ¥20,435,758 million.

Also, could calculate as follows:

Cost of Goods Sold (LIFO)..	¥ 20,452,338
Change in LIFO reserve (¥30,360 – ¥13,780).................	(16,580)
Cost of Goods Sold (FIFO)	¥ 20,435,758

8.49 (Bayer Group; interpreting restructuring disclosures.)

a. Restructuring Provision... 134
    Cash.. 134

Assets	=	Liabilities	+	Shareholders' Equity	(Class.)
–134		–134			

To record utilizations.

8.49 a. continued.

Restructuring Provision..   31
    Reversal of Restructuring Expense.......................   31

Assets	=	Liabilities	+	Shareholders' Equity	(Class.)
		−31		+31	IncSt → RE

To record reversal.

b. Journal entry to record additions to Restructuring Provision during 2007:

Restructuring Expense   128
    Restructuring Provision...   128

Assets	=	Liabilities	+	Shareholders' Equity	(Class.)
		+128		−128	IncSt → RE

To record €128 million of restructuring charges made during 2007.

Beginning Balance of Restructuring Provision + Additions = Utilizations + Net Other Effects + Reversals + Ending Balance of Restructuring Provision €196 + Additions = €134 + €5 + €31 + €154.

Additions = €128 million.

         Odd-numbered Solutions

This page is intentionally left blank

CHAPTER 9

LONG-LIVED TANGIBLE AND INTANGIBLE ASSETS

Questions, Exercises, and Problems: Answers and Solutions

9.1 See the text or the glossary at the end of the book.

9.3 The central concept underlying GAAP for these three items is the ability to identify and reliably measure expected future benefits. Expenditures to research new drugs may give rise to future benefits, but identifying the existence of those future benefits while research progresses is problematic. Thus, GAAP in the United States requires immediate expensing of research and development expenditures. The external market transaction for a patent on a new drug validates both the existence and fair value of the patent. GAAP, therefore, recognizes the patent as an asset. In-process R&D has characteristics of the previous two cases. Whether the in-process project will yield future benefits is uncertain, suggesting that firms should expense such expenditures at the time of acquisition. However, an external market transaction between independent parties suggests the existence of future benefits, supporting recognition of an asset until such time as the status of the research project becomes more certain. FASB *Statement No. 141 (Revised)* requires firms to recognize as an asset the fair value of in-process R&D acquired in a corporate acquisition, placing greater weight on the evidence provided by the external market transaction than on the uncertainty of future benefits.

9.5 A long-lived asset with a finite life is expected to provide benefits for a limited amount of time. Benefits will eventually decline to zero, either because of physical use, obsolescence, or disposal. Firms depreciate or amortize assets with a finite life. Note that firms must estimate the finite life in most cases (except for benefit periods limited by contract). An asset with an infinite life is one that is expected to last forever. GAAP assumes that all assets eventually wear out, become obsolete, or are sold. Thus, GAAP does not allow firms to assume long-lived assets have an infinite life. GAAP treats assets that have an extended life, but for which the length of that life is highly uncertain, as having an indefinite life. GAAP does not require firms to depreciate or amortize assets with an indefinite life but must test those assets annually for possible asset impairment.

9.7   The treatment of this change in depreciable life would depend on the reason for and the materiality of the change. The change in this case appears prompted by new governmental regulations imposed on the airline industry. If the change in expected life is material, the firm can make a strong case for recognizing an asset impairment loss and revising its depreciation going forward. If the impact is not material, the airline might treat the change in depreciable life as a change in an estimate and spread the effect of the change over the current and future years. The purpose of this question is to demonstrate that judgments are often required in applying GAAP.

9.9   Generally accepted accounting principles compares the undiscounted cash flows from an asset to its carrying value to determine if an impairment loss has occurred. The rationale is that an impairment loss has not occurred if a firm will receive cash flows in the future at least equal to the carrying value of the asset. Receiving such cash flows will permit the firm to recover the carrying value. This criterion ignores the time value of money. Cash received earlier has more economic value than cash received later, but this criterion ignores such differences.

9.11   An asset impairment loss that arises during a period results from a decline in fair value due to some external event. Using undiscounted, instead of discounted, cash flows to signal an impairment loss ignores the decline in fair value that occurred. Firms will not recognize the asset impairment loss as long as the undiscounted cash flows exceed the carrying value of the asset.

9.13   (Outback Steakhouse; calculating acquisition costs of long-lived assets.)

The relative market values of the land and building are 20% (= $52,000/$260,000) for the land and 80% (= $208,000/$260,000) for the building. We use these percentages to allocate joint cost of the land and building.

	Land	**Building**
Purchase Price of Land and Building.........	$ 52,000	$ 208,000
Legal Costs Split 20% and 80%..................	2,520	10,080
Renovation Costs.......................................	--	35,900
Property and Liability Insurance Costs during Renovation Split 20% and 80%	800	3,200
Property Taxes during Renovation Split 20% and 80%..	1,000	4,000
Total...	$ 56,320	$ 261,180

Note: One might argue that the split of the insurance and property taxes should recognize the increase in market value of the building as a result of the renovation and use some other percentages besides 20% and 80%. Note also that the insurance and property taxes for the period after opening are expenses of the first year of operation.

9.15   (Bolton Company; cost of self-constructed assets.)

Land: $70,000 + $2,000 (14) = $72,000.

Factory Building: $200,000 (1) + $12,000 (2) + $140,000 (3) + $6,000 (5) −
$7,000 (7) + $10,000 (8) + $8,000 (9) + $3,000[a] (10) + $8,000 (11) + $4,000
(13) + $1,000[a] (15) = $385,000.

Office Building: $20,000 + $13,000 (4) = $33,000.

Site Improvements: $5,000 (12).

> [a]The firm might expense these items. It depends on the rationality of
> the firm's "self-insurance" policy.
>
> Item (6) is omitted because of *SFAS No. 34*.
>
> Item (16) is omitted because no arm's length transaction occurred in
> which the firm earned a profit.

9.17   (Bulls Eye Stores; calculating interest capitalized during construction.)

Capitalized Interest on Borrowing Directly Related to Construction: .06 x $2,000,000	$ 120,000
Capitalized Interest of Other Borrowing: .07 x $1,400,000	98,000
Total Interest Capitalized	$ 218,000

9.19   (Alcoa; calculations for various depreciation methods.)

	Year 1	Year 2	Year 3
a. Straight-Line (Time) Method ($88,800 − $4,800)/6 = $14,000.	$14,000	$14,000	$14,000
b. Straight-Line (Use) Method $84,000/30,000 = $2.80 per hour.	$12,600	$14,000	$15,400

9.21   (Thompson Financial; change in depreciable life and salvage value.)

Carrying Value on January 1, 2008: $10,000,000 − {2 x [($10,000,000 −
$1,000,000)/6]} = $7,000,000. Depreciation expense for 2008 based on the
new depreciable life and salvage value is $3,200,000 [= ($7,000,000 −
$600,000)/2].

9.23   (Disney World; distinguishing repairs versus betterments.)

Repair: (1.00/1.20 x $30,200) + $86,100 + (1.00/1.25 x $26,900) + $12,600 =
$145,387.

Betterment: (.20/1.20 x $30,200) + (.25/1.25 x $26,900) = $10,413.

9.25   (Kieran Corporation; computing the amount of impairment loss.)

	Carrying Value	Undis- counted Cash Flows	Impair- ment Loss Recog- nized	Fair Value	Amount of Loss
Land	$ 550,000	$ 575,000	No	$ 550,000	$ 0
Buildings	580,000	600,000	No	580,000	0
Equipment	1,200,000	950,000	Yes	800,000	400,000
Goodwill	500,000[a]	--	Yes	270,000	230,000
Total	$ 2,830,000			$ 2,200,000	$ 630,000

[a]$500,000 = $2,400,000 - $400,000 - $600,000 - $900,000.

After recognizing the impairment losses on the property, plant, and equipment, the carrying value of Kieran Corporation is $2,430,000 (= $550,000 for land + $580,000 for buildings + $800,000 for equipment + $500,000 for goodwill). The carrying value of $2,430,000 exceeds the fair value of the entity of $2,200,000, so a goodwill impairment loss may have occurred (Step 1 of goodwill impairment test). The fair value column above shows the allocation of the $2,200,000 fair value to identifiable assets, with the residual of $270,000 attributed to goodwill. The carrying value of the goodwill of $500,000 exceeds its implied fair value of $270,000, so Kieran Corporation recognizes an impairment loss on the goodwill of $230,000 (Step 2 of goodwill impairment test).

9.27   (Wilcox Corporation; working backwards to derive proceeds from disposition of plant assets.)

Cost of Equipment Sold: $400,000 + $230,000 - $550,000 = $80,000.
Accumulated Depreciation
  on Equipment Sold: $180,000 + $50,000 - $160,000 = $70,000.
Carrying Value of Equip-
  ment Sold: $80,000 - $70,000 = $10,000.
Proceeds of Sale: $10,000 + $4,000 = $14,000.

9.29   (Moon Macrosystems; recording transactions involving tangible and intangible assets.)

a. Office Equipment 400,000
    Computer Software 40,000
        Cash   440,000

9.29 a. continued.

Assets	=	Liabilities	+	Shareholders' Equity	(Class.)
+400,000					
+40,000					
−440,000					

b. Office Equipment 20,000
    Computer Software 10,000
       Cash..   30,000

Assets	=	Liabilities	+	Shareholders' Equity	(Class.)
+20,000					
+10,000					
−30,000					

c. **2006 and 2007**
    Depreciation Expense [($400,000 + $20,000 −
       $40,000)/10] 38,000
    Amortization Expense [($40,000 + $10,000)/4] 12,500
       Accumulated Depreciation......................................   38,000
       Computer Software   12,500

Assets	=	Liabilities	+	Shareholders' Equity	(Class.)
−38,000				−38,000	IncSt → RE
−12,500				−12,500	IncSt → RE

d. Impairment Loss of Computer Software
       ($40,000 + $10,000 − $12,500 − $12,500)............ 25,000
       Computer Software...   25,000

Assets	=	Liabilities	+	Shareholders' Equity	(Class.)
−25,000				−25,000	IncSt → RE

e. Depreciation Expense [($400,000 + $20,000 −
       $38,000 − $38,000 − $56,000)/12].......................... 24,000
       Accumulated Depreciation..................................   24,000

Assets	=	Liabilities	+	Shareholders' Equity	(Class.)
−24,000				−24,000	IncSt → RE

        Odd-numbered Solutions

9.29 continued.

f. Depreciation Expense 24,000
      Accumulated Depreciation 24,000

Assets	=	Liabilities	+	Shareholders' Equity	(Class.)
−24,000				−24,000	IncSt → RE

Cash 260,000
Accumulated Depreciation ($38,000 + $38,000 +
   $24,000 + $24,000) 124,000
Loss on Sale of Office Equipment 36,000
   Office Equipment 420,000

Assets	=	Liabilities	+	Shareholders' Equity	(Class.)
+260,000				−36,000	IncSt → RE
+124,000					
−420,000					

9.31   (Recognizing and measuring impairment losses.)

a. The loss occurs because of an adverse action by a governmental entity. The undiscounted cash flows of $50 million are less than the carrying value of the building of $60 million. An impairment loss has therefore occurred. The fair value of the building of $32 million is less than the carrying value of $60 million. Thus, the amount of the impairment loss is $28 million (= $60 million − $32 million). The journal entry to record the impairment loss is (in millions):

Loss from Impairment 28
Accumulated Depreciation 20
   Building 48

Assets	=	Liabilities	+	Shareholders' Equity	(Class.)
+20				−28	IncSt → RE
−48					

This entry records the impairment loss, eliminates the accumulated depreciation, and writes down the building to its fair value of $32 million (= $80 − $48).

b. The undiscounted cash flows of $70 million exceed the carrying value of the building of $60 million. Thus, no impairment loss occurs according to the definition in FASB *Statement No. 144*. An **economic** loss occurred but U.S. GAAP does not recognize it.

9.31 continued.

c. The loss arises because the accumulated costs significantly exceed the amount originally anticipated. The carrying value of the building of $25 million exceeds the undiscounted future cash flows of $22 million. Thus, an impairment loss has occurred. The impairment loss recognized equals $9 million (= $25 million – $16 million). The journal entry is (in millions):

Loss from Impairment... 9
    Construction in Process... 9

Assets	=	Liabilities	+	Shareholders' Equity	(Class.)
–9				–9	IncSt → RE

d. The loss occurs because of a significant decline in the fair value of the patent. FASB *Statement No. 142* requires calculation of the impairment loss on the patent before computing the impairment loss on goodwill. The undiscounted future cash flows of $18 million are less than the carrying value of the patent of $20 million. Thus, an impairment loss occurred. The amount of the loss is $8 million (= $20 million – $12 million). The journal entry to record the loss is:

Loss from Impairment... 8
    Patent... 8

Assets	=	Liabilities	+	Shareholders' Equity	(Class.)
–8				–8	IncSt → RE

The second step is to determine if an impairment loss on the goodwill occurred. The fair value of the entity is $25 million. The carrying value after writing down the patent is $27 million (= $12 million for patent and $15 million for goodwill). Thus, a goodwill impairment loss occurred. If the fair value of the patent is $12 million, the market value of the goodwill is $13 million. The impairment loss on goodwill is therefore $2 million (= $15 million – $13 million). The journal entry is:

Loss from Impairment... 2
    Goodwill... 2

Assets	=	Liabilities	+	Shareholders' Equity	(Class.)
–2				–2	IncSt → RE

9.31 continued.

e. The loss occurs because of a significant change in the business climate for Chicken Franchisees. One might question whether this loss is temporary or permanent. Evidence from previous similar events (for example, Tylenol) suggests that consumers soon forget or at least forgive the offending company. The FASB reporting standard discusses but rejects the use of a permanency criterion in identifying impairment losses. Thus, an impairment loss occurs in this case because the future undiscounted cash flows of $6 million from the franchise rights are less than the carrying value of the franchise rights of $10 million. The amount of the impairment loss is $7 million (= $10 million − $3 million). The journal entry is (in millions):

Impairment Loss.. 7
    Franchise Rights 7

Assets	=	Liabilities	+	Shareholders' Equity	(Class.)
−7				−7	IncSt → RE

This entry assumes that Chicken Franchisees does not use an Accumulated Amortization account.

9.33 (General Mills; interpreting disclosures regarding long-lived assets.) (Amounts in Millions)

a. General Mills purchased software for its internal use from a software developer. General Mills expects to receive future benefits from using the software and the acquisition cost provides evidence of the amount of expected future benefits.

b. Yes. The computer software has a finite life because of technological obsolescence and would be depreciated.

c. Average Total Life: .5($5,806 − $54 − $252 + $6,096 − $61 − $276)/$421 = 13.4 years.

Average Age: .5($2,809 + $3,082)/$421 = 7.0 years.

d. Yes. The accumulated depreciation account increased by $273 (= $3,082 − $2,809). Depreciation expense increased accumulated depreciation by $421. Thus, the accumulated depreciation on assets sold or abandoned was $148 (= $273 − $421).

e. General Mills has grown heavily by corporate acquisitions. Intangibles comprise 57.9% (= $10,529/$18,184) of total assets. Because GAAP does not require firms to recognize internally developed intangibles, these intangibles arise from corporate acquisitions.

9.33 continued.

  f. Yes. The amount for brands and goodwill increased. Because firms cannot write up assets for increases in fair value, the increased amounts suggest a small acquisition during the year.

  g. Patents have a 20-year legal life and, therefore, have a finite life. Trademarks are subject to renewal at the end of their legal life as long as a firm continues to use them. General Mills must intend not to renew these trademarks.

  h. General Mills must expect the brand names to have an indefinite life. The firm would need to provide evidence based on past experience for its brand names and from industry experience to convince its independent accountants that the timing of any cessation of benefits is highly uncertain.

  i. General Mills shows amounts in its Construction in Progress account. Thus, General Mills must capitalize a portion of interest expense. The reported amount is the net of total interest cost minus the amount capitalized in Construction in Progress.

9.35 (Hewlett-Packard Company; interpreting disclosures regarding long-lived assets.) (Amounts in Millions)

  a. Average Total Life: .5($15,024 − $534 + $16,411 − $464)/$1,922 = 7.9 years.

   Average Age: .5($8,161 + $8,613)/$1,922 = 4.4 years.

  b. Yes. The Accumulated Depreciation account increased $452 (= $8,613 − $8,161). Depreciation increased the Accumulated Depreciation account by $1,922. Thus, the accumulated depreciation on assets sold or abandoned was $1,470 (= $452 − $1,922).

  c. Customer Contracts have a specific term and, therefore, have a finite life. Core Technology likely involves technologies related to the design of computer hardware and software in general and is not product specific. Given the pace of change in the computer industry, even core technologies change over time. HP would likely encounter difficulties in convincing its independent accountants that core technologies do not have a finite, albeit uncertain, life. Patents have a 20-year life, although the technological life in the computer industry is much shorter. Trademarks are renewable as long as a firm continues to use them. HP must expect to discontinue using the trademarks.

  d. Average Remaining Total Life: .5($4,612 + $6,122)/$783 = 6.9 years.

   Average Age: .5($2,682 + $3,465)/$783 = 3.9 years.

9.35 continued.

e. At the time of the acquisition, the Compaq name was highly recognizable. HP likely had no difficulty convincing its independent accountants that the brand name had an indefinite life. Given the elapsed time since the acquisition and the merging of Compaq products into HP's line of offerings, one wonders whether HP will write off the brand name at some point.

f. Yes. The amount of each intangible, except the Compaq brand name, increased during 2007. HP allocated a portion of the purchase price to these intangibles, with most of the increase involving goodwill.

CHAPTER 10

NOTES, BONDS, AND LEASES

Questions, Exercises, and Problems: Answers and Solutions

10.1   See the text or the glossary at the end of the book.

10.3   Applying the effective interest method using the historical market interest rate gives a constant amount of interest expense only if a firm initially issued bonds at face value. If a firm issued bonds at a discount or a premium to face value, then the amount of interest expense will change each period. A statement that applies to all bonds, whether issued at face value, a discount, or a premium, is that using the historical market interest rate in applying the effective interest method gives a constant rate of interest expense as a percentage of the liability at the beginning of the period. That constant rate is the historical market interest rate.

10.5   The initial issue prices will differ. Although the present value of the $1,000,000 face amount of these bonds will be the same for the two issues, the present value of the coupon payments will differ because the 9% coupon bonds requires larger cash outflows each year than the 7% coupon bonds.

10.7   The statement is still correct. Instead of repaying the bonds at maturity, the firm repurchases them in the market. The amount paid to repurchase the bonds depends on market interest rates at the time, but that amount is independent of whether the firm used the historical market interest rate or the current market interest rate to account for the bonds while they were outstanding.

10.9   The minimum contractual lease payments do not include the rental based on sales. If sales are zero, the lease payment will be zero. Thus, the "minimum" payment is zero. The present value of the "small fixed amount" will not likely exceed 90% of the fair market value of the property. The ten-year lease is also likely less than 75% of the useful life of the building.

10.11   The distinction depends upon which criteria of the lease made it a capital lease. The major difference is that at the end of a lease term the asset reverts to the lessor in a capital lease, whereas at the end of the installment payments, the asset belongs to the purchaser. The criteria for capitalizing a lease are such that the expected value of the asset when it reverts to the lessor is small, but misestimates can occur. In most other respects, capital leases and installment purchases are similar in economic substance.

Odd-numbered Solutions

10.13 Using the operating lease method for financial reporting permits the lessee to keep the lease liability off the balance sheet and report less cumulative expenses than the capital lease method. The lessee prefers the capital lease for income tax reporting because it reports more cumulative expenses than the operating lease method and therefore minimizes the present value of income tax payments.

10.15 (Hagar Company; amortization schedule for note where stated interest rate differs from historical market rate of interest.)

a. **Amortization Schedule for a Three-Year Note with a Maturity Value of $40,000, Calling for 6% Annual Interest Payments, Yield of 8% per Year**

Year	Carrying Value Start of Year	Interest Expense for Period	Payment	Interest Added to Carrying Value	Carrying Value End of Year
(1)	(2)	(3)a	(4)	(5)	(6)
1	$37,938	$ 3,035	$ 2,400	$ 635	$38,573
2	38,573	3,086	2,400	686	39,259
3	39,259	3,141	2,400	741	40,000

a(3) = (2) X .08.

b. Computer.. 37,938
   Note Payable... 37,938

Assets	= Liabilities	+	Shareholders' Equity	(Class.)
+37,938	+37,938			

To record purchase of computer.

Annual Journal Entry for Interest and Principal

Interest Expense............. Amount in Col. (3)
   Cash .... Amount in Col. (4)*
   Note Payable............... Amount in Col. (5)*

Assets	= Liabilities	+	Shareholders' Equity	(Class.)
−Amt (4)	+Amt (5)		−Amt (3)	IncSt → RE

*In third year, the firm also debits Note Payable and credits Cash for $40,000.

10.17   (Computing the issue price of bonds.)

     a. $1,000,000 x .14205[a] .... $ 142,050

         [a]Present value of $1 for 40 periods at 5%.

     b. $50,000 x 23.11477[a] .... $ 1,155,739

         [a]Present value of annuity for 40 periods at 3%.

     c. $50,000 x 19.79277[a] .... $ 989,639
          $1,000,000 x .20829[b]   208,290
                                                      $ 1,197,929

         [a]Present value of annuity for 40 periods at 4%.
         [b]Present value of $1 for 40 periods at 4%.

     d. $30,000 x 12.46221[a] .... $ 373,866
          $40,000 x 12.46221[a] x .37689[b]   187,875
          $1,000,000 x .14205[c]   142,050
                                                      $ 703,791

         [a]Present value of annuity for 20 periods at 5%.
         [b]Present value of $1 for 20 periods at 5%.
         [c]Present value of $1 for 40 periods at 5%.

10.19   (Seward Corporation; amortization schedule for bonds.)

     a. $100,000 x .74622[a] .... $ 74,622
          $4,000 x 5.07569[b]   20,303
           Issue Price .... $ 94,925

         [a]Table 2, 5% column and 6-period row.
         [b]Table 4, 5% column and 6-period row.

Odd-numbered Solutions

10.19 continued.

b.

Six-Month Period	Liability at Start of Period	Interest at 5% for Period	Cash Payment	Increase in Carrying Value of Liability	Liability at End of Period
1	$94,925	$ 4,746	$ 4,000	$ 746	$ 95,671
2	95,671	4,784	4,000	784	96,455
3	96,455	4,823	4,000	823	97,278
4	97,278	4,864	4,000	864	98,142
5	98,142	4,907	4,000	907	99,049
6	99,049	4,951[a]	4,000	951	100,000
Total..................		$ 29,075	$ 24,000	$ 5,075	

[a]Does not equal .05 x $99,049 due to rounding.

c. **January 2, 2008**
Cash... 94,925
    Bonds Payable... 94,925

Assets	=	Liabilities	+	Shareholders' Equity	(Class.)
−94,925		+94,925			

To record issue of bonds.

June 30, 2008
Interest Expense... 4,746
    Cash Payable... 4,000
    Bonds Payable... 746

Assets	=	Liabilities	+	Shareholders' Equity	(Class.)
−4,000		+746		−4,746	IncSt → RE

To record interest expense for first six months, the
cash payment, and the increase in the liability for
the difference.

10.19 c. continued.

December 31, 2008

Interest Expense... 4,784

    Cash..   4,000

    Bonds Payable...   784

Assets	=	Liabilities	+	Shareholders' Equity	(Class.)
–4,000		+784		–4,784	IncSt → RE

To record interest expense for the second six months, the cash payment, and the increase in the liability for the difference.

d. Bonds Payable (.20 x $98,142)................................... 19,628

    Loss on Retirement of Bonds...................................   772

        Cash..   20,400

Assets	=	Liabilities	+	Shareholders' Equity	(Class.)
–20,400		–19,628		–772	IncSt → RE

10.21 (Robinson Company; accounting for bonds using amortized cost measurement based on the historical market interest rate.)

    a. $5,000,000 x .37689[a]... $ 1,884,450

        $200,000 x 12.46221[b]   2,492,442

          Issue Price .... $ 4,376,892

    [a]Table 2, 5% column and 20-period row.

    [b]Table 4, 5% column and 20-period row.

    b. .05 x $4,376,892 = $218,845.

    c. .05($4,376,892 + $218,845 – $200,000) = $219,787.

    d. $4,376,892 + $218,845 – $200,000 + $219,787 – $200,000 = $4,415,524.

10.21 continued.

    e. $5,000,000 x .41552[a] .... $ 2,077,600
        $200,000 x 11.68959[b] .... <u>2,337,918</u>
          Present Value... <u>$ 4,415,518</u>

[a]Table 2, 5% column and 18-period row.
[b]Table 4, 5% column and 18-period row.

The difference between the carrying value in Part *d.* and the present value in Part *e.* results from rounding present value factors.

10.23   (Stroud Corporation; accounting for bonds using the fair value option based on the current market interest rate.)

    a. January 1, 2008: The carrying value of these bonds is $10,000,000, their issue price. The issue price equals the face value because the coupon rate and the required market yield both equal 6%.

June 30, 2008:
$10,000,000 x .5598676[a] .... $ 5,598,676
$300,000 x 14.197818[b] .... <u>4,259,346</u>
                                                        <u>$ 9,858,022</u>

[a]Present value of $1 for 19 periods at 3.1%.
[b]Present value of an annuity for 19 periods at 3.1%.

December 31, 2008:
$10,000,000 x .557435[a] .... $ 5,574,350
$300,000 x 13.411061[b] .... <u>4,023,318</u>
                                                        <u>$ 9,597,668</u>

[a]Present value of $1 for 18 periods at 3.3%.
[b]Present value of an annuity for 18 periods at 3.3%.

    b. Interest Expense: .03 x $10,000,000 = $300,000.

        Unrealized Gain: $141,978 (= $10,000,000 – $9,858,022).

    c. Interest Expense: .031 x $9,858,022 = $303,599. The carrying value of the bonds at the end of the second six months before computing the unrealized gain or loss is $9,861,621 (= $9,858,022 + $303,599 – $300,000).

        Unrealized Gain: $263,953 (= $9,861,621 – $9,597,668).

10.23 continued.

d. **January 1, 2008**
Cash...10,000,000
   Bonds Payable...   10,000,000

Assets	=	Liabilities	+	Shareholders' Equity	(Class.)
+10,000,000		+10,000,000			

To record issue of $10 million bonds at face value.

June 30, 2008
Interest Expense 300,000
   Cash   300,000

Assets	=	Liabilities	+	Shareholders' Equity	(Class.)
−300,000				−300,000	IncSt → RE

To record interest expense for the first six months.

June 30, 2008
Bonds Payable.. 141,978
   Unrealized Gain from Revaluation of Bonds.........   141,978

Assets	=	Liabilities	+	Shareholders' Equity	(Class.)
		−141,978		+141,978	IncSt → RE

To revalue bonds to current fair value.

December 31, 2008
Interest Expense 303,599
   Cash   300,000
   Bonds Payable...   3,599

Assets	=	Liabilities	+	Shareholders' Equity	(Class.)
−300,000		+3,599		−303,599	IncSt → RE

To record interest expense for the second six months.

10.23 d. continued.

December 31, 2008

Bonds Payable... 263,953

    Unrealized Gain on Revaluation of Bonds.............   263,953

Assets	=	Liabilities	+	Shareholders' Equity	(Class.)
		−263,953		+263,953	IncSt → RE

To revalue bonds to current fair value.

10.25 (Boeing and American; applying the capital lease criteria.)

a. This lease is a capital lease because the lease period of 20 years exceeds 75% of the expected life of the aircraft. The lease does not meet any other capital lease criteria. The aircraft reverts to Boeing at the end of 20 years. The present value of the lease payments when discounted at 10% is $51.1 million ($6 million X 8.51356), which is less than $54 million (= 90% of the fair value of $60 million).

b. This lease is a capital lease because the present value of the lease payments of $54.8 million (= $7.2 million X 7.60608) exceeds 90% of the $60 million fair value of the aircraft.

c. The lease is not a capital lease. The present value of the required lease payments of $36.9 million (= $5.5 million X 6.71008) is less than $54 million (= 90% of the fair value of the aircraft). The life of the lease is less than 75% of the expected useful life of the aircraft. The purchase option price coupled with the rental payments provides Boeing with a present value of all cash flows exceeding $62.4 million [= ($5.5 million X 6.71008) + ($55 million X .46319)]. This amount exceeds the usual sales price of $60 million, so there does not appear to be a bargain purchase option.

d. This lease is not a capital lease. The present value of the minimum required lease payments is $50.9 million (= $6.2 million X 8.20141). The fee contingent on usage could be zero, so the calculations exclude it. The life of the lease is less than 75% of the useful life of the aircraft. The aircraft reverts to Boeing at the end of the lease period.

10.27 (Sun Microsystems; preparing lessor's journal entries for an operating lease and a capital lease.)

a. This lease is a capital lease. The life of the lease equals the expected useful life of the property. The present value of the lease payments of $12,000 [= $4,386.70 + ($4,386.70 X 1.73554)] equals the fair value of the leased asset.

10.27 continued.

b. **Beginning of Each Year**

Cash... 4,386.70
    Rental Fees Received in Advance............................. 4,386.70

Assets	=	Liabilities	+	Shareholders' Equity	(Class.)
+4,386.70		+4,386.70			

To record cash received in advance from lessee.

End of Each Year

Rental Fees Received in Advance............................... 4,386.70
    Rent Revenue... 4,386.70

Assets	=	Liabilities	+	Shareholders' Equity	(Class.)
		−4,386.70		+4,386.70	IncSt → RE

To record rent revenue for each year.

Depreciation Expense 2,400.00
    Accumulated Depreciation.. 2,400.00

Assets	=	Liabilities	+	Shareholders' Equity	(Class.)
−2,400.00				−2,400.00	IncSt → RE

To record annual depreciation (= $7,200/3).

c. **January 1, 2008**

Cash... 4,386.70
Lease Receivable (= $4,386.70 x 1.73554)................. 7,613.30
    Sales Revenue... 12,000.00

Assets	=	Liabilities	+	Shareholders' Equity	(Class.)
+4,386.70				+12,000.00	IncSt → RE
+7,613.30					

To record "sale" of workstation.

10.27 c. continued.

Cost of Goods Sold.. 7,200.00

    Inventory 7,200.00

Assets	=	Liabilities	+	Shareholders' Equity	(Class.)
–7,200.00				–7,200.00	IncSt → RE

To record cost of workstation "sold".

December 31, 2008
Lease Receivable (= .10 x $7,613.30)........................ 761.33

    Interest Revenue... 761.33

Assets	=	Liabilities	+	Shareholders' Equity	(Class.)
+761.33				+761.33	IncSt → RE

To record interest revenue for 2008.

January 1, 2009
Cash... 4,386.70

    Lease Receivable.. 4,386.70

Assets	=	Liabilities	+	Shareholders' Equity	(Class.)
+4,386.70					
–4,386.70					

To record cash received at the beginning of 2009.
The carrying value of the receivable is now $3,987.93
(= $7,613.30 + $761.33 – $4,386.70).

December 31, 2009
Lease Receivable (= .10 x $3,987.93)........................ 398.77

    Interest Revenue... 398.77

Assets	=	Liabilities	+	Shareholders' Equity	(Class.)
+398.77				+398.77	IncSt → RE

To record interest revenue for 2009. Interest revenue
is slightly less than .10 x $3,987.93 due to rounding of
present value factors. The carrying value of the receivable is now $4,386.70 (= $3,987.93 + $398.77).

10.27 c. continued.

January 1, 2010

Cash.. 4,386.70
   Lease Receivable... 4,386.70

Assets	=	Liabilities	+	Shareholders' Equity	(Class.)
+4,386.70					
−4,386.70					

To record cash received for 2010.

10.29   (Aggarwal Corporation; accounting for long-term bonds.)

  a. **Interest Expense**
First Six Months: .05 x $301,512 = $15,076.
Second Six Months: .05($301,512 + $15,076) = $15,829.
Carrying value of bonds on December 31, 2008: $301,512 + $15,076 +
   $15,829 = $332,417.

  b. **Carrying Value of Bonds on December 31, 2007**
Interest:
   $35,000 x 8.11090 = $ 283,882   (Table 4, 10 periods and 4%)
Principal:
   $1,000,000 x .67556 =   675,560   (Table 2, 10 periods and 4%)
   Total............................ $ 959,442

Carrying Value of Bonds, December 31, 2007......................... $ 959,442
Add Interest Expense for 2008 x
Subtract Coupon Payments during 2008.................................. (70,000)
Carrying Value of Bonds, December 31, 2008.......................... $ 966,336

Interest expense for 2008 is $76,894.

  c. **Carrying Value of Bonds on July 1, 2008**
Carrying Value of Bonds, December 31, 2007...................... $ 1,305,832
Plus Interest Expense for First Six Months of 2008: .03
  x $1,305,832... 39,175
Subtract Coupon Payment during First Six Months of
  2008 .... (45,000)
Carrying Value of Bonds, July 1, 2008.............................. $ 1,300,007
Carrying Value of One-Half of Bonds................................ $ 650,004

10.29 c. continued.

July 1, 2008

Bonds Payable	650,004	
Cash		526,720
Gain on Bonds Retirement		123,284

Assets	=	Liabilities	+	Shareholders' Equity	(Class.)
−526,720		−650,004		+123,284	IncSt → RE

d. **Interest Expense for Second Six Months**
.03 x $650,004 = $19,500.

10.31   (Understanding and using bond tables.)

a. The coupon rate on these bonds of 8% compounded semiannually equals the historical market interest rate of 8% compounded semiannually. The initial issue price therefore equals the face value. The carrying value increases each period for interest expense equal to 4% of the carrying value of the liability at the beginning of the period and decreases for 4% of the face value of the liability. Because the carrying value equals the face value throughout the life of the bonds, the carrying value remains at face value.

b. The coupon rate on these bonds is 8% compounded semiannually. When the historical market interest rate exceeds the coupon rate, the bonds will have a carrying value greater than face value. When the historical market interest rate is less than the coupon rate, the bonds will have a carrying value less than face value.

c. Firms amortize any initial issue premium as a reduction in interest expense and a reduction in the bond liability over the life of the bonds. Firms amortize any initial issue discount as an increase in interest expense and an increase in the bond liability over the life of the bonds.

d. $1,000,000 x 111.7278% = $1,117,278. Note that the rows indicate *years* to maturity, not the total number of periods.

e. $1,000,000 x 110.6775% = $1,106,775.

f.
Cash Payment for Interest	$	80,000
Decrease in Carrying Value of Liability during 2013:		
$1,000,000 x (110.6775% − 110.4205%)		(2,570)
Interest Expense	$	77,430

10.31 f. continued.

Interest Expense, First Six Months: .035 x ($1,000,000 x
110.6775%).. $ 38,737
Interest Expense, Second Six Months: .035 x ($1,000,000
x 110.5512%)... 38,693
Interest Expense... $ 77,430

g. Carrying Value of Liability: $1,000,000 x 107.1062%....... $ 1,071,062
Market Value of Liability: $1,000,000 x 101.3711%.......... 1,013,711
Unrealized Gain Increasing Retained Earnings.................... $ 57,351

h. Interest expense for first six months is $39,535 (= .078/2 x $1,013,711).
The carrying value of the liability at the end of the first six months
before recognizing any unrealized gain or loss is $1,013,246 (=
$1,013,711 + $39,535 – $40,000) = $1,000,000 x 101.3246%.

Unrealized Gain:
Carrying Value before Unrealized Gain............................... $ 1,013,246
Market Value on June 30, 2023: $1,000,000 x
98.0548%.. 980,548
Unrealized Gain.. $ 32,698

i. Interest expense for the second six months is $40,692 (= .083/2 x
$980,548). The carrying value of the liability at the end of the second six
months before recognizing any unrealized gain or loss is $981,240 (=
$980,548 + $40,692 – $40,000) = $1,000,000 x 98.1240%.

Unrealized Gain:
Carrying Value before Unrealized Gain............................... $ 981,240
Market Value on December 31, 2023: $1,000,000 x
93.920% 939,200
Unrealized Gain.. $ 42,040

10.33 (IBM and Adair Corporation; accounting for lease by lessor and lessee.)

a. **January 1, 2008**
Cash.. 10,000
Note Payable.. 10,000

Assets	=	Liabilities	+	Shareholders' Equity	(Class.)
+10,000		+10,000			

Odd-numbered Solutions

10.33 a. continued.

| Computer | 10,000 | |
| Cash | | 10,000 |

Assets	=	Liabilities	+	Shareholders' Equity	(Class.)
+10,000					
−10,000					

December 31, 2008

| Depreciation Expense | 3,333 | |
| Accumulated Depreciation | | 3,333 |

Assets	=	Liabilities	+	Shareholders' Equity	(Class.)
−3,333				−3,333	IncSt → RE

Interest Expense (.08 X $10,000)	800	
Note Payable (Plug)	3,080	
Cash ($10,000/2.57710)		3,880

Assets	=	Liabilities	+	Shareholders' Equity	(Class.)
−3,880		−3,080		−800	IncSt → RE

December 31, 2009

| Depreciation Expense | 3,333 | |
| Accumulated Depreciation | | 3,333 |

Assets	=	Liabilities	+	Shareholders' Equity	(Class.)
−3,333				−3,333	IncSt → RE

Interest Expense [.08 X ($10,000 − $3,080)]	554	
Note Payable (Plug)	3,326	
Cash		3,880

Assets	=	Liabilities	+	Shareholders' Equity	(Class.)
−3,880		−3,326		−554	IncSt → RE

b. **January 1, 2008**
No entry.

10.33 b. continued.

December 31, 2008

Rent Expense.. 3,810
    Cash.. 3,810

Assets	=	Liabilities	+	Shareholders' Equity	(Class.)
−3,810				−3,810	IncSt → RE

December 31, 2009

Rent Expense.. 3,810
    Cash.. 3,810

Assets	=	Liabilities	+	Shareholders' Equity	(Class.)
−3,810				−3,810	IncSt → RE

c. ### January 1, 2008

Leased Asset... 10,000
    Lease Liability... 10,000

Assets	=	Liabilities	+	Shareholders' Equity	(Class.)
+10,000		+10,000			

December 31, 2008

Depreciation Expense 3,333
    Accumulated Depreciation..................................... 3,333

Assets	=	Liabilities	+	Shareholders' Equity	(Class.)
−3,333				−3,333	IncSt → RE

Interest Expense (.07 x $10,000).............................. 700
Lease Liability (Plug)... 3,110
    Cash ($10,000/2.62432)... 3,810

Assets	=	Liabilities	+	Shareholders' Equity	(Class.)
−3,810		−3,110		−700	IncSt → RE

10.33 c. continued.

December 31, 2009

Depreciation Expense 3,333

Accumulated Depreciation 3,333

Assets	=Liabilities	+	Shareholders' Equity	(Class.)
–3,333			–3,333	IncSt → RE

Interest Expense [.07 x ($10,000 – $3,110)] 482

Lease Liability (Plug) 3,328

Cash 3,810

Assets	=Liabilities	+	Shareholders' Equity	(Class.)
–3,810	–3,328		–482	IncSt → RE

d. **January 1, 2008**

Cash 10,000

Sales Revenue 10,000

Assets	=Liabilities	+	Shareholders' Equity	(Class.)
+10,000			+10,000	IncSt → RE

Cost of Goods Sold 6,000

Inventory 6,000

Assets	=Liabilities	+	Shareholders' Equity	(Class.)
–6,000			–6,000	IncSt → RE

December 31, 2008 and 2009

No entries necessary.

e. **January 1, 2008**

Computer Equipment 6,000

Inventory 6,000

Assets	=Liabilities	+	Shareholders' Equity	(Class.)
+6,000				
–6,000				

10.33 e. continued.

December 31, 2008

Depreciation Expense..			2,000	
Accumulated Depreciation....................................				2,000

Assets	=	Liabilities	+	Shareholders' Equity	(Class.)
−2,000				−2,000	IncSt → RE

Cash..			3,810	
Rent Revenue..				3,810

Assets	=	Liabilities	+	Shareholders' Equity	(Class.)
+3,810				+3,810	IncSt → RE

December 31, 2009

Depreciation Expense..			2,000	
Accumulated Depreciation....................................				2,000

Assets	=	Liabilities	+	Shareholders' Equity	(Class.)
−2,000				−2,000	IncSt → RE

Cash..			3,810	
Rent Revenue..				3,810

Assets	=	Liabilities	+	Shareholders' Equity	(Class.)
+3,810				+3,810	IncSt → RE

f. **January 1, 2008**

Lease Receivable...			10,000	
Sales Revenue..				10,000

Assets	=	Liabilities	+	Shareholders' Equity	(Class.)
+10,000				+10,000	IncSt → RE

Cost of Goods Sold..			6,000	
Inventory				6,000

Assets	=	Liabilities	+	Shareholders' Equity	(Class.)
−6,000				−6,000	IncSt → RE

10.33 f. continued.

December 31, 2008

Cash	3,810	
Interest Revenue (see Part *c*.)		700
Lease Receivable		3,110

Assets	=	Liabilities	+	Shareholders' Equity	(Class.)
+3,810				+700	IncSt → RE
−3,110					

December 31, 2009

Cash	3,810	
Interest Revenue (see Part *c*.)		482
Lease Receivable		3,328

Assets	=	Liabilities	+	Shareholders' Equity	(Class.)
+3,810				+482	IncSt → RE
−3,328					

g. **Lessee**

Borrow and Purchase	2008	2009	2010	Total
Depreciation Expense	$ 3,333	$ 3,333	$ 3,334	$ 10,000
Interest Expense	800	554	286	1,640
	$ 4,133	$ 3,887	$ 3,620	$ 11,640

Operating Lease				
Rent Expense	$ 3,810	$ 3,810	$ 3,810	$ 11,430

Capital Lease				
Depreciation Expense	$ 3,333	$ 3,333	$ 3,334	$ 10,000
Interest Expense	700	482	248	1,430
	$ 4,033	$ 3,815	$ 3,582	$ 11,430

10.33 continued.

h. **Lessor**

	2008	2009	2010	Total
Sale				
Sales Revenue.................	$10,000	$ --	$ --	$ 10,000
Cost of Goods Sold...........	(6,000)	--	--	(6,000)
	$ 4,000	$ --	$ --	$ 4,000
Operating Lease				
Rent Revenue..................	$ 3,810	$ 3,810	$ 3,810	$ 11,430
Depreciation Expense.....	(2,000)	(2,000)	(2,000)	(6,000)
	$ 1,810	$ 1,810	$ 1,810	$ 5,430
Capital Lease				
Sales Revenue.................	$10,000	$ --	$ --	$ 10,000
Cost of Goods Sold...........	(6,000)	--	--	(6,000)
Interest Revenue.............	700	482	248	1,430
	$ 4,700	$ 482	$ 248	$ 5,430

10.35 (Northern Airlines; financial statement effects of capital and operating leases.) (Amounts in Millions)

a.
Capital Lease Liability, December 31, 2007............................	$ 1,088
Plus Interest Expense (Plug).......................................	102
Plus New Capital Leases Signed[a]...................................	0
Less Cash Payment on Capital Leases..................................	(263)
Capital Lease Liability, December 31, 2008...........................	$ 927

[a]A comparison of the commitments under capital leases on December 31, 2007 and December 31, 2008 indicates that Northern Airlines did not sign any new capital leases during 2008.

b. $102/$1,088 = 9.375\%$.

c.
Capitalized Leased Asset, December 31, 2007	$ 1,019
Plus New Capital Leases Signed[a].................................	0
Less Depreciation on Capital Leases (Plug)...........................	(154)
Capital Leased Asset, December 31, 2008	$ 865

[a]See Footnote [a] to Part a. above.

10.35 continued.

d. **December 31, 2008**
Interest Expense.. 102
Lease Liability... 161
   Cash.. 263

Assets	=	Liabilities	+	Shareholders' Equity	(Class.)
−263		−161		−102	IncSt → RE

To record interest expense on capital leases, the cash
payment, and decrease in the capital lease liability for
the difference.

December 31, 2008
Depreciation Expense 154
   Accumulated Depreciation.................................... 154

Assets	=	Liabilities	+	Shareholders' Equity	(Class.)
−154				−154	IncSt → RE

To recognize depreciation expense on capitalized
leased asset for 2008.

e. **December 31, 2008**
Rent Expense.. 1,065
   Cash.. 1,065

Assets	=	Liabilities	+	Shareholders' Equity	(Class.)
−1,065				−1,065	IncSt → RE

To recognize rent expense on operating leases for
2008.

10.35 continued.

f.

Present Value of Operating Lease Commitment on
December 31, 2007

Year	Payments	Present Value Factor at 10.0%	Present Value
2008	$ 1,065	.90909	$ 968
2009	$ 1,039	.82645	859
2010	$ 973	.75131	731
2011	$ 872	.68301	596
2012	$ 815	.62092	506
After			
2012	$ 7,453[a]	5.81723[b] x .62092[c]	2,944
Total			$ 6,604

[a]Assume that the firm pays the $7,453 at the rate of $815 a year for 9.145 (= $7,453/$815) periods at 10%.

[b]Factor for the present value of an annuity of $815 million for 9.145 periods at 10%.

[c]Factor for the present value of $1 for five periods at 10%.

Present Value of Operating Lease Commitment on
December 31, 2008

Year	Payments	Present Value Factor at 10.0%	Present Value
2009	$ 1,098	.90909	$ 998
2010	$ 1,032	.82645	853
2011	$ 929	.75131	698
2012	$ 860	.68301	587
2013	$ 855	.62092	531
After			
2013	$ 6,710[a]	5.26685[b] x .62092[c]	2,796
Total			$ 6,463

[a]Assume that the firm pays the $6,710 at the rate of $855 a period for 7.848 (= $6,710/$855) periods.

[b]Factor for the present value of an annuity of $855 million for 7.848 periods at 10%.

[c]Factor for the present value of $1 for five periods at 10%.

10.35 continued.

    g. **Long-Term Debt Ratio Based on Reported Amounts:**
        December 31, 2007: $13,456/$29,495 = 45.6%
        December 31, 2008: $12,041/$29,145 = 41.3%

    h. **Long-Term Debt Ratio Including Capitalization of Operating Leases:**
        December 31, 2007: ($13,456 + $6,604 − $968)/($29,495 + $6,604) =
               52.9%
        December 31, 2008: ($12,041 + $6,463 − $998)/($29,145 + $6,463) =
               49.2%

10.37   (GSB Corporation; measuring interest expense.)

The Carrying value of a liability changes during a period as follows:

Beginning Balance + Interest Expense − Cash Payment = Ending Balance

Substituting the known information:
    BB + .05BB − $4,400 = $110,000

Solving for BB:
    1.05BB = $114,400
       BB = $108,952

Thus, interest expense for this last six month period equals $5,447.62 (= .05 x $108,952).

CHAPTER 11

LIABILITIES: OFF-BALANCE-SHEET FINANCING, RETIREMENT BENEFITS, AND INCOME TAXES

Questions, Exercises, and Problems: Answers and Solutions

11.1   See the text or the glossary at the end of the book.

11.3   The financial components approach records the benefits to each entity as an asset and the obligations of each entity as a liability. Although accountants must make a judgment about whether the seller of an asset retains most of the benefits and risks (the asset and the related financing appear on the balance sheet) or whether the purchaser obtains most of the benefits and risks (the seller removes the asset and does not record a liability on the balance sheet), each entity records assets and liabilities for any benefits obtained and risks incurred. Absent the financial components approach, the recording would reflect an all-or-nothing approach.

11.5   The use of a special purpose entity enhances the ability of a firm to demonstrate that it has transferred control of the receivables to the purchaser. Whether the transferor has in fact transferred control depends on its relation to the special purpose entity and its rights and obligations related to the receivables. The special purpose entity at least permits separation of the receivables from the transferring entity.

11.7   Laws require firms to contribute funds to an independent trustee to manage on behalf of employees. The employer cannot use these funds for its general corporate purposes.

11.9   Firms typically have multiple pension plans for their different groups of employees (for example, wage earners versus corporate officers, domestic employees versus non-domestic employees). Some plans have assets that exceed liabilities and other plans have liabilities that exceed assets. Netting all pension plans results in loss of information about the mix of overfunded and underfunded plans.

11.11   GAAP requires firms to increase pension expense for the increase in the pension obligation that results from the passage of time (that is, the interest cost). Firms must generate earnings from investments sufficient to fund this increase in present value. Earnings from pension investments offset the interest cost, explaining why GAAP requires a subtraction for earnings from investments.

11.13 Income tax expense equals income taxes payable currently plus (minus) the income taxes the firm expects to pay (save) in the future when revenues and expenses that appear in book income now appear in tax returns later.

11.15 Deferred tax assets (liabilities) arise when a firm recognizes revenue (expense) earlier for tax purposes than book purposes or expenses (revenues) later for tax purposes than for book purposes. Deferred tax assets (liabilities) provide for lower (higher) taxable income in the future relative to book income and, therefore, future tax savings (costs).

11.17 Analysts often forecast earnings and need to make some assumption about a firm's average, or effective, tax rate in future periods. The information in the tax reconciliation helps the analysts in judging whether reconciling items in recent years will likely continue or not.

11.19 (Cypres Appliance Store; using accounts receivable to achieve off-balance-sheet financing.)

a. (1) **January 2, 2008**

Cash... 92,593
    Bank Loan Payable......................................   92,593

Assets	=	Liabilities	+	Shareholders' Equity	(Class.)
+92,593		+92,593			

To record bank loan.

December 31, 2008

Cash... 100,000
    Accounts Receivable....................................   100,000

Assets	=	Liabilities	+	Shareholders' Equity	(Class.)
+100,000					
−100,000					

To record collections from customers.

Interest Expense (= .08 x $92,593).................. 7,407
Bank Loan Payable.. 92,593
    Cash   100,000

Assets	=	Liabilities	+	Shareholders' Equity	(Class.)
−100,000		−92,593		−7,407	IncSt → RE

To record interest expense on loan for 2008 and repayment of the loan.

11.19 a. continued.

(2) Cash				92,593
Loss from Sale of Accounts Receivable				7,407
Accounts Receivable				100,000

Assets	= Liabilities	+	Shareholders' Equity	(Class.)
+92,593			−7,407	IncSt → RE
−100,000				

To record sale of accounts receivable; an alternative title for the loss account is interest expense.

b. Both transactions result in an expense of $7,407 for 2008 for this financing. Both transactions result in an immediate increase in cash. Liabilities increase for the collateralized loan, whereas an asset decreases for the sale.

c. Cypres Appliance Store must attempt to shift credit and interest rate risk to the bank. The bank should have no rights to demand additional receivables if interest rates increase or uncollectible accounts appear. Likewise, Cypres Appliance Store should have no rights to buy back the accounts receivable if interest rates decline. The bank of course will not both lend on the receivables and purchase the receivables at the same price because it incurs different amounts of risk in each case.

11.21 (Preparing journal entry for pension plan.) (Amounts in Millions)

2008

Pension Expense	1,050	
Pension Asset ($46,203 − $45,582)	621	
Pension Liability ($45,183 − $43,484)	1,699	
Cash		526
Other Comprehensive Income (Actuarial Gains and Losses: $960 gain + $1,101 amortization)		2,061
Other Comprehensive Income (Excess of Actual Return over Expected Return on Investments: $4,239 − $3,456)		783

11.21 continued.

Assets	=	Liabilities	+	Shareholders' Equity	(Class.)
+621		−1,699		−1,050	IncSt → RE
−526				+2,061	OCI → AOCI
				+783	OCI → AOCI

To record pension expense and pension funding for 2008, eliminate the net pension liability at the beginning of the year, recognize the net pension asset at the end of the year, and recognize other comprehensive income for the change in actuarial and performance gains and losses.

11.23   (Preparing journal entry for health care plan.) (Amounts in Millions)

2008

Health Care Expense...	2,183
Health Care Liability [($30,863 − $5,460) − ($39,274 − $6,497)]	7,374
Other Comprehensive Income (Actuarial Gains and Losses: $9,485 gain + $41 amortization).....	9,526
Other Comprehensive Income (Excess of Actual Return over Expected Return on Investments: $510 − $479)...	31

Assets	=	Liabilities	+	Shareholders' Equity	(Class.)
		−7,374		−2,183	IncSt → RE
				+9,526	OCI → AOCI
				+31	OCI → AOCI

To record health care expense for 2008, the reduction in the health care liability, and other comprehensive income for the change in actuarial and performance gains and losses.

11.25   (Preparing journal entries for income tax expense.) (Amounts in Millions)

a.   **2006**

Income Tax Expense 272

Income Tax Receivable.. 96

    Deferred Tax Liability..   368

Assets	=	Liabilities	+	Shareholders' Equity	(Class.)
+96		+368		−272	IncSt → RE

To record income tax expense, a claim for a refund in taxes paid previously, and the increase in the deferred tax liability for 2006.

2007

Income Tax Expense 341

Deferred Tax Liability.. 74

    Income Tax Payable   415

Assets	=	Liabilities	+	Shareholders' Equity	(Class.)
		−74		−341	IncSt → RE
		+415			

To record income tax expense, income tax payable, and the decrease in the deferred tax liability for 2007.

2008

Income Tax Expense 390

    Income Tax Payable   46

    Deferred Tax Liability..   344

Assets	=	Liabilities	+	Shareholders' Equity	(Class.)
		+46		−390	IncSt → RE
		+344			

To record income tax expense, income tax payable, and the increase in the deferred tax liability for 2008.

b. The firm operated at a net taxable loss for 2006 and likely received a refund of taxes paid in previous years due to net operating loss carryforward provisions in the income tax law. The net taxable loss likely occurred because the firm acquired new equipment for which accelerated depreciation deductions for tax purposes exceeded straight-line depreciation for financial reporting. The increase in the deferred tax liability for 2006 supports this explanation. 2007 was a profitable year for both financial and tax reporting. The decrease in the deferred tax liability for temporary depreciation differences suggests that the firm reduced its capital expenditures sufficiently during 2007 to permit straight-line depreciation for financial reporting to exceed accelerated depreciation for tax reporting. 2008 was similar to 2006 except that accelerated depreciation for tax purposes resulted in low but positive taxable income and again led to an increase in the deferred tax liability. Note that income before taxes for financial reporting increased each year in line with the increase in income tax expense because of the stable effective tax rate.

11.27 (Lilly Company; reconstructing information about income taxes.)

LILLY COMPANY
Illustrations of Timing Differences and Permanent Differences

	Financial Statements	Type of Difference	Income Tax Return
Operating Income Except Depreciation	$427,800 (6)	--	$427,800 (4)
Depreciation	(322,800) (g)	Temporary	(358,800) (3)
Municipal Bond Interest	85,800 (5)	Permanent	--
Taxable Income	--		$ 69,000 (2)
Pretax Book Income	$190,800 (g)		
Income Taxes Payable at 40%			$ 27,600 (g)
Income Tax Expense at 40% of $105,000 = $427,800 − $322,800, Which Is Income Excluding Permanent Differences	(42,000) (g)		
Net Income	$148,800 (1)		

11.27 continued.

Order and derivation of computations:
(g) Given.
(1) $148,800 = $190,800 − $42,000.
(2) $69,000 = $27,600/.40.
(3) Temporary difference for depreciation is ($42,000 − $27,600)/.40 = $36,000. Because income taxes payable are less than income tax expense, we know that depreciation deducted on tax return exceeds depreciation expense on financial statements. Thus, the depreciation deduction on the tax return is $358,800 = $322,800 + $36,000.
(4) $427,800 = $358,800 + $69,000.
(5) Taxable income on financial statements is $105,000 = $42,000/.40. Total financial statement income before taxes, including permanent differences, is $190,800. Hence, permanent differences are $190,800 − $105,000 = $85,800.
(6) $190,800 + $322,800 − $85,800 = $427,800. See also (4), for check.

11.29 (Federated Department Stores; interpreting disclosures regarding sales of receivables.)

a. Exhibit 11.2 in the text contains the GAAP criteria to qualify a transfer of receivables as a sale.

1. The receivables are isolated from the transferor: the receivables are in the possession and ownership of Citibank.

2. The receivables are transferred to an entity that has the right to pledge or exchange the receivables: Federated Department Stores (Federated) has not placed restrictions on the receivables that constrain Citibank from doing what it pleases with the receivables.

3. The transferor does not maintain control over the receivables: Citibank incurs interest rate, credit, and bankruptcy risk, controls which customers receive credit, and services the credit accounts.

b. Federated benefits from the increased sales revenue that the credit cards provide without incurring interest rate, credit, and bankruptcy risk. Federated also does not incur the administrative cost of the credit card operation. Federated loses control over which of its customers can obtain credit cards, perhaps losing sales it would otherwise obtain if Federated controlled the granting of credit. The disclosures in Exhibit 11.16 in the text do not indicate the nature of any other marketing provisions but perhaps Citibank advertises its association with Federated and, thereby, enhances the Federated brand name.

Odd-numbered Solutions

11.29 continued.

    c.   These special purpose entities likely enhanced Federated's ability to isolate the receivables that it sold to GE Capital Consumer Co. and, thereby, qualify the transfers as sales instead of collateralized borrowing. Federated appears to have maintained a closer association with the credit cards under the arrangement with GE Capital Consumer Co. than under the new arrangement with Citibank. The arrangement with GE Capital Consumer Co. appears to primarily involve financing services, whereas the new arrangement involves a shift of the credit card operation to Citibank.

11.31   (Interpreting retirement plans disclosures.) (Amounts in Millions)

    a.   The firm increased the discount rate it used to compute the pension and health care obligations from 5.7% to 5.8%, thereby reducing the present value of these obligations and resulting in an actuarial gain. Also, the firm reduced the initial health care cost trend rate from 10% to 9%, which reduced the health care obligation and resulted in an actuarial gain. Offsetting these two factors is a change in the assumed rate of compensation increases, which increases the pension obligation and offsets the actuarial gains from the preceding two factors. Note that the firm amortized an actuarial loss from previous years in computing its net pension expense and net health care expense. The question does not address this amortization but only the actuarial gain that arose in 2008.

    b.   The actual return on investments (disclosed in the change in fair value of plan assets) exceeded the expected return on investments (disclosed in the computation of net pension expense) each year.

    c.   The firm contributed cash to the health care plan each year equal to the benefits paid. Thus, the health care plan has no assets to invest on which to generate a return. Common terminology refers to such funding arrangements as *pay as you go*.

    d.

Prior Service Cost, End of 2007	$ 5
Plus Increase in Prior Service Cost during 2008 from Plan Amendments	11
Less Amortization of Prior Service Cost during 2008	(3)
Prior Service Cost, End of 2008	$ 13

    e.

Net Actuarial Loss, End of 2007	$ 2,285
Less Decrease in Actuarial Loss during 2008 from Actuarial Gain in Pension Obligation	(163)
Less Amortization of Actuarial Loss during 2008	(164)
Less Excess of Actual Return over Expected Return on Pension Investments ($513 – $391)	(122)
Prior Service Credit, End of 2008	$ 1,836

11.31 continued.

f.
Prior Service Credit, End of 2007...	$ 114
Less Amortization of Prior Service Cost during 2008	(13)
Prior Service Credit, End of 2008..	$ 101

g.
Net Actuarial Loss, End of 2007..	$ 419
Less Decrease in Actuarial Loss from Actuarial Gain in Pension Obligation during 2008	(34)
Less Amortization of Actuarial Loss during 2008..................	(21)
Net Actuarial Loss, End of 2008...	$ 364

h. **2008**

Pension Expense...	340	
Pension Liability (Noncurrent Liabilities: $2,753 – $729)..	2,024	
Other Comprehensive Income (Prior Service Cost: $13 – $5)..	8	
Other ($7 – $3)..	4	
Cash...		19
Pension Asset (Noncurrent Assets: $2,068 – $185)...		1,883
Pension Liability (Current Liabilities: $25 – $0)..		25
Other Comprehensive Income (Actuarial Loss: $2,285 – $1,836)...		449

Assets	=	Liabilities	+	Shareholders' Equity	(Class.)
+4		–2,024		–340	IncSt → RE
–19		+25		–8	OCI → AOCI
–1,883				+449	OCI → AOCI

To record pension expense, pension funding, and the change in balance sheet accounts relating to the pension plan for 2008.

11.31 continued.

    i. **2008**

Health Care Expense 126

Health Care Liability (Noncurrent Liabilities:
$1,312 – $1,270) 42

Other Comprehensive Income (Prior Service Cost:
$114 – $101) 13

Other 49

    Cash 75

    Health Care Liability (Current Liabilities:
$100 – $0) 100

    Other Comprehensive Income (Actuarial Loss:
$419 – $364) 55

Assets	=	Liabilities	+	Shareholders' Equity	(Class.)
+49		−42		−126	IncSt → RE
−75		+100		−13	OCI → AOCI
				+55	OCI → AOCI

To record health care expense, health care funding,
and the change in balance sheet accounts relating to
the health care plan for 2008.

11.33   (Interpreting income tax disclosures.) (Amounts in Millions)

    a. **2007**

Income Tax Expense 699

Deferred Income Taxes 39

    Income Tax Payable 738

Assets	=	Liabilities	+	Shareholders' Equity	(Class.)
+39	or	−39		−699	IncSt → RE
		+738			

To record income tax expense, income tax payable,
and a debit change in deferred income taxes for 2007.

11.33 continued.

b. **2008**

Income Tax Expense 742
    Income Tax Payable 736
    Deferred Income Taxes 6

Assets	=	Liabilities	+	Shareholders' Equity	(Class.)
		+736		−742	IncSt → RE
−6	or	+6			

To record income tax expense, income tax payable, and the credit change in deferred income taxes for 2008.

c. The first line of the tax reconciliation assumes that governmental entities tax income before income taxes at 35%. However, 35% is only the U.S. federal tax rate. State and local taxes (net of any tax savings from subtracting state and local taxes in computing U.S. federal taxable income) increase the effective tax rate above 35%.

d. Nondeductible items increase the effective tax rate, despite their appearing with other reconciling items with a negative sign in this case. The first line of the tax reconciliation assumes that all costs or expenses save income taxes at a 35% tax rate. If firms cannot deduct a particular cost or expense for tax purposes, the effective tax rate on income before income taxes increases.

e. A recognized pension liability or health care liability suggests that a firm has recognized more pension or health care expense than the firm has contributed cash. The contribution of cash gives rise to an income tax deduction. Thus, taxable income exceeds book income, resulting in a deferred tax asset for the higher taxes paid currently. A recognized prepaid pension asset suggests that a firm has contributed more cash to the pension fund than it had recognized as pension expense. Thus, book income exceeds taxable income, resulting in a deferred tax liability for the delayed payment of taxes.

f. GAAP requires firms using the accrual basis of accounting to recognize sales allowances as an expense in the period of sale, whereas firms cannot deduct sales allowances in computing taxable income until making actual expenditures. Thus, a growing firm will likely record higher taxable income than book income and recognize a deferred tax asset for the early payment of taxes.

11.33 continued.

g. This firm increased the deferred tax asset for expected benefits from tax loss and tax credit carryforwards. If the entity that realized the tax losses is not yet profitable, uncertainty exists as to whether this firm will benefit from the tax losses and tax credit carryforwards, creating the need for a valuation allowance. Some of the other items in deferred tax assets may relate to the unprofitable entity, leading as well to uncertainty about the ability to realize those tax benefits.

h. The decreasing amount of deferred tax liability for temporary depreciation differences suggests that book depreciation exceeds tax depreciation. The likely explanation is that this firm reduced its expenditures on depreciable assets, resulting in more assets in the later years of their lives when straight-line depreciation for book purposes exceeds accelerated depreciation for tax purposes than assets in their early years when accelerated depreciation exceeds straight-line depreciation. Cumulative depreciation for tax purposes still exceeds cumulative depreciation for book purposes because this firm reports a deferred tax liability.

i. This firm is the lessor. The reporting of a deferred tax liability indicates that cumulative book income exceeds cumulative taxable income. This firm likely accounts for these leases as capital leases for financial reporting and operating leases for tax reporting. The capital lease method results in the lessor reporting a gain in the year the parties sign the lease, whereas the operating lease method spreads the income over the term of the lease.

11.35 (Interpreting income tax disclosures.) (Amounts in Millions)

a. **2006**

Income Tax Expense 1,146
    Income Tax Payable 1,052
    Deferred Income Taxes.. 94

Assets	=	Liabilities	+	Shareholders' Equity	(Class.)
		+1,052		−1,146	IncSt → RE
−94	or	+94			

To record income tax expense, income tax payable, and the change in deferred income taxes for 2006.

11.35 continued.

b. **2007**

Income Tax Expense	1,452
Deferred Income Taxes	122
Income Tax Payable	1,574

Assets	=	Liabilities	+	Shareholders' Equity	(Class.)
−122	or	−122		−1,452	IncSt → RE
		+1,574			

To record income tax expense, income tax payable,
and the change in deferred income taxes for 2007.

c. **2008**

Income Tax Expense	1,710
Deferred Income Taxes	201
Income Tax Payable	1,911

Assets	=	Liabilities	+	Shareholders' Equity	(Class.)
−201	or	−201		−1,710	IncSt → RE
		+1,911			

To record income tax expense, income tax payable,
and the change in deferred income taxes for 2008.

d. The deferred tax amounts in Exhibit 11.24 in the text relate not only to amounts affecting income tax expense of the current period but also to tax effects of items included in other balance sheet items. For example, when firms debit or credit other comprehensive income when initially recognizing or subsequently amortizing prior service costs and actuarial gains and losses of pension and health care plans, the firms must credit or debit other comprehensive income for the income tax effects of these items. The deferred tax amounts in Exhibit 11.24 in the text include the tax effects of all temporary differences, not just those affecting income tax expense of the current period.

e. The first line of the tax reconciliation assumes that governmental entities tax income before income taxes at 35%. However, 35% is only the U.S. federal tax rate. State and local taxes (net of any tax savings from subtracting state and local taxes in computing U.S. federal taxable income) increase the effective tax rate above 35%.

11.35 continued.

f. The deferred tax asset for health care benefits suggests that this firm has an underfunded health care plan. This firm has recognized more health care expenses than it has contributed cash to the health care benefits plan. The cash contribution triggers an income tax deduction for computing taxable income. This firm has prepaid income taxes because health care expense for tax is less than book, giving rise to the deferred tax asset. The deferred tax liability for pension care benefits suggests that this firm has an overfunded pension plan. The firm has recognized less pension expenses than it has contributed cash to the pension benefits plan. The cash contribution triggers an income tax deduction for computing taxable income. The firm has delayed paying income taxes because pension expense for tax exceeds pension expense for book, giving rise to the deferred tax liability.

g. A steady deferred tax liability for temporary depreciation differences suggests that depreciation using the accelerated method for tax purposes approximately equals straight-line depreciation for book purposes. This equality generally occurs around the mid-point of assets' lives. The relatively flat deferred tax amount suggests that this firm replaces depreciable assets at approximately the same rate as they wear out.

h. This firm is profitable and more likely than not to realize the benefits of deferred tax assets.

11.37 (Shiraz Company; attempts to achieve off-balance-sheet financing.)

[The chapter does not give sufficient information for the student to know the GAAP answers. The six items are designed to generate a lively discussion.]

Transfer of Receivables with Recourse *SFAS No. 140* sets out the following criteria to treat a transfer of receivables with recourse as a sale: (1) the arrangement separates the receivables from the seller (Shiraz), (2) the purchaser of the receivables (Credit Company) is free to sell or exchange the receivables without undue restrictions placed by the seller, and (3) the seller does not maintain effective control over the receivables.

Shiraz Company retains control of the future economic benefits. If interest rates decrease, Shiraz can borrow funds at the lower interest rate and repurchase the receivables. Because the receivables carry a fixed interest return, Shiraz enjoys the benefit of the difference between the fixed interest return on the receivables and the lower borrowing cost. If interest rates increase, Shiraz will not repurchase the receivables. Credit Company bears the risk of interest rate increases because of the fixed interest return

11.37 continued.

on the receivables. The right of Shiraz to repurchase the receivables restricts the ability of Credit Company to sell or exchange the receivables. The control of who benefits from interest rate changes and who bears the risk resides with Shiraz. Shiraz, therefore, maintains effective control of the receivables. Shiraz Company also bears credit risk in excess of the allowance. Thus, this transaction does not meet the last two criteria as a sale. Shiraz Company should report the transaction as a collateralized loan.

Product Financing Arrangement *SFAS No. 49* (1981) provides that firms recognize product financing arrangements as liabilities if (1) the arrangement requires the sponsoring firm (Shiraz) to purchase the inventory at specified prices and (2) the payments made to the other entity (Credit Company) cover all acquisition, holding, and financing costs.

Shiraz Company agrees to repurchase the inventory at a fixed price, thereby incurring the risk of changing prices. The purchase price formula includes a fixed interest rate, so Shiraz enjoys the benefits or incurs the risk of interest rate changes. Shiraz also controls the benefits and risk of changes in storage costs. Thus, Shiraz treats this product financing arrangement as a collateralized loan.

Throughput Contract *SFAS Statement No. 49* (1981) treats throughput contracts as executory contracts and does not require their recognition as a liability. Note, however, the similarity between a product financing arrangement (involving inventory) and a throughput contract (involving a service). Shiraz Company must pay specified amounts each period regardless of whether it uses the shipping services. The wording of the problem makes it unclear as to whether the initial contract specifies a selling price (railroad bears risk of operating cost increases) or whether the selling price is the railroad's current charges for shipping services each period (Shiraz bears risk of operating cost increases). It seems unlikely that the railroad would accept a fixed price for all ten years. Thus, it appears that Shiraz incurs a commitment to make highly probable future cash payments in amounts that cover the railroad's operating and financing costs. This transaction has the economic characteristics of a collateralized loan, even though GAAP permits treatment as an executory contract.

Construction Joint Venture The construction loan will appear as a liability on the books of Chemical, the joint entity. Shiraz will recognize the fair value of its loan guarantee as a liability. Shiraz and Mission each own 50% but Shiraz appears to have the residual owners' equity because in return for guaranteeing the debt of Chemical, it can buy out Mission for a fixed cost-based price if the venture turns out well. (Chapter 13 discusses consolidated financial statements and variable interest entities.)

GAAP treats the commitment to pay one-half of the operating and debt service costs as an executory contract, similar to the throughput contract. Even though the probability of making future cash payments is high, GAAP concludes that a liability does not arise until the firm receives future benefits from Chemical.

11-15

11.37 continued.

Research and Development Partnership *SFAS No. 68* (1982) requires firms to recognize financings related to research and development (R & D) as liabilities if (1) the sponsoring firm (Shiraz) must repay the financing regardless of the outcome of the R & D work, or (2) the sponsoring firm, even in the absence of a loan guarantee, bears the risk of failure of the R & D effort.

Shiraz guarantees the bank loan in this case regardless of the outcome of the R & D effort and therefore must recognize a liability (satisfies first criterion above). It does not matter whether Shiraz has an option or an obligation to purchase the results of the R & D effort.

If Shiraz did not guarantee the bank loan, then the second criterion above determines whether Shiraz recognizes a liability. If Shiraz has the option to purchase the results of the R & D work, it does not bear the risk of failure and need not recognize a liability. If Shiraz has the obligation to purchase the results, it recognizes a liability for the probable amount payable. The problem does not make it clear whether the amount payable includes the unpaid balance of the loan or merely the value of the R & D work (which could be zero). It seems unlikely that the bank would lend funds for the R & D work without some commitment or obligation by Shiraz to repay the loan.

Hotel Financing Shiraz Company will recognize a liability for the fair value of its guarantee, which is likely to be less than the amount of the loan. It appears in this case that the probability of Shiraz having to make payments under the loan guarantee is low. The hotel is profitable and probably generating cash flows. In addition, the bank can sell the hotel in the event of loan default to satisfy the unpaid balance of the loan. Thus, Shiraz's loan guarantee is a third level of defense against loan default. If default does occur and the first two lines of defense prove inadequate to repay the loan in full, then Shiraz would recognize a liability for the unpaid portion.

CHAPTER 12

MARKETABLE SECURITIES AND DERIVATIVES

Questions, Exercises, and Problems: Answers and Solutions

12.1   See the text or the glossary at the end of the book.

12.3   Firms acquire trading securities primarily for their short-term profit potential. Including the unrealized holding gain or loss in income provides the financial statement user with relevant information for assessing the performance of the trading activity. Firms acquire securities available for sale to support an operating activity (for example, investment of temporarily excess cash) instead of primarily for their profit potential. Deferring recognition of any gain or loss until sale treats securities available for sale the same as inventories, equipment and other assets. Excluding the unrealized gain or loss from earnings also reduces earnings volatility.

12.5   A derivative is a hedge when the firm bears a risk such that the change in the value of the derivative attempts to offset the change in the value of the firm as time passes. We distinguish an attempt at hedging from an effective hedge or even from a partially effective hedge. A firm attempting to hedge by holding a derivative has a hedge, even though that hedge may be only partially effective. When the firm acquires a derivative that is completely ineffective, that is, zero correlated with the hedged item, then we would say the firm does not hold a hedge, even though the firm says it attempts to reduce risk.

Under this interpretation, a derivative is not a hedge when changes in the fair value of the derivative do not at least partially offset other changes in firm value occurring at the same time.

If the firm chooses not to use hedge accounting when it could, the fluctuations in the fair value of the derivative appear in income, not offset by the changes in fair value of the hedged item. We would say that choosing not to use hedge accounting reduces opportunity for manipulation rather than that it increases it because firms cannot offset gains and losses on the derivative against losses and gains on the hedged item.

12.7   Firms do not recognize the fair value of the commitment except to the extent that firms recognize the fair value of the derivative that is hedging that commitment. Thus, firms recognize a portion of the commitment relating to the hedging activity but not the full fair value of that commitment. Firms also do not recognize the asset that the firm will receive when it satisfies the commitment.

12.9   To qualify for hedge accounting, there must be an expectation that the derivative will be effective in hedging a particular risk. Obtaining a derivative that will be highly effective in hedging a particular risk may be costly. A firm might be satisfied with obtaining a derivative that will hedge a significant portion of the risk, accepting the likelihood that the derivative will not be fully effective. Because firms must report gains and losses when derivatives are not highly effective, they may not wish to classify a derivative as a hedge and have to report such information. Another explanation is that the firm wishes to speculate on movements in interest rates, foreign exchange rates, or commodity prices. That is, firms acquire certain derivatives for trading gains and not to hedge a business risk.

12.11   (Classifying securities.)

a. Securities available for sale; current asset.

b. Debt securities held to maturity; noncurrent asset.

c. Securities available for sale; current asset.

d. Securities available for sale; noncurrent asset.

e. Trading securities; current asset.

f. Securities available for sale; noncurrent asset (although a portion of these bonds might appear as a current asset).

12.13   (Murray Company; accounting for bonds held to maturity.)

a. Present Value of Periodic Payments: $3,000 x 6.73274[a] = $ 20,198
    Present Value of Maturity Amount: $100,000 x .73069[b] =   73,069
    Total .... $ 93,267

[a]Present value of an annuity for 8 periods at 4%.
[b]Present value of $1 for 8 periods at 4%.

12.13 continued.

    b. See Schedule 12.1 below.

Schedule 12.1
Amortization Table for $100,000 Bonds with Interest Paid Semiannually at 6% and Priced to Yield 8% Compounded Semiannually
(Exercise 13)

Period	Balance at Beginning of Period	Interest Revenue for Period	Cash Received	Portion of Payment Increasing Carrying Value	Balance at End of Period
1	$93,267	$3,731	$3,000	$731	$ 93,998
2	$93,998	$3,760	$3,000	$760	$ 94,758
3	$94,758	$3,790	$3,000	$790	$ 95,548
4	$95,548	$3,822	$3,000	$822	$ 96,370
5	$96,370	$3,855	$3,000	$855	$ 97,225
6	$97,225	$3,889	$3,000	$889	$ 98,114
7	$98,114	$3,925	$3,000	$925	$ 99,038
8	$99,038	$3,962	$3,000	$962	$ 100,000

    c. **January 1, 2008**

Marketable Debt Securities.. 93,267

    Cash   93,267

Assets	=	Liabilities	+	Shareholders' Equity	(Class.)
–93,267					
+93,267					

June 30, 2008

Cash... 3,000

Marketable Debt Securities.. 731

    Interest Revenue..   3,731

Assets	=	Liabilities	+	Shareholders' Equity	(Class.)
+3,000				+3,731	IncSt → RE
+731					

12.13 c. continued.

December 31, 2008

Cash..	3,000	
Marketable Debt Securities..	760	
Interest Revenue..		3,760

Assets	=	Liabilities	+	Shareholders' Equity	(Class.)
+3,000				+3,760	IncSt → RE
+760					

d. December 31, 2011

Cash..	3,000	
Marketable Debt Securities..	962	
Interest Revenue..		3,962

Assets	=	Liabilities	+	Shareholders' Equity	(Class.)
+3,000				+3,962	IncSt → RE
+962					

December 31, 2011

Cash..	100,000	
Marketable Debt Securities		100,000

Assets	=	Liabilities	+	Shareholders' Equity	(Class.)
+100,000					
−100,000					

12.15   (Elston Corporation; accounting for securities available for sale.)

10/15/2008

Marketable Securities (Security A).................................	28,000	
Cash		28,000

Assets	=	Liabilities	+	Shareholders' Equity	(Class.)
+28,000					
−28,000					

To record acquisition of shares of Security A.

12.15 continued.

11/02/2008

Marketable Securities (Security B)................................. 49,000

    Cash   49,000

Assets	=	Liabilities	+	Shareholders' Equity	(Class.)
+49,000					
−49,000					

To record acquisition of shares of Security B.

12/31/2008

Cash 1,000

    Dividend Revenue   1,000

Assets	=	Liabilities	+	Shareholders' Equity	(Class.)
+1,000				+1,000	IncSt → RE

To record dividend received from Security B.

12/31/2008

Unrealized Holding Loss on Security A Available for
    Sale (Other Comprehensive Income) 3,000

    Marketable Securities (Security A).......................   3,000

Assets	=	Liabilities	+	Shareholders' Equity	(Class.)
−3,000				−3,000	OCInc → AOCInc

To record unrealized holding loss on Security A.

12/31/2008

Marketable Securities (Security B)................................. 6,000

    Unrealized Holding Gain on Security B Available
        for Sale (Other Comprehensive Income)   6,000

Assets	=	Liabilities	+	Shareholders' Equity	(Class.)
+6,000				+6,000	OCInc → AOCInc

To record unrealized holding gain on Security B.

12.15 continued.

2/10/2009

Cash	24,000	
Realized Loss on Sale of Securities Available for Sale (= $24,000 − $28,000)...	4,000	
Marketable Securities (Security A)......................		25,000
Unrealized Holding Loss on Security A Available for Sale (Other Comprehensive Income)...		3,000

Assets	=	Liabilities	+	Shareholders' Equity	(Class.)
+24,000				−4,000	IncSt → RE
−25,000				+3,000	OCInc → AOCInc

To record sale of Security A.

12/31/2009

Cash	1,200	
Dividend Revenue		1,200

Assets	=	Liabilities	+	Shareholders' Equity	(Class.)
+1,200				+1,200	IncSt → RE

To record dividend received from Security B.

12/31/2009

Unrealized Holding Gain on Security B Available for Sale (Other Comprehensive Income).......................	2,000	
Marketable Securities (Security B) (= $53,000 − $55,000)		2,000

Assets	=	Liabilities	+	Shareholders' Equity	(Class.)
−2,000				−2,000	OCInc → AOCInc

To revalue Security B to market value.

12.15 continued.

7/15/2010

Cash...	57,000	
Unrealized Holding Gain on Security B Available for Sale (= \$6,000 − \$2,000) (Other Comprehensive Income)...	4,000	
Marketable Securities (Security B)......................		53,000
Realized Gain on Sale of Securities Available for Sale (= \$57,000 − \$49,000)................................		8,000

Assets	=	Liabilities	+	Shareholders' Equity	(Class.)
+57,000				+8,000	IncSt → RE
−53,000				−4,000	OCInc → AOCInc

To record sale of Security B.

12.17   (Fischer/Black Co.; working backwards from data on marketable securities transaction.)

a. $21,000 = $18,000 + $3,000.

b. $18,000, the amount credited to Marketable Securities in the journal entry which the student might think of as $21,000 acquisition cost, derived above, less $3,000 of Unrealized Holding Loss.

c. $5,000 loss from the debit for Realized Loss.

12.19   (Reconstructing events from journal entries.)

a.   The fair value of a marketable security classified as available for sale is $4,000 less than its carrying value and the firm increases the Unrealized Holding Loss account on the balance sheet.

b.   A firm sells marketable securities classified as either trading securities or as securities available for sale in the same period as it purchased the securities for an amount that is $200 (= $1,100 − $1,300) less than was originally paid for them.

c.   The fair value of marketable securities classified as available for sale is $750 more than its carrying value and the firm increases the Unrealized Holding Gain account on the balance sheet.

d.   A firm sells marketable securities classified as either trading securities or as securities available for sale in the same period that it purchased the securities for an amount that is $100 (= $1,800 − $1,700) more than was originally paid for them.

12.21   (Turner Corporation; accounting for forward foreign exchange contract as a fair value hedge.)

a.   The amount that Turner Corporation would receive if the contract were settled on December 31, 2008 is $1,020 (= $52,000 − $50,980). The present value of $1,020 discounted back six months at 8% per year is $981 (= $1,020 x .96154). Turner Corporation would report this amount as an asset.

b.   Turner Corporation would also report a commitment to purchase the equipment for $981. The firm would not report a liability for the full purchase price; the commitment is an executory contract. It recognizes the commitment only to the extent of the derivative on the asset side of the balance sheet.

c.   The fair value of the foreign exchange contract on June 30, 2009 just before settlement is the amount of cash Turner Corporation will receive from the counterparty, which is $3,757 (= $54,737 − $50,980).

d.   **June 30, 2009**

Equipment	50,980	
Commitment to Purchase Equipment	3,757	
Cash		54,737

Assets	=	Liabilities	+	Shareholders' Equity	(Class.)
+50,980		−3,757			
−54,737					

e.   **June 30, 2009**

Cash	3,757	
Forward Foreign Exchange Contract		3,757

Assets	=	Liabilities	+	Shareholders' Equity	(Class.)
+3,757					
−3,757					

12.23   (Dostal Corporation; journal entries and financial statement presentation of short-term securities available for sale.)

a.   **2/05/2008**

Marketable Securities (Security A)	60,000	
Cash		60,000

Assets	=	Liabilities	+	Shareholders' Equity	(Class.)
+60,000					
−60,000					

12.23 a. continued.

8/12/2008

Marketable Securities (Security B).............................. 25,000

    Cash 25,000

Assets	=	Liabilities	+	Shareholders' Equity	(Class.)
+25,000					
−25,000					

12/31/2008

Marketable Securities (Security A) (= \$66,000 − \$60,000)... 6,000

    Unrealized Holding Gain on Security A
    Available for Sale (Other Comprehensive
    Income)... 6,000

Assets	=	Liabilities	+	Shareholders' Equity	(Class.)
+6,000				+6,000	OCInc → AOCInc

Unrealized Holding Loss on Security B Available for Sale (Other Comprehensive Income) 5,000

    Marketable Securities (Security B)
    (= \$20,000 − \$25,000).. 5,000

Assets	=	Liabilities	+	Shareholders' Equity	(Class.)
−5,000				−5,000	OCInc → AOCInc

1/22/2009

Marketable Securities (Security C)............................ 82,000

    Cash 82,000

Assets	=	Liabilities	+	Shareholders' Equity	(Class.)
+82,000					
−82,000					

12.23 a. continued.

2/25/2009

Marketable Securities (Security D)............................	42,000	
Cash		42,000

Assets	=Liabilities	+	Shareholders' Equity	(Class.)
+42,000				
−42,000				

3/25/2009

Marketable Securities (Security E)............................	75,000	
Cash		75,000

Assets	=Liabilities	+	Shareholders' Equity	(Class.)
+75,000				
−75,000				

6/05/2009

Cash..	72,000	
Unrealized Holding Gain on Security A Available for Sale (Other Comprehensive Income)	6,000	
Marketable Securities (Security A)....................		66,000
Realized Gain on Sale of Securities Available for Sale		12,000

Assets	=Liabilities	+	Shareholders' Equity	(Class.)
+72,000			+12,000	IncSt → RE
−66,000			−6,000	OCInc → AOCInc

6/05/2009

Cash..	39,000	
Realized Loss on Sale of Securities Available for Sale..	3,000	
Marketable Securities (Security D)....................		42,000

Assets	=Liabilities	+	Shareholders' Equity	(Class.)
+39,000			−3,000	IncSt → RE
−42,000				

12.23 a. continued.

12/31/2009

Unrealized Holding Loss on Security C Available for Sale (Other Comprehensive Income)..............	3,000	
Marketable Securities (Security C) (= $79,000 – $82,000).....................................		3,000

Assets	=Liabilities	+	Shareholders' Equity	(Class.)
–3,000			–3,000	OCInc → AOCInc

12/31/2009

Marketable Securities (Security E) (= $80,000 – $75,000)...	5,000	
Unrealized Holding Gain on Security E Available for Sale (Other Comprehensive Income)..		5,000

Assets	=Liabilities	+	Shareholders' Equity	(Class.)
+5,000			+5,000	OCInc → AOCInc

b. **Balance Sheet on December 31, 2008**

Marketable Securities at Fair Value...	$	86,000
Net Unrealized Holding Gain on Securities Available for Sale ($6,000 – $5,000)...	$	1,000

Note

Marketable Securities on December 31, 2008 had an acquisition cost of $85,000 and a fair value of $86,000. Gross unrealized gains total $6,000 and gross unrealized losses total $5,000.

c. **Balance Sheet on December 31, 2009**

Marketable Securities at Fair Value...	$	179,000
Net Unrealized Holding Loss on Securities Available for Sale...	$	(3,000)

Note

Marketable Securities on December 31, 2009 had an acquisition cost of $182,000 and a fair value of $179,000. Gross unrealized gains total $5,000 and gross unrealized losses total $8,000. Proceeds from sales of marketable securities totaled $111,000 during 2009. These sales resulted in gross realized gains of $12,000 and gross realized losses of $3,000. The net unrealized holding loss on securities available for sale changed as follows during 2009:

12.23 c. continued.

Balance, December 31, 2008 .... $ 1,000 Cr.
Accumulated Other Comprehensive Income (Unrealized Holding Gain on Securities Sold)........................ (6,000) Dr.
Change in Net Unrealized Loss on Securities Held at
Year End ($5,000 – $3,000)... 2,000 Cr.
Balance, December 31, 2009 .... $ (3,000) Dr.

12.25 (Moonshine Mining Company; analysis of financial statement disclosures for securities available for sale.) (Amounts in Thousands)

a. $10,267 loss = $11,418 – $21,685.

b. $2,649 gain = $8,807 – $6,158.

c. $12,459 = $21,685 – $6,158 – $3,068.

d. None. The unrealized holding loss on current marketable securities of $2,466 (= $4,601 – $7,067) and the unrealized holding gain on noncurrent marketable securities of $2,649 (= $8,807 – $6,158) appear in the shareholders' equity section of the balance sheet.

12.27 (Analysis of financial statement disclosures related to marketable securities and quality of earnings.) (Amounts in Millions)

a. Cash.. 37,600
Realized Loss on Sale of Securities Available for
Sale.. 113
Realized Gain on Securities Available for
Sale.. 443
Marketable Securities... 37,270[a]

Assets	=	Liabilities	+	Shareholders' Equity	(Class.)
+37,600				–113	IncSt → RE
–37,270[a]				+443	IncSt → RE

[a]$14,075 + $37,163 – $13,968 = $37,270.

Marketable Securities... 262
Unrealized Holding Loss on Securities Available
for Sale (= $37,270 – $37,008) (Other Comprehensive Income)... 262

Assets	=	Liabilities	+	Shareholders' Equity	(Class.)
+262				+262	OCInc → AOCInc

12.27 continued.

b. Balance, December 31, 2008 (= $957 – $510)................... $ 447 Cr.
Net Unrealized Holding Loss on Securities Sold (from
   Part a.).. 262 Cr.
Increase in Net Unrealized Holding Gain on Securities
   Held on December 31, 2009 (Plug)..................................... 518 Cr.
Balance, December 31, 2009 (= $1,445 – $218)............... $ 1,227 Cr.

c. Interest and Dividend Revenue .... $ 1,081
Net Realized Gain on Securities Sold from Market
   Price Changes Occurring during 2009:
   (= $37,600 – $37,008)... 592
Net Unrealized Holding Gain on Securities Held on
   December 31, 2009 (from Part b.) 518
Total Income .... $ 2,191

d. The bank sold marketable securities during 2009, which had net
unrealized holding losses of $262 million as of December 31, 2009. The
sale of these securities at a gain suggests that fair prices increased
substantially ($592 million) during 2009. The substantial increase in
the net unrealized holding gain of $518 lends support to this conclusion
about market price increases. The bank could have increased its
income still further by selecting securities for sale that had unrealized
holding *gains* as of December 31, 2008. If prices continued to increase
on such securities during 2009 prior to sale, the realized gain would have
been even larger than the reported net realized gain of $330 million (=
$443 – $113). Firms with securities available for sale with unrealized
holding gains can manage income by choosing which items to sell. This
will not affect comprehensive income, but until analysts focus on
comprehensive income, rather than net income, managements will be
tempted to manage the net income figure.

12.29 (Owens Corporation; accounting for forward foreign exchange contract as a
fair value hedge and a cash flow hedge.)

a. **October 1, 2008:** The purchase commitment and the forward foreign
exchange contract are mutually unexecuted contracts as of October 1,
2008. GAAP provisions do not require firms to recognize mutually
unexecuted contracts in the accounts.

December 31, 2008: The change in the value of the undiscounted cash
flows related to the purchase commitment and the forward foreign
exchange contract is $1,800 [= (60,000 x $1.35) – (60,000 x $1.32)].
The present value of $1,800 discounted at 8% for six months is $1,731
(= $1,800 x .96154).

12.29 a. continued.

December 31, 2008
Loss on Firm Commitment... 1,731
    Commitment to Purchase Equipment...................   1,731

Assets	=	Liabilities	+	Shareholders' Equity	(Class.)
		+1,731		−1,731	IncSt → RE

To record a loss in net income on a previously un-recognized firm commitment because the U.S. dollar decreased in value relative to the euro.

December 31, 2008
Forward Foreign Exchange Contract......................... 1,731
    Gain on Forward Foreign Exchange Contract......   1,731

Assets	=	Liabilities	+	Shareholders' Equity	(Class.)
+1,731				+1,731	IncSt → RE

To measure the foreign exchange contract at fair value and recognize a gain in net income.

June 30, 2009
Interest Expense... 69
    Commitment to Purchase Equipment...................   69

Assets	=	Liabilities	+	Shareholders' Equity	(Class.)
		+69		−69	IncSt → RE

To recognize interest on the commitment because of the passage of time: $69 = .04 \times \$1,731$.

June 30, 2009
Forward Foreign Exchange Contract......................... 69
    Interest Revenue...   69

Assets	=	Liabilities	+	Shareholders' Equity	(Class.)
+69				+69	IncSt → RE

To record interest on the foreign contract because of the passage of time: $69 = .04 \times \$1,731$.

12.29 a. continued.

The change in the value of the purchase commitment and the forward foreign exchange contract due to exchange rate changes between December 31, 2008 and June 30, 2009 is $3,000 [= (60,000 X $1.40) − (60,000 X $1.35)].

June 30, 2009

Loss on Firm Commitment.. 3,000
    Commitment to Purchase Equipment...................   3,000

Assets	=	Liabilities	+	Shareholders' Equity	(Class.)
		+3,000		−3,000	IncSt → RE

To record a loss on the purchase commitment because the value of the U.S. dollar declined relative to the euro.

June 30, 2009

Forward Foreign Exchange Contract........................... 3,000
    Gain on Forward Foreign Exchange Contract   3,000

Assets	=	Liabilities	+	Shareholders' Equity	(Class.)
+3,000				+3,000	IncSt → RE

To record the increase in the fair value of the forward foreign exchange contract because the U.S. dollar declined in value relative to the euro.

June 30, 2009

Equipment 79,200
Commitment to Purchase Equipment........................ 4,800
    Cash   84,000

Assets	=	Liabilities	+	Shareholders' Equity	(Class.)
+79,200		−4,800			
−84,000					

To record the amount paid in U.S. dollars to acquire €60,000 [$84,000 = (€60,000 X $1.4)], to eliminate the balance in the Commitment to Purchase Equipment account of $4,800 (= $1,731 + $69 + $3,000), and to record the acquisition cost of the equipment for $79,200.

12.29 a. continued.

June 30, 2009

Cash.. 4,800
    Forward Foreign Exchange Contract.................... 4,800

Assets	=	Liabilities	+	Shareholders' Equity	(Class.)
+4,800					
–4,800					

To record cash received from the counterparty and eliminate the balance in the Forward Foreign Exchange account of $4,800 (= $1,731 + $69 + $3,000).

b. Owens Corporation would not recognize changes in the value of the purchase commitment. The entries for changes in the fair value of the forward foreign exchange contract would affect other comprehensive income each period instead of net income. On June 30, 2009, Accumulated Other Comprehensive Income would have a balance of $4,800 (= $1,731 + $69 + $3,000). The entry on this date to purchase the equipment would involve a debit to Other Comprehensive Income instead of the Commitment to Purchase Equipment account as shown in Part a. above.

c. To treat this hedge as a fair value hedge, Owens Corporation must desire to protect the value of the equipment. Perhaps Owens Corporation has committed to resell the equipment to a customer on June 30, 2009 for a fixed price in U.S. dollars and wants to protect its expected profit margin from the sale. To treat this hedge as a cash flow hedge, Owens Corporation must desire to protect the amount of cash it pays to the European supplier.

12.31 (Avery Corporation; accounting for an interest rate swap as a cash flow hedge.)

January 1, 2008

Equipment.. 50,000
    Note Payable... 50,000

Assets	=	Liabilities	+	Shareholders' Equity	(Class.)
+50,000		+50,000			

To record the acquisition of equipment by giving a $50,000 note payable with a variable interest rate of 6%.

12.31 continued.

December 31, 2008

Interest Expense 3,000
    Cash   3,000

Assets	=	Liabilities	+	Shareholders' Equity	(Class.)
−3,000				−3,000	IncSt → RE

To recognize interest expense and cash payment at the
variable interest rate of 6%: $3,000 = .06 x $50,000.

The fair value of the swap agreement on December 31, 2008 after the
counterparty resets the interest rate to 8% is $1,783 (= $1,000 x 1.78326).
This amount is the present value of the $1,000 that the counterparty will
pay Avery Corporation on December 31 of 2009 and December 31 of 2010
if the interest rate remains at 8%.

December 31, 2008

Swap Contract 1,783
    Gain on Revaluation of Swap Contract   1,783

Assets	=	Liabilities	+	Shareholders' Equity	(Class.)
+1,783				+1,783	OCInc → AOCInc

To measure the swap contract at fair value and recognize
an asset on the balance sheet and a gain in other comprehensive income.

December 31, 2009

Interest Expense 4,000
    Cash   4,000

Assets	=	Liabilities	+	Shareholders' Equity	(Class.)
−4,000				−4,000	IncSt → RE

To recognize interest expense and cash payment at the
variable interest rate: $4,000 = .08 x $50,000.

Avery Corporation must also recognize interest on the swap contract
because of the passage of time.

12.31 continued.

December 31, 2009

Swap Contract.. 143

    Interest on Swap Contract.. 143

Assets	=	Liabilities	+	Shareholders' Equity	(Class.)
+143				+143	OCInc → AOCInc

To record interest for the increase in the carrying value
of the swap contract for the passage of time: $143 = .08
x $1,783.

Avery Corporation receives from the counterparty the $1,000 [= $50,000 x
(.08 – .06)] required by the swap contract. The entry is:

December 31, 2009

Cash 1,000

    Swap Contract... 1,000

Assets	=	Liabilities	+	Shareholders' Equity	(Class.)
+1,000					
−1,000					

To record cash received from the counterparty because
the interest rate increased from 6% to 8%.

December 31, 2009

Other Comprehensive Income.. 1,000

    Interest Expense 1,000

Assets	=	Liabilities	+	Shareholders' Equity	(Class.)
				−1,000	OCInc → AOCInc
				+1,000	IncSt → RE

To reclassify a portion of other comprehensive income to
net income for the hedged portion of interest expense on
the note payable.

At this point the swap contract account has a debit balance of $926 (=
$1,783 + $143 – $1,000). Other comprehensive income related to this
transaction, likewise, has a credit balance of $926.

12.31 continued.

Resetting the interest rate on December 31, 2009 to 4% changes the fair value of the swap contract from an asset to a liability. The present value of the $1,000 that Avery Corporation will pay to the counterparty at the end of 2010 when discounted at 4% is $962 (= $1,000 x .96154). The entry to revalue to swap contract is:

December 31, 2009

Loss on Revaluation of Swap Contract	1,888	
Swap Contract (Asset)		926
Swap Contract (Liability)		962

Assets	=	Liabilities	+	Shareholders' Equity	(Class.)
−926		+962		−1,888	OCInc → AOCInc

To measure the swap contract at fair value and recognize a liability on the balance sheet and a loss in other comprehensive income.

December 31, 2010

Interest Expense	2,000	
Cash		2,000

Assets	=	Liabilities	+	Shareholders' Equity	(Class.)
−2,000				−2,000	IncSt → RE

To recognize interest expense and cash payment at the variable interest rate of 4%: $2,000 = .04 x $50,000.

December 31, 2010

Interest on Swap Contract	38	
Swap Contract		38

Assets	=	Liabilities	+	Shareholders' Equity	(Class.)
		+38		−38	OCInc → AOCInc

To record interest for the increase in the carrying value of the swap contract for the passage of time: $38 = .04 x $962.

12.31 continued.

December 31, 2010
Swap Contract.. 1,000
   Cash 1,000

Assets	=	Liabilities	+	Shareholders' Equity	(Class.)
−1,000		−1,000			

To record cash paid to the counterparty because the interest rate decreased from 10% to 4%.

December 31, 2010
Interest Expense 1,000
   Other Comprehensive Income...................................... 1,000

Assets	=	Liabilities	+	Shareholders' Equity	(Class.)
				−1,000	IncSt → RE
				+1,000	OCInc → AOCInc

To reclassify a portion of other comprehensive income to net income for the hedged portion of interest expense on the note payable.

December 31, 2010
Note Payable.. 50,000
   Cash 50,000

Assets	=	Liabilities	+	Shareholders' Equity	(Class.)
−50,000		−50,000			

To record repayment of note payable at maturity.

The Swap Contract account has a balance of zero on December 31, 2010 (= $962 + $38 − $1,000). Thus, Avery Corporation need make no entry to close out the swap contract account.

CHAPTER 13

INTERCORPORATE INVESTMENTS IN COMMON STOCK

Questions, Exercises, and Problems: Answers and Solutions

13.1   See the text or the glossary at the end of the book.

13.3   Dividends represent revenues under the fair-value method, or a return of capital under the equity method, or eliminated under the consolidation method.

13.5   When control is present, a parent and a subsidiary operate as a single economic entity. Eliminating intercompany profit and loss in these cases reflects transactions of the economic entity with all other entities. When significant influence is present, the investor and investee operate as economic entity to a lesser extent than when control is present. Thus, the concept of operating as an economic entity, in part, justifies eliminating intercompany profit and loss on equity method investments. Also, the ability to exert significant influence places the firms in a related party arrangement where prices set on intercompany transactions may not reflect arms-length dealings.

13.7   Under the equity method, the change each period in the net assets, or shareholders' equity, of the subsidiary appears on the one line, Investment in Subsidiary, on the balance sheet. When the parent consolidates the subsidiary, changes in the individual assets and liabilities that comprise the net asset change appear in the individual consolidated assets and liabilities. Likewise, under the equity method, the investor's interest in the investee's earnings appears in one line on the income statement, Equity in Earnings of Unconsolidated Subsidiary. When the parent consolidates the subsidiary, the individual revenues and expenses of the subsidiary appear in consolidated revenues and expenses.

13.9   If Company A owns less than, or equal to, 50% of Company B's voting stock, it is a minority investor in Company B. If Company A owns more than 50% of Company C, it is a majority investor in Company C. The entities holding the remainder of the voting stock of Company C are minority investors. Their minority, or noncontrolling, interest appears on the consolidated balance sheet of Company A and Company C.

Odd-numbered Solutions

13.11   Failing to eliminate the Investment in Subsidiary account will result in double counting the net assets of the subsidiary in the consolidated balance sheet, once as the Investment account on the parent's books and once as the individual net assets on the subsidiary's books.

13.13   One can envision scenarios where the equity method or proportionate consolidation better reflects the relation between the joint owners and the joint venture. For example, assume a joint venture in which one of the joint owners manages day-to-day operations and the other joint owner(s) simply takes part in making strategic decisions. In this case, the equity method may better reflect the relation for the less active owner(s). As another example assume one joint owner manages operations in the United States and another joint owner manages operations in Europe. In this case, the assets, markets, pricing, and other factors are separate. Proportionate consolidation may better reflect the relation for the joint owners.

13.15   (Hanna Company; equity method entries.)

Investment in Stock of Denver Company...................... 550,000
   Cash 550,000

Assets	=	Liabilities	+	Shareholders' Equity	(Class.)
+550,000					
−550,000					

To record acquisition of common stock.

Investment in Stock of Denver Company...................... 120,000
   Equity in Earnings of Denver Company................... 120,000

Assets	=	Liabilities	+	Shareholders' Equity	(Class.)
+120,000				+120,000	IncSt → RE

To accrue 100% share of Denver Company's earnings.

Cash or Dividends Receivable.. 30,000
   Investment in Stock of Denver Company................. 30,000

Assets	=	Liabilities	+	Shareholders' Equity	(Class.)
+30,000					
−30,000					

To accrue dividends received or receivable.

13.17 (Wood Corporation; journal entries to apply the equity method of accounting for investments in securities.)

January 2

Investment in Securities (Knox)...	350,000
Investment in Securities (Vachi)..	196,000
Investment in Securities (Snow)...	100,000
Cash	646,000

Assets	=	Liabilities	+	Shareholders' Equity	(Class.)
+350,000					
+196,000					
+100,000					
−646,000					

December 31

Investment in Securities (Knox)..	35,000
Investment in Securities (Vachi)...	12,000
Investment in Securities (Snow)...................................	4,800
Equity in Earnings of Affiliates...................................	42,200

Assets	=	Liabilities	+	Shareholders' Equity	(Class.)
+35,000				+42,200	IncSt → RE
+12,000					
−4,800					

(.50 x $70,000) + (.30 x $40,000) − (.20 x $24,000) = $42,200.

December 31

Cash	19,500
Investment in Securities (Knox)...................................	15,000
Investment in Securities (Vachi).................................	4,500

Assets	=	Liabilities	+	Shareholders' Equity	(Class.)
+19,500					
−15,000					
−4,500					

(.50 x $30,000) + (.30 x $15,000) = $19,500.

13.19   (Laesch Company; working backwards to consolidation relations.)

    a. $70,000 = ($156,000 − $100,000)/.80.

    b. 72.7 percent = ($156,000 − $100,000)/$77,000.

    c. $56,000 = ($156,000 − $100,000).

13.21   (CAR Corporation; consolidation policy and principal consolidation concepts.)

    a. CAR Corporation should consolidate Alexandre du France Software Systems and R Credit Corporation or, under exceptional circumstances, use the fair value method.

    b.

Charles Electronics	(.75 x $120,000) =	$ 90,000
Alexandre du France Software Systems...	(.80 x 60,000) =	48,000
R Credit Corporation	(.90 x 144,000) =	129,600
Total Income from Subsidiaries		$267,600

    c. Noncontrolling Interest shown under accounting assumed in problem:

Charles Electronics	(.25 x $120,000) =	$30,000
Alexandre du France Software Systems...	(None) =	--
R Credit Corporation	(None) =	--
		$30,000

CAR Corporation subtracts the noncontrolling interest in computing net income.

    d. Charles Electronics, no increase because already consolidated.

Alexandre du France Software Systems increase by 80% of net income less dividends:

$$.80 \times (\$96,000 − \$60,000) = \$28,800.$$

R Credit Corporation, no increase because equity method results in the same income statement effects as do consolidated statements. Net income of CAR Corporation would be:

$1,228,800 = $1,200,000 (as reported) + $28,800 (increase).

    e. Noncontrolling Interest shown if CAR Corporation consolidated all companies:

Charles Electronics	(.25 x $120,000) =	$ 30,000
Alexandre du France Software Systems..	(.20 x 96,000) =	19,200
R Credit Corporation	(.10 x 144,000) =	14,400
		$ 63,600

13.23 (Alpha/Omega; working backwards from data which has eliminated intercompany transactions.)

a. $80,000 = $450,000 + $250,000 − $620,000.

b. $30,000 is Omega's cost; $20,000 is Alpha's cost; $20,000 original cost to Alpha.

Markup on the goods sold from Alpha to Omega, which remain in Omega's inventory, is $10,000 (= $60,000 + $50,000 − $100,000).
Because Alpha priced the goods with markup 50% over its costs, the cost to Alpha to produce goods with markup of $10,000 is $20,000 and the total sales price from Alpha to Omega is $30,000 (= $10,000 + $20,000).

13.25 (Effect of equity method versus consolidation.)

a. (1) When Parent uses the equity method, it recognizes 80% of the net income of Sub. When Parent prepares consolidated financial statements with Sub, it recognizes 100% of the revenues, expenses, and net income of Sub and then subtracts the 20% noncontrolling interest share of net income. Thus, net income is the same whether Parent uses the equity method or consolidates Sub.

(2) Liabilities in the numerator increase by the amount of the liabilities of Sub. Assets in the denominator decrease by the amount in the investment account and increase by the amount of Sub's assets. In this case where there is no excess purchase price, the denominator increases by the liabilities (= assets of Sub minus shareholders' equity) of Sub. Equal increases in the numerator and denominator of a ratio that is initially less than 1.0 result in an increase in the ratio.

b. (1) The Parent or investor's share of Sub's net income declines, regardless of whether the amount appears on the single line, Equity in Earnings of Sub, or on multiple revenue and expense lines.

(2) Total assets decrease when using the equity method because the investor invests less. Total assets do not decrease when preparing consolidated financial statements because Parent eliminates its Investment in Sub account and consolidates 100% of Sub's assets, regardless of its ownership percentage.

(3) The liabilities of Sub do not appear on Parent's balance sheet when it uses the equity method, regardless of the ownership percentage.

(4) Total liabilities do not change when preparing consolidated financial statements because Parent consolidates 100% of Sub's liabilities, regardless of its ownership percentage.

13-5

13.25 b. continued.

    (5) Shareholders' equity decreases when using the equity method because Parent owns less of the net income, dividends, and shareholders' equity of Sub. The shareholders' equity on the consolidated balance sheet is the shareholders' equity of Parent only. Parent eliminates the shareholders' equity of Sub when preparing consolidated financial statements in its entry to eliminate the Investment in Sub account and recognize the noncontrolling interest.

    (6) Assets and liabilities do not change with the decrease in ownership percentage, because consolidated financial statements reflect 100% of Sub's assets and liabilities. The change in the ownership percentage affects the amount of the noncontrolling interest in Sub's net assets.

13.27   (Parrot Corporation; accounting for a joint venture.)

a.

	Equity Method	Proportionate Consolidation
Current Assets	$ 300	$ 400
Property, Plant and Equipment (Net)	500	800
Investment in Joint Venture (Equity Method	200	--
Total Assets	$ 1,000	$ 1,200
Current Liabilities	$ 250	$ 325
Long-Term Debt	450	575
Total Liabilities	$ 700	$ 900
Shareholders' Equity	$ 300	$ 300
Total Liabilities and Shareholders' Equity	$ 1,000	$ 1,200

b. (1) **Equity Method**
Liabilities to Assets Ratio: $700/$1,000 = 70%.
Debt-Equity Ratio: $450/$300 = 150%.

    (2) **Consolidation**
Liabilities to Assets Ratio: $900/$1,200 = 75%.
Debt-Equity Ratio: $575/$300 = 191.7%.

c. The liabilities to asset ratio is larger with proportionate consolidation, because the joint venture has a higher proportion of liabilities in its capital structure than does Parrot Corporation. Although the joint venture has a lower debt-equity ratio than Parrot Corporation, consolidation results in an increase in the numerator of the debt-equity ratio with no change in the denominator, so the ratio increases.

13.29 (Company P and Company S; preparing a consolidated balance sheet.)

a.

	Company P	Company S	Consolidated
Assets			
Cash..	$ 36,000	$ 26,000	$ 62,000
Accounts and Notes Receivable........................	180,000	50,000	213,600
Inventories............................	440,000	250,000	690,000
Investment in Company S (Using the Equity Method).............................	726,000	--	--
Property, Plant and Equipment (Net).............	600,000	424,000	1,080,000
Total Assets.................	$ 1,982,000	$ 750,000	$ 2,045,600
Liabilities and Shareholders' Equity			
Accounts and Notes Payable.............................	$ 110,000	$ 59,000	$ 152,600
Other Liabilities..................	286,000	21,000	307,000
Common Stock....................	1,200,000	500,000	1,200,000
Additional Paid-In Capital..............................	--	100,000	--
Retained Earnings...............	386,000	70,000	386,000
Total Liabilities and Shareholders' Equity..........................	$ 1,982,000	$ 750,000	$ 2,045,600

The elimination entries (not required) are as follows:

Common Stock...	500,000	
Additional Paid-In Capital..	100,000	
Retained Earnings..	70,000	
Property, Plant and Equipment....................................	56,000	
Investment in Company S.......................................		726,000

Assets	=	Liabilities	+	Shareholders' Equity	(Class.)
+56,000				–500,000	ContriCap
–726,000				–100,000	ContriCap
				–70,000	RE

To eliminate the investment account, the shareholders' equity accounts of Company S, and recognize the unamortized excess acquisition cost.

13.29 a. continued.

Accounts and Notes Payable... 16,400
    Accounts and Notes Receivable............................ 16,400

Assets	=	Liabilities	+	Shareholders' Equity	(Class.)
−16,400		−16,400			IncSt → RE

To eliminate intercompany note.

b. The unamortized excess acquisition cost on December 31, 2009 is $56,000. With eight years remaining on the building's useful life, the annual depreciation is $7,000 (= $56,000/8). Thus, the excess acquisition on January 1, 2008 was $70,000 [= $56,000 + (2 x $7,000)]. The computation of the acquisition cost on January 1, 2008 is as follows:

Common Stock of Company S .... $ 500,000
Additional Paid-In Capital of Company S 100,000
Retained Earnings of Company S.............................. 40,000
Excess Acquisition Cost.. 70,000
Acquisition Cost.. $ 710,000

c. Acquisition Cost on January 1, 2008....................... $ 710,000
Company P's Share of the Increase in Retained Earnings
    of Company S for 2008 and 2009; ($70,000 − $40,000).... 30,000
Less Amortization of Excess Acquisition Cost for 2008
    and 2009 .... (14,000)
Carrying Value on December 31, 2009...................... $ 726,000

13.31 (Parent Company and Sub Company; equity method and consolidated financial statements with noncontrolling interest.)

	Parent Company	Sub Company	Consolidated
Assets			
Cash	$ 38,000	$ 12,000	$ 50,000
Accounts Receivable	63,000	32,000	95,000
Investment in Sub Company (Using Equity Method)	105,600	--	--
Other Assets	296,400	160,000	456,400
Total Assets	$503,000	$204,000	$601,400
Liabilities and Share-holders' Equity			
Accounts Payable	$ 85,000	$ 32,000	$117,000
Bonds Payable	150,000	40,000	190,000
Total Liabilities	$235,000	$ 72,000	$307,000
Noncontrolling Interest in Net Assets of Sub Company	$ --	$ --	$ 26,400
Common Stock	20,000	50,000	20,000
Retained Earnings	248,000	82,000	248,000
Total Shareholders' Equity	$268,000	$132,000	$294,400
Total Liabilities and Share-holders' Equity	$503,000	$204,000	$601,400
Sales Revenue	$800,000	$145,000	$945,000
Equity in Earnings of Sub Company	16,000	--	--
Cost of Goods Sold	(620,000)	(85,000)	(705,000)
Selling and Administrative Expense	(135,000)	(30,000)	(165,000)
Income Tax Expense	(24,000)	(10,000)	(34,000)
Net Income of Consolidated Entity	$ 37,000	$ 20,000	$ 41,000
Noncontrolling Interest in Net Income of Sub Company	--	--	(4,000)
Net Income	$ 37,000	$ 20,000	$ 37,000

The elimination and reclassification entry (not required) is as follows:

Common Stock	40,000	
Retained Earnings	65,600	
Investment in Sub Company		105,600

13.31 continued.

Assets	=	Liabilities	+	Shareholders' Equity	(Class.)
−105,600				−40,000	ContriCap
				−65,600	RE

To eliminate investment account and Parent Company's
share of the shareholders' equity of Sub Company.

Alternative elimination entries using amounts before closing entries are as
follows:

Common Stock..	40,000	
Retained Earnings...	56,000	
Equity in Earnings of Sub Company...............................	16,000	
Dividend Declared..		6,400
Investment in Sub Company......................................		105,600

Assets	=	Liabilities	+	Shareholders' Equity	(Class.)
−105,600				−40,000	ContriCap
				−56,000	RE
				−16,000	IncSt → RE
				+6,400	RE

To eliminate investment account and Parent Company's
share of the shareholders' equity of Sub Company.

Common Stock..	10,000	
Retained Earnings...	16,400	
Noncontrolling Interest in Net Assets of Sub		
Company...		26,400

Assets	=	Liabilities	+	Shareholders' Equity	(Class.)
				−10,000	ContriCap
				−16,400	RE
				+26,400	MinInt

To recognize the noncontrolling interest in Sub Company.

13.31 continued.

An alternative elimination entry using amounts before closing entries is as follows:

Common Stock...	10,000	
Retained Earnings..	14,000	
Noncontrolling Interest in Net Income of Sub		
Company..	4,000	
Dividend Declared..		1,600
Noncontrolling Interest in Net Assets of Sub		
Company..		26,400

Assets	=	Liabilities	+	Shareholders' Equity	(Class.)
				−10,000	ContriCap
				−14,000	RE
				−4,000	IncSt → RE
				+1,600	RE
				+26,400	MinInt

To recognize the noncontrolling interest in Sub Company.

13.33   (Smithfield Foods; accounting for joint ventures.)

a.

	Equity Method	Proportionate Consolidation	Full Consolidation
Assets			
Current Assets	$ 2,733.7	$ 3,417.6	$ 4,101.6
Investments in Joint Ventures	420.8	--	--
Other Noncurrent Assets....	3,814.1	4,471.6	5,129.1
Total Assets....................	$ 6,968.6	$ 7,889.2	$ 9,230.7
Liabilities and Shareholders' Equity			
Current Liabilities.................	$ 1,361.2	$ 1,834.9	$ 2,308.7
Noncurrent Liabilities	3,352.7	3,799.6	4,246.5
Total Liabilities	$ 4,713.9	$ 5,634.5	$ 6,555.2
Joint Owners' Interest in Net Assets of Joint Ventures	$ --	$ --	$ 420.8
Shareholders' Equity.............	2,254.7	2,254.7	2,254.7
Total Shareholders' Equity	$ 2,254.7	$ 2,254.7	$ 2,675.5
Total Liabilities and Shareholders' Equity....	$ 6,968.6	$ 7,889.2	$ 9,230.7

13.33 a. continued.

Income Statement

Sales	$ 11,911.1	$ 13,367.5	$ 14,823.9
Equity in Earnings of Joint Ventures	10.9	--	--
Expenses	(11,733.6)	(13,179.1)	(14,624.6)
Net Income of Consolidated Entity	$ 188.4	$ 188.4	$ 199.3
Joint Owner's Interest in Net Income of Joint Ventures	--	--	(10.9)
Net Income	$ 188.4	$ 188.4	$ 188.4

The work sheet entries for proportionate consolidation and full consolidation (not required) are as follows:

Proportionate Consolidation
Using Post-Closing Amounts:

Shareholders' Equity	115.0	
Other Noncurrent Assets	305.8	
Investment in Joint Ventures		420.8

Assets	= Liabilities	+	Shareholders' Equity	(Class.)
+305.8			−115.0	ContriCap and RE
−420.8				

To eliminate the investment account, the shareholders' equity account of the joint ventures, and recognize the excess of acquisition cost over carrying value of net assets of joint ventures.

Using Pre-Closing Amounts:

Shareholders' Equity	104.1	
Equity in Earnings of Joint Ventures	10.9	
Other Noncurrent Assets	305.8	
Investment in Joint Ventures		420.8

Assets	= Liabilities	+	Shareholders' Equity	(Class.)
+305.8			−104.1	ContriCap and RE
−420.8			−10.9	IncSt → RE

To eliminate the investment account, the shareholders' equity account of the joint ventures, and recognize the excess of acquisition cost over carrying value of net assets of joint ventures.

13.33 a. continued.

Full Consolidation
In addition to the entries above to eliminate the investment account, the following entries recognize the interest of the other joint owners.

Using Post-Closing Amounts:

Shareholders' Equity........................	115.0
Other Noncurrent Assets.............................	305.8
Joint Owners' Interest in Net Assets of Joint	
Ventures...	420.8

Assets	=	Liabilities	+	Shareholders' Equity	(Class.)
+305.8				−115.0	ContriCap and RE
				+420.8	Jt.Int.

To recognize the joint owners' interest in the joint ventures and recognize the excess carrying value of net assets of joint ventures.

Using Pre-Closing Amounts:

Shareholders' Equity........................	104.1
Joint Owners' Interest in Earnings of Joint Ven-	
tures	10.9
Other Noncurrent Assets.............................	305.8
Joint Owners' Interest in Net Asset of Joint	
Ventures...	420.8

Assets	=	Liabilities	+	Shareholders' Equity	(Class.)
+305.8				−104.1	ContriCap and RE
				−10.9	IncSt → RE
				+420.8	Jt.Int.

To recognize the joint owners' interest in the joint ventures and recognize the excess carrying value of net assets of joint ventures.

13.33 continued.

b. **Equity Method**
   (1) Liabilities to Assets Ratio: $4,713.9/$7,268.6 = 64.9%.
   (2) Debt-Equity Ratio: $3,352.7/$2,254.7 = 148.7%.
   (3) Net Income to Sales Percentage: $188.4/$11,911.1 = 1.6%.

Proportionate Consolidation
   (1) Liabilities to Assets Ratio: $5,634.5/$7,889.2 = 71.4%.
   (2) Debt-Equity Ratio: $3,799.6/$2,254.7 = 148.7%.
   (3) Net Income to Sales Percentage: $188.4/$13,367.5 = 1.4%.

Full Consolidation
   (1) Liabilities to Assets Ratio: $6,555.2/$9,230.7 = 71.0%.
   (2) Debt-Equity Ratio: $4,246.5/$2,675.5 = 158.7%.
   (3) Net Income to Sales Percentage: $188.4/$14,823.9 = 1.3%.

c. Full consolidation is inappropriate, because Smithfield Foods does not control the joint ventures. Whether the equity method or proportionate consolidation better reflects the operating relations between Smithfield Foods and the joint ventures depends on the involvement and responsibilities of each joint owner. If the other joint owners manage day-to-day operations and Smithfield Foods provides only strategic oversight, then the equity method seems more appropriate. If Smithfield Foods operates the joint ventures, or at least approximately 50 percent of the assets of the joint ventures, then proportionate consolidation seems more appropriate.

CHAPTER 14

SHAREHOLDERS' EQUITY: CAPITAL CONTRIBUTIONS, DISTRIBUTIONS, AND EARNINGS

Questions, Exercises, and Problems: Answers and Solutions

14.1 See the text or the glossary at the end of the book.

14.3 Redeemable preferred stock will appear as a liability if it is subject to mandatory redemption on a particular date or upon occurrence of a specified event certain to occur. Redeemable preferred stock will appear in shareholders' equity if it is subject to redemption fully at the option of the issuing firm. Redeemable preferred stock will appear between liabilities and shareholders' equity if redemption is dependent on an event not certain to occur. The latter classification is appropriate if either the issuing firm or the shareholders' have a redemption option.

14.5 The greater the volatility of the stock price, the larger is the potential excess of the market price over the exercise price on the exercise date and the greater the benefit to the employee. The longer the time between the grant date and the exercise date, the more time that elapses for the market price to increase. Offsetting the value of this increased benefit element is the longer time to realize the benefit, which reduces the present value of the option. Stock option valuation models discount the expected benefit element in a stock option to a present value. The larger the discount rate, the smaller is the present value of the benefit.

14.7 The accounting for each of these transactions potentially involves transfers between contributed capital and retained earnings accounts and clouds the distinction between capital transactions and income transactions. The accounting for stock options results in a reduction in net income and retained earnings and an increase in contributed capital. The accounting for stock dividends results in a reduction in retained earnings and an increase in contributed capital. The purchase of treasury stock represents a reduction in both contributed capital and accumulated earnings. The reissuance of treasury stock at a "loss" may result in a debit to both contributed capital and retained earnings. Thus, the Common Stock and Additional Paid-in Capital accounts do not reflect just capital transactions and Retained Earnings does not reflect just income transactions.

14.9   The managers of a firm have knowledge of the plans and risks of the firm that external investors may not possess. Although laws prevent firms from taking advantage of this "inside information," inclusion of gains from treasury stock transactions in net income might motivate firms to buy and sell treasury stock to improve reported earnings. Excluding these gains from net income removes this incentive. Also, the accounting for the acquisition of treasury stock (that is, a reduction from total shareholders' equity) has the same effect on shareholders' equity as a retirement of the capital stock. The reissue of the treasury stock for more than its acquisition cost does not result in a gain any more than the issue of common stock for more than par value represents a gain.

14.11   The FASB suggests that the distinction between performance-related (subject to significant influence by management) and non-performance-related (subject to external influences not controllable by management) items drives the exclusion. The real reason, however, we suspect, has to do with the volatility of some of the items of other comprehensive income. Including all unrealized gains and losses on securities held in net income will cause reported earnings to fluctuate (in response to fluctuations in market prices) more than it would otherwise. Many, probably most, managers prefer to report stable net income in contrast to fluctuating net income. All else equal, the less risky the net income stream—that is, the less volatile is reported net income—the higher will be the market price of the firm's shares.

14.13   (The Washington Post Company; classification of redeemable preferred stock.)

           This redeemable preferred stock will appear between liabilities and shareholders' equity on the balance sheet because its redemption is subject to an event not certain to occur. Neither the company nor the preferred shareholder might initiate redemption.

14.15   (Intel; accounting for stock options.)

           The value of the stock options on December 31, 2007, is $142.434 (= 24.6 x $5.79) million. Intel amortizes this value as an expense of $47.478 (= $142.434/3) million for 2008, 2009, and 2010. Intel recognizes no additional expense when employees exercise their options in 2012.

14.17   (Watson Corporation; journal entries for employee stock options.)

December 31, 2009, 2010, and 2011

Compensation Expense (= $75,000/3)..............................	25,000	
Additional Paid-in Capital (Stock Options)...............		25,000

14.17 continued.

Assets	=	Liabilities	+	Shareholders' Equity	(Class.)
				−25,000	IncSt → RE
				+25,000	ContriCap

April 30, 2012
Cash (= 15,000 x $25).. 375,000
Additional Paid-in Capital (Stock Options) [=
    (15,000/20,000) x $75,000]....................................... 56,250
      Common Stock (= 15,000 x $10)........................... 150,000
      Additional Paid-in Capital [= $56,250 +
        (15,000 x $15)]... 281,250

Assets	=	Liabilities	+	Shareholders' Equity	(Class.)
+375,000				−56,250	ContriCap
				+150,000	ContriCap
				+281,250	ContriCap

September 15, 2013
Cash (= 5,000 x $25).. 125,000
Additional Paid-in Capital (Stock Options) [= (5,000/
    20,000) x $75,000] 18,750
      Common Stock (= 5,000 x $10)............................. 50,000
      Additional Paid-in Capital [= $18,750 +
        (5,000 x $15)]... 93,750

Assets	=	Liabilities	+	Shareholders' Equity	(Class.)
+125,000				−18,750	ContriCap
				+50,000	ContriCap
				+93,750	ContriCap

14.19   (Symantec; accounting for conversion of bonds.)

Carrying Value Method
Convertible Bonds Payable 10,255,000
    Common Stock (= 100,000 x $10).............................. 1,000,000
    Additional Paid-in Capital (Plug)................................. 9,255,000

Assets	=	Liabilities	+	Shareholders' Equity	(Class.)
		−10,225,000		+1,000,000	ContriCap
				+9,255,000	ContriCap

14.19 continued.

Fair Value Method

Convertible Bonds Payable	10,255,000	
Loss on Conversion of Bonds (Plug).................................	245,000	
Common Stock (= 100,000 x $10).............................		1,000,000
Additional Paid-in Capital (= 100,000 x $95)...........		9,500,000

Assets	=	Liabilities	+	Shareholders' Equity	(Class.)
		−10,255,000		−245,000	IncSt → RE
				+1,000,000	ContriCap
				+9,500,000	ContriCap

14.21　(Altus Pharmaceuticals; journal entries for stock warrants.)

December 7, 2002

Cash	46,180,000	
Convertible Preferred Stock......................................		43,450,000
Additional Paid-in Capital (Stock Warrants)......		2,730,000

Assets	=	Liabilities	+	Shareholders' Equity	(Class.)
+46,180,000				+43,450,000	ContriCap
				+2,730,000	ContriCap

To record issuance of convertible preferred stock with stock warrants.

January 15, 2007

Convertible Preferred Stock..	62,533,000	
Common Stock (5,269,705 x $.01).......................		52,697
Additional Paid-in Capital		62,480,303

Assets	=	Liabilities	+	Shareholders' Equity	(Class.)
				−62,533,000	ContriCap
				+52,697	ContriCap
				+62,480,303	ContriCap

To record conversion of preferred stock with accumulated dividends into common stock. $62,533,000 = $43,450,000 + $19,083,000.

14.23   (Watt Corporation; journal entries for dividends.)

a. **March 31, 2008**
Retained Earnings (Dividends Declared)..................... 10,000
    Dividends Payable 10,000

Assets	=	Liabilities	+	Shareholders' Equity	(Class.)
		+10,000		−10,000	RE

$10,000 = 20,000 x $.50.

b. **April 15, 2008**
Dividends Payable... 10,000
    Cash 10,000

Assets	=	Liabilities	+	Shareholders' Equity	(Class.)
−10,000		−10,000			

c. **June 30, 2008**
Retained Earnings (Dividends Declared) (= 2,000 x $20)... 40,000
    Common Stock (= 2,000 x $15) 30,000
    Additional Paid-in Capital................................. 10,000

Assets	=	Liabilities	+	Shareholders' Equity	(Class.)
				−40,000	RE
				+30,000	ContriCap
				+10,000	ContriCap

d. **September 30, 2008**
Retained Earnings (Dividends Declared)................... 11,000
    Dividends Payable 11,000

Assets	=	Liabilities	+	Shareholders' Equity	(Class.)
		+11,000		−11,000	RE

$11,000 = 22,000 x $.50.

14.23 continued.

e. **October 15, 2008**

Dividends Payable.. 11,000

    Cash 11,000

Assets	=Liabilities	+	Shareholders' Equity	(Class.)
−11,000	−11,000			

f. **December 31, 2008**

Additional Paid-in Capital.................................... 165,000

    Common Stock (= 11,000 x $15)........................ 165,000

Assets	=Liabilities	+	Shareholders' Equity	(Class.)
			−165,000	ContriCap
			+165,000	ContriCap

14.25   (Melissa Corporation; journal entries for treasury stock transactions.)

a. Treasury Stock—Common 120,000

    Cash (= 10,000 x $12)................................... 120,000

Assets	=Liabilities	+	Shareholders' Equity	(Class.)
−120,000			−120,000	ContriCap

b. Bonds Payable 72,000

    Treasury Stock—Common (= 6,000 x $12)........... 72,000

Assets	=Liabilities	+	Shareholders' Equity	(Class.)
	−72,000		+72,000	ContriCap

c. Treasury Stock—Common 300,000

    Cash (= 20,000 x $15)................................... 300,000

Assets	=Liabilities	+	Shareholders' Equity	(Class.)
−300,000			−300,000	ContriCap

14.25 continued.

d. Land... 540,000
      Treasury Stock—Common [= (4,000 x $12) +
        (20,000 x $15)]... 348,000
      Common Stock (= 6,000 x $5)................................... 30,000
      Additional Paid-in Capital.. 162,000

Assets	=Liabilities +	Shareholders' Equity	(Class.)
+540,000		+348,000	ContriCap
		+30,000	ContriCap
		+162,000	ContriCap

14.27 (Uncertainty Corporation; journal entries to correct errors and adjust for changes in estimates.)

a. Retained Earnings... 12,000
      Patent (or Accumulated Amortization)................ 12,000

Assets	=Liabilities +	Shareholders' Equity	(Class.)
−12,000		−12,000	RE

To correct error from neglecting to amortize patent during previous year.

b. Accumulated Depreciation.. 7,000
      Retained Earnings.. 4,000
      Retained Earnings.. 3,000

Assets	=Liabilities +	Shareholders' Equity	(Class.)
+7,000		+4,000	RE
		+3,000	RE

To correct error in recording the sale of a machine by eliminating the balance in accumulated depreciation relating to the machine sold and converting a $4,000 loss on the sale to a $3,000 gain.

14.27 continued.

c. Depreciation Expense.. 50,000
    Accumulated Depreciation 50,000

Assets	=	Liabilities	+	Shareholders' Equity	(Class.)
–50,000				–50,000	IncSt → RE

To record depreciation expense for 2008. Carrying value on January 1, 2008 is $1,600,00 [= $2,400,000 – ($80,000 x 10)]. The revised annual depreciation is $50,000 (= $1,600,000/32).

d. Bad Debt Expense... 10,000
    Allowance for Uncollectible Accounts 10,000

Assets	=	Liabilities	+	Shareholders' Equity	(Class.)
–10,000				–10,000	IncSt → RE

To adjust the balance in the allowance account to the amount needed to cover estimated uncollectibles.

14.29 (Journal entries for the issuance of common stock.)

a. Inventory 175,000
  Land 220,000
  Building.. 1,400,000
  Equipment 405,000
    Common Stock (= 20,000 x $10) 200,000
    Additional Paid-in Capital 2,000,000

Assets	=	Liabilities	+	Shareholders' Equity	(Class.)
+175,000				+200,000	ContriCap
+220,000				+2,000,000	ContriCap
+1,400,000					
+405,000					

b. Cash (= 10,000 x $100)... 1,000,000
    Redeemable Preferred Stock..................................... 1,000,000

Assets	=	Liabilities	+	Shareholders' Equity	(Class.)
+1,000,000		+1,000,000			

14.29 continued.

c. Cash (= 5,000 x $24)... 120,000
    Additional Paid-in Capital (Common Stock War-
        rants) (= 5,000 x $8)... 40,000
            Common Stock (= 5,000 x $1)............................. 5,000
            Additional Paid-in Capital.................................. 155,000

Assets	=	Liabilities	+	Shareholders' Equity	(Class.)
+120,000				−40,000	ContriCap
				+5,000	ContriCap
				+155,000	ContriCap

d. Preferred Stock (= 10,000 x $50)................................. 500,000
        Common Stock (= 20,000 x $10)............................. 200,000
        Additional Paid-in Capital 300,000

Assets	=	Liabilities	+	Shareholders' Equity	(Class.)
				−500,000	ContriCap
				+200,000	ContriCap
				+300,000	ContriCap

14.31   (Fisher Company; reconstructing transactions involving shareholders' equity.)

a. $60,000 par value/$10 per share = 6,000 shares.

b. $7,200/360 = $20 per share.

c. 600 − 360 = 240 shares.

d. If the Additional Paid-in Capital is $31,440, then $30,000 [= 6,000 x ($15 − $10)] represents contributions in excess of par value on original issue of 6,000 shares. Then, $1,440 (= $31,440 − $30,000) represents the credit to Additional Paid-in Capital when it reissued the treasury shares.
    The $1,440 represents 240 shares reissued times the excess of reissue price over acquisition price:

$$240(\$X - \$20) = \$1,440, \text{ or } X = \$26.$$

The shares were reissued for $26 each.

14.31 continued.

e. (1) Cash (= 6,000 x $15).. 90,000
     Common Stock ($10 Par Value)..................... 60,000
     Additional Paid-in Capital 30,000

Assets	=	Liabilities	+	Shareholders' Equity	(Class.)
+90,000				+60,000	ContriCap
				+30,000	ContriCap

(2) Treasury Stock—Common 12,000
     Cash (= 600 x $20)....................................... 12,000

Assets	=	Liabilities	+	Shareholders' Equity	(Class.)
−12,000				−12,000	ContriCap

(3) Cash (= 240 x $26)...................................... 6,240
     Treasury Stock—Common (= 240 x $20) 4,800
     Additional Paid-in Capital 1,440

Assets	=	Liabilities	+	Shareholders' Equity	(Class.)
+6,240				+4,800	ContriCap
				+1,440	ContriCap

(4a) Cash.. 10,000
     Securities Available for Sale 6,000
     Realized Gain on Sale of Securities Available for Sale... 4,000

Assets	=	Liabilities	+	Shareholders' Equity	(Class.)
+10,000				+4,000	IncSt → RE
−6,000					

(4b) Securities Available for Sale.............................. 2,000
     Unrealized Holding Gain on Securities
     Available for Sale (Accumulated Other
     Comprehensive Income).............................. 2,000

Assets	=	Liabilities	+	Shareholders' Equity	(Class.)
+2,000				+2,000	OCInc → AOCInc

14.31 continued.

    f. The realized gain appears in the income statement and the unrealized gain appears in a statement of other comprehensive income or in reconciliation of accumulated other comprehensive income.

14.33   (Lowe Corporation; accounting for stock options.)

Compensation expense reduces net income each year as follows:

2008: zero compensation because all benefits occur after the granting of the stock option.

2009:	.5(5,000 x $2.40)	$ 6,000
2010:	[.5(5,000 x $2.40) + .5(6,000 x $3.00)]	15,000
2011:	[.5(6,000 x $3.00) + .5(7,000 x $3.14)]	19,990
2012:	[.5(7,000 x $3.14) + .5(8,000 x $3.25)]	23,990
	Total Compensation Expense	$ 64,980

14.35   (Microsoft Corporation; reconstructing transactions affecting shareholders' equity.) (Amounts in Millions)

(1) Cash 6,763

        Common Stock and Additional Paid-in

           Capital 6,763

Assets	=	Liabilities	+	Shareholders' Equity	(Class.)
+6,763				+6,763	ContriCap

To issue common stock for cash.

(2) Common Stock and Additional Paid-in Capital 6,162

        Retained Earnings 21,212

           Cash 27,374

Assets	=	Liabilities	+	Shareholders' Equity	(Class.)
−27,374				−6,162	ContriCap
				−21,212	RE

To repurchase common stock for more than its initial issue price.

14.35 continued.

(3) Compensation Expense 889

      Additional Paid-in Capital 889

Assets	=	Liabilities	+	Shareholders' Equity	(Class.)
				−889	IncSt → RE
				+889	ContriCap

(4) Revenues and Gains Net of Expenses and Losses. 14,065

      Retained Earnings... 14,065

Assets	=	Liabilities	+	Shareholders' Equity	(Class.)
				−14,065	IncSt → RE
				+14,065	RE

To close revenues, gain, expense, and loss accounts to retained earnings.

(5) Retained Earnings... 3,837

      Cash 3,837

Assets	=	Liabilities	+	Shareholders' Equity	(Class.)
−3,837				−3,837	RE

To declare and pay cash dividends.

(6) Marketable Securities... 326

      Net Unrealized Gains and Losses on Marketable Securities... 326

Assets	=	Liabilities	+	Shareholders' Equity	(Class.)
+326				+326	OCInc → AOCInc

To record net unrealized gains and losses for changes in fair value of marketable securities.

14.35 continued.

    (7) Derivative Securities   14

              Net Unrealized Gains and Losses on

                 Derivatives   14

Assets	=	Liabilities	+	Shareholders' Equity	(Class.)
+14	or	−14		+14	OCInc → AOCInc

14.37   (Anheuser-Busch Companies; journal entries for changes in shareholders' equity.) (Amounts in Millions)

    (1) Cash 292.3

              Common Stock 8.8

              Additional Paid-in Capital 283.5

Assets	=	Liabilities	+	Shareholders' Equity	(Class.)
+292.3				+8.8	ContriCap
				+283.5	ContriCap

To record the issuance of common stock to employees under stock option plans.

    (2) Compensation Expense 136.3

              Additional Paid-in Capital 136.1

              Treasury Stock—Common 2

Assets	=	Liabilities	+	Shareholders' Equity	(Class.)
				−136.2	IncSt → RE
				+136.1	ContriCap
				+.2	ContriCap

To record the amortized cost of *employees stock* options. The reason for the *credit* to *Treasury Stock is not explained* by Anheuser-Busch.

    (3) Revenues, Gains, Expenses, and Losses 2,115.3

              Retained Earnings 2,115.3

Assets	=	Liabilities	+	Shareholders' Equity	(Class.)
				−2,115.3	IncSt → RE
				+2,115.3	RE

14.37 continued.

(4) Retained Earnings.. 932.4
      Cash 932.4

Assets	=	Liabilities	+	Shareholders' Equity	(Class.)
−932.4				−932.4	RE

To record the declaration and payment of cash dividends.

(5) Treasury Stock—Common 2,707.2
      Cash 2,707.2

Assets	=	Liabilities	+	Shareholders' Equity	(Class.)
−2,707.2				−2,707.2	ContriCap

To record repurchase of common stock held as treasury stock.

(6) Net Unrealized Gains and Losses on Marketable
      Securities.. .3
         Marketable Securities 3

Assets	=	Liabilities	+	Shareholders' Equity	(Class.)
−.3				−.3	OCInc → AOCInc

To record net unrealized loss on marketable securities.

(7) Net Unrealized Gains and Losses on Cash Flow
      Hedges... 2.0
         Derivative Securities 2.0

Assets	=	Liabilities	+	Shareholders' Equity	(Class.)
−2.0	or	+2.0		−2.0	OCInc → AOCInc

To record net unrealized loss on cash flow hedges.

14.37 continued.

    (8) Pension Liability.. 205.2

           Pension Liability Adjustment......................................   205.2

Assets	=	Liabilities	+	Shareholders' Equity	(Class.)
		+205.2		+205.2	OCInc → AOCInc

To reduce pension liability for a reduction in the minimum pension liability or for changes in actuarial assumptions, actuarial performance, or prior cost and increase in other comprehensive income.

14.39   (Layton Ball Corporation; case introducing earnings-per-share calculations for a complex capital structure.)

    a. $\dfrac{\$9,500}{2,500} = \$3.80$ per share.

    b.   1,000 options X $15 = $15,000 cash raised.

$$\dfrac{\$15,000 \text{ new cash}}{\$25 \text{ per share}} = 600 \text{ shares assumed purchased.}$$

Total number of shares increases by 400 (= 1,000 – 600).

$$\dfrac{\$9,500}{2,500 + 400} = \$3.276 \text{ per share.}$$

    c.   2,000 warrants X $30 = $60,000 cash raised.

$$\dfrac{\$60,000 \text{ new cash}}{\$25 \text{ per share}} = 2,400 \text{ shares purchased.}$$

Total number of shares decreases by 400 (= 2,000 – 2,400).

$$\dfrac{\$9,500}{2,500 - 400} = \$4.524 \text{ per share.}$$

14.39 continued.

d. Before taxes, each converted bond saves $40 in annual interest expense. After taxes, the savings in expense and increase in income is only $24 [= $(1 - .40) \times \$40$].

There are 100 bonds outstanding; each is convertible into 10 shares. Thus, the new earnings per share figure is:

$$\frac{\$9,500 + \$24 \text{ savings per bond} \times 100 \text{ bonds}}{2,500 + 10 \text{ shares per bond} \times 100 \text{ bonds}} = \frac{\$11,900}{3,500 \text{ shares}} =$$

$3.40 per share.

e. The warrants are antidilutive and should be ignored if we seek the maximum possible dilution of earnings per share.

$$\frac{\$9,500 + \$2,400 \text{ (Increase from interest savings)}}{2,500 + 1,000 \text{ (bond conversion)} + 400 \text{ (option exercise)}} = \frac{\$11,900}{3,900} =$$

$3.05 per share.

f. Probably the Wall Street Journal should use the earnings per share that results in the maximum possible dilution. It should clearly ignore antidilutive securities. Do not conclude from the presentation in this problem that one can check the dilution characteristics of potentially dilutive securities one by one and know for sure which combination of assumed exercise and conversions leads to the minimum earnings per share figure.

CHAPTER 15

STATEMENT OF CASH FLOWS: ANOTHER LOOK

Problems and Cases: Answers and Solutions

15.1   (Effects of transactions on statement of cash flows.)

a.   The journal entry to record this transaction is:

Retained Earnings...   15,000
    Dividends Payable   3,000
    Cash   12,000

	Δ**Cash**	**=**	Δ**L**	**+**	Δ**SE**	**–**	Δ**N\$A**
Financing	–$12,000	=	$3,000	+	–$15,000	–	$0

The credit to the Cash account reduces Line (11) by $12,000. Paying dividends is a financing activity, so Line (10) increases by $12,000.

b.   The journal entry to record this transaction is:

Cash...   75,000
    Bank Loan Payable...   75,000

	Δ**Cash**	**=**	Δ**L**	**+**	Δ**SE**	**–**	Δ**N\$A**
Financing	+$75,000	=	$75,000	+	$0	–	$0

The debit to the Cash account increases Line (11) by $75,000. Borrowing is a financing activity so Line (8) increases by $75,000.

15.1 continued.

c. The journal entry to record this transaction is:

Cash..	20,000	
Accumulated Depreciation.......................................	35,000	
Machinery..		40,000
Gain on Sale of Machinery.....................................		15,000

	ΔCash	=	ΔL	+	ΔSE	−	ΔN$A
Investing	$20,000	=	$0	+	$15,000	−	−$5,000

The debit to the Cash account results in an increase in Line (11) of $20,000. Selling machinery is an investing activity so Line (6) increases by $20,000. The gain on the sale increases net income on Line (3) by $15,000. Because the full cash proceeds is an investing activity, Line (5) increases by $15,000 to subtract from net income a revenue that did not provide an operating source of cash.

d. The journal entry for this transaction is:

Rent Expense...	28,000	
Cash...		28,000

	ΔCash	=	ΔL	+	ΔSE	−	ΔN$A
Operations	−$28,000	=	$0	+	−$28,000	−	$0

The credit to the Cash account reduces Line (11) by $28,000. The recognition of rent expense reduces net income on Line (3) by $28,000. Expenditure matched the expense, so Line (2) shows an increase in the amount subtracted of $28,000.

e. The journal entry to record this transaction is:

Marketable Securities..	39,000	
Cash...		39,000

	ΔCash	=	ΔL	+	ΔSE	−	ΔN$A
Investing	−$39,000	=	$0	+	$0	−	$39,000

The credit to the Cash account reduces Line (11) by $39,000. Purchasing marketable securities is an investing transaction so Line (7) increases by $39,000.

f. The journal entry to record this transaction is:

Accumulated Depreciation.. 14,000
    Truck.. 14,000

	ΔCash	=	ΔL	+	ΔSE	−	ΔN$A
	$0	=	$0	+	$0	−	$0

Because this transaction affects neither the Cash account nor net income, it does not appear on the statement of cash flows.

g. The journal entry to record this event is:

Unrealized Holding Loss of Marketable Secur-
    ities (Other Comprehensive Income)................... 8,000
        Marketable Securities....................................... 8,000

	ΔCash	=	ΔL	+	ΔSE	−	ΔN$A
	$0	=	$0	+	−$8,000	−	−$8,000

Because this entry does not affect either the Cash account or net income, it does not appear on the statement of cash flows. The firm discloses in a supplementary schedule or note the write down of marketable equity securities totaling $8,000.

h. The journal entry to record this transaction is:

Interest Expense... 15,000
    Bonds Payable... 500
    Cash 14,500

	ΔCash	=	ΔL	+	ΔSE	−	ΔN$A
Operations	−$14,500	=	$500	+	−$15,000	−	$0

The credit to the Cash account results in a decrease in Line (11) of $14,500. The recognition of interest expense reduces net income on Line (3) by $15,000. Because the firm used only $14,500 of cash for this expense, Line (4) increases by $500 for the portion of the expense that did not use cash. Line (2) increased the amount to be subtracted by the amount of the expense paid in cash, $14,500.

15.1 continued.

    i.   The journal entry for this event is:

Goodwill Impairment Loss.. 22,000
    Goodwill..   22,000

ΔCash	=	ΔL	+	ΔSE	–	ΔN$A
$0	=	$0	+	–$22,000	–	–$22,000

This entry does not involve the Cash account so Line (11) does not change. The recognition of the impairment loss reduces net income on Line (3) by $22,000. Because this loss requires no cash outflow, Line (4) increases by $22,000 to convert net income to cash flow from operations.

15.3   (Effects of transactions on statement of cash flows.)

    a.   The journal entry to record this event is:

Contracts in Process 15,000
    Contract Revenue   15,000

ΔCash	=	ΔL	+	ΔSE	–	ΔN$A
$0	=	$0	+	$15,000	–	$15,000

This entry does not affect the Cash account so Line (11) does not change. The recognition of contract revenue increases net income on Line (3) by $15,000. Because this revenue does not result in a change in cash, Line (5) increases by $15,000 to convert net income to cash flow from operations.

    b.   The journal entry to record this transaction is:

Land 50,000
    Donated Capital..   50,000

ΔCash	=	ΔL	+	ΔSE	–	ΔN$A
$0	=	$0	+	$50,000	–	$50,000

This transaction affects neither the Cash account [Line (11)] nor net income [Line (3)] and, therefore, does not appear on the statement of cash flows. The firm discloses in a supplementary schedule or note the donation of land by a governmental agency totaling $50,000.

15.3 continued.

c. The journal entry to record this event is:

Unrealized Holding Loss on Investments in
    Securities (Other Comprehensive Income)........ 8,000
        Investments in Securities 8,000

ΔCash	=	ΔL	+	ΔSE	−	ΔN$A
$0	=	$0	+	−$8,000	−	−$8,000

This transaction affects neither the Cash account [Line (11)] nor net income [Line (3)] so would not appear on the statement of cash flows. The firm discloses in a supplementary schedule or note the write down of marketable equity investments totaling $8,000.

d. The journal entry to record the recognition of depreciation is:

Inventories.. 60,000
    Accumulated Depreciation 60,000

The journal entry to record the sale of the inventory items is:

Cost of Goods Sold.. 60,000
    Inventories.. 60,000

ΔCash	=	ΔL	+	ΔSE	−	ΔN$A
$0	=	$0	+	−$60,000	−	−$60,000

These entries do not affect the Cash account so Line (11) does not change. The recognition of cost of goods sold containing depreciation reduces net income on Line (3) by $60,000. Because this expense does not use cash, Line (4) increases by $60,000 to convert net income to cash flow from operations.

e. The journal entry to record this transaction is:

Warranty Expense... 35,000
    Estimated Warranty Liability............................. 35,000

ΔCash	=	ΔL	+	ΔSE	−	ΔN$A
$0	=	$35,000	+	−$35,000	−	$0

This entry does not affect the Cash account so Line (11) does not change. The recognition of warranty expense reduces net income on Line (3) by $35,000. Because this expense does not use cash, Line (4) increases by $35,000 to convert net income to cash flow from operations.

15.3 continued.

f. The journal entry to record this transaction is:

Estimated Warranty Liability.................................. 28,000
   Cash...   28,000

	ΔCash	=	ΔL	+	ΔSE	−	ΔN$A
Operations	−$28,000	=	−$28,000	+	$0	−	$0

The credit to the Cash account reduces Line (11) by $28,000. Honoring warranties is an operating item so Line (2) increases the amount to be subtracted. This entry does not affect net income on Line (3) this period. Thus, Line (5) increases by $28,000 to convert net income to cash flow from operations.

g. The journal entry to record this event is:

Income Tax Expense 80,000
Deferred Tax Liability.................................... 20,000
   Cash..   100,000

	ΔCash	=	ΔL	+	ΔSE	−	ΔN$A
Operations	−$100,000	=	−$20,000	+	−$80,000	−	$0

The credit to the Cash account results in a reduction in Line (11) of $100,000. Line (2) increases the amount to be subtracted by $100,000. The recognition of income tax expense reduces net income on Line (3) by $80,000. Because the firm used more cash this period than the amount of income tax expense, Line (5) increases by $20,000 when converting net income to cash flow from operations.

h. The journal entry to record this event is:

Loss from Writedown of Inventories 18,000
   Inventories..   18,000

	ΔCash	=	ΔL	+	ΔSE	−	ΔN$A
	$0	=	$0	+	−$18,000	−	−$18,000

This entry does not affect the Cash account so Line (11) does not change. The recognition of the writedown reduces net income on Line (3) by $18,000. Because the writedown did not use cash, Line (4) increases by $18,000 to convert net income to cash flow from operations.

15.5 (Metals Company deriving direct method cash flow from operations using data from T-account work sheet.) (All Dollar Amounts in Millions) (Based on financial statements of Alcoa.)

(a) (The letters here correspond to the column header-letters in the exhibit below.) Copy Income Statement and Cash Flow from Operations

(b) Copy Information from T-Account Work Sheet Next to Related Income Statement Item

(c)–(d) Sum Across Rows to Derive Direct Receipts and Expenditures

Operations	Indirect Method	Changes in Related Balance Sheet Accounts from T-Account Work Sheet	Direct Method	From Operations: Receipts Less Expenditures
	(a)	(b)	(c)	(d)	
Sales Revenues	$20,465.0	$74.6	= Accounts Receivable Decrease	20,539.6	Receipts from Customers
Gain on Sale of Marketable Equity Securities	20.8	(20.8)	Gain Produces No Operating Cash	-	
Equity in Earnings of Affiliates	214.0	(47.1)	Alcoa's Share of Earnings Retained by Affiliates	166.9	Receipts for Equity Method Investments
Cost of Goods Sold	(9,963.3)	664.0 / 33.9 / (198.9)	Depreciation on Manufacturing Facilities / = Accounts Payable Increase / = Increase in Inventories	(9,464.3)	Payments for Inventory
General and Administrative Expenses	(5,570.2)	(40.3) / (110.8)	= Prepayments Increase / = Decrease in Other Current Liabilities	(5,721.3)	Payments for General and Administrative Services
Interest Expense	(2,887.3)	-		(2,887.3)	Payments for Interest
Income Tax Expense	(911.6)	82.0	Deferred Income Taxes Uses no Cash this Period	(829.6)	Payment for Income Taxes
Net Income	= $1,367.4	= 1,367.4	Totals.........	$1,804.0	= Cash Flow from Operations

$1,804.0 = Cash Flow from Operations Derived via Indirect Method

Derived via Direct Method

15.7 (Warren Corporation; preparing a statement of cash flows.)

a.

	Cash		
	√ 223,200		

Operations

Net Income	(5)	234,000
Loss on Sale of Machinery	(1b)	15,600
Amortize Patent	(2b)	5,040
Decrease in Accounts Receivable	(7)	18,000
Bad Debt Expense	(8)	2,400
Decrease in Inventories	(9)	66,000
Depreciation Expense	(11)	106,800
Amortize Leasehold Improvements	(12)	10,800
Increase in Accounts Payable	(13)	153,360

Investing

Sale of Machinery	(1b)	57,600	463,200	(1a)	Acquisition of Machinery
			2,400	(2a)	Payment for Patent Defense
			180,000	(10)	Acquisition of Securities

Financing

		13,200	(3)	Retirement of Preferred Stock
		60,000	(15)	Provision for Current Portion of Serial Bonds

	√ 174,000	

15.7 a. continued.

	Accounts Receivable			Allowance for Un-collectible Accounts				Inventory	
√	327,600					20,400	√	√ 645,600	
		3,600 (6)	(6)	3,600		2,400	(8)		66,000 (9)
		18,000 (7)							
√	306,000					19,200	√	√ 579,600	

Securities Held for Plant Expansion		Machinery and Equipment (Cost)		Accumulated Depreciation	
√ -0-		√ 776,400			446,400 √
(10) 180,000		(1a) 463,200	127,200 (1b)	(1b) 54,000	106,800 (11)
√ 180,000		√ 1,112,400			499,200 √

Leasehold Improvements		Allowance for Amortization		Patents	
√ 104,400			58,800 √	√ 36,000	
			10,800 (12)	(2a) 2,400	5,040 (2b)
√ 104,400			69,600 √	√ 33,360	

Accounts Payable		Dividends Payable		Bonds Payable (Current)	
	126,000 √		-- √		60,000 √
	153,360 (13)		48,000 (4)	(15) 60,000	60,000 (14)
	279,360 √		48,000 √		60,000 √

6% Serial Bonds Payable		Preferred Stock		Common Stock	
	360,000 √		120,000 √		600,000 √
(14) 60,000		(3) 12,000			
	300,000 √		108,000 √		600,000 √

Retained Earnings	
	321,600 √
(4) 48,000	234,000 (5)
(3) 1,200	
	506,400 √

15.7 continued.

b.

WARREN CORPORATION
Statement of Cash Flows
For the Year Ending June 30, 2009

Operations:

Net Income	$234,000	
Loss on Sale of Machinery	15,600	
Depreciation	106,800	
Amortization of Leasehold Improvements	10,800	
Amortization of Patents	5,040	
Bad Debt Expense	2,400	
Decrease in Accounts Receivable	18,000	
Decrease in Inventories	66,000	
Increase in Accounts Payable	153,360	
Cash Flow from Operations		$612,000
Investing:		
Sale of Machinery	$ 57,600	
Payment of Legal Fee for Patent Defense	(2,400)	
Acquisition of Securities for Plant Expansion	(180,000)	
Acquisition of Machinery	(463,200)	
Cash Flow from Investing		(588,000)
Financing:		
Retirement of Serial Bonds	$ (60,000)	
Retirement of Preferred Stock	(13,200)	
Cash Flow from Financing		(73,200)
Net Change in Cash		$ (49,200)
Cash, January 1, 2009		223,200
Cash, June 30, 2009		$174,000

15.9 (Biddle Corporation; preparing a statement of cash flows.)

a.

Cash					
√	45,000				

Operations

Income from Continuing Operations	(14)	60,500	6,000	(3)	Gain on Retirement of Bonds Net of Income Taxes
Loss on Sale of Equipment	(4)	2,000	35,000	(7)	Increase in Accounts Receivable
Depreciation	(9)	10,000			
Amortization	(10)	1,500			
Increase in Accounts Payable	(11)	30,000	20,000	(8)	Increase in Inventories
Deferred Income Taxes	(13)	20,000	5,000	(12)	Decrease in Accrued Liabilities

Investing

Sale of Equipment	(4)	9,500	42,500	(6)	Acquisition of Land

Financing

			19,000	(3)	Retirement of Bonds, Including Income Taxes
			1,000	(5)	Dividends
√	50,000				

Accounts Receivable—Net		Inventories		Land	
√ 70,000		√ 110,000		√ 100,000	
(7) 35,000		(8) 20,000		(2) 20,000	
				(6) 42,500	
√ 105,000		√ 130,000		√ 162,500	

15.9 a. continued.

Plant and Equipment	
√ 316,500	
	26,500 (4)
√ 290,000	

Accumulated Depreciation	
	50,000 √
(4) 15,000	10,000 (9)
	45,000 √

Patents	
√ 16,500	
	1,500(10)
√ 15,000	

Accounts Payable	
	100,000 √
	30,000(11)
	130,000 √

Accrued Liabilities	
	105,000 √
(12) 5,000	
	100,000 √

Deferred Income Taxes	
	50,000 √
	20,000(13)
	70,000 √

Long-term Bonds	
	90,000 √
(3) 25,000	
	65,000 √

Common Stock	
	105,000 √
	10,500 (1)
	9,500 (2)
	125,000 √

Additional Paid-in Capital	
	85,000 √
	21,000 (1)
	10,500 (2)
	116,500 √

Retained Earnings	
	73,000 √
(1) 31,500	60,500 (14)
(5) 1,000	
	101,000 √

15.9 continued.

b.

BIDDLE CORPORATION
Statement of Cash Flows
For the Year Ended December, 2009

Operations:
Income from Continuing Operations	$ 54,500	
Loss on Sale of Equipment	2,000	
Depreciation	10,000	
Amortization	1,500	
Deferred Income Taxes	20,000	
Increase in Accounts Payable	30,000	
Increase in Accounts Receivable	(35,000)	
Increase in Inventories	(20,000)	
Decrease in Accrued Liabilities	(5,000)	
Cash Flow from Operations		$ 58,000
Investing:		
Sale of Equipment	$ 9,500	
Acquisition of Land	(42,500)	
Cash Flow from Investing		(33,000)
Financing:		
Retirement of Bonds	$ (19,000)	
Dividends	(1,000)	
Cash Flow from Financing		(20,000)
Net Change in Cash		$ 5,000
Cash, January 1, 2009		45,000
Cash, December 31, 2009		$ 50,000

Supplementary Information
During 2009, Biddle Corporation issued common stock with a market value of $20,000 in the acquisition of land.

15.11 (Airlines Corporation; preparing and interpreting the statement of cash flows.) (Based on financial statements of UAL.)

a. T-account work sheet for 2008.

	Cash		
√	1,087		

	Operations		
(1)	324	106	(4)
(3)	517	147	(7)
(11)	56	39	(8)
(15)	42	67	(9)
(17)	12	49	(16)

	Investing		
(4)	1,199	1,568	(2)
(10)	40	957	(6)

	Financing		
(12)	325	110	(13)
(18)	4	98	(19)
√	465		

Marketable Securities			Accounts Receivable			Inventories	
√	--		√	741		√	210
(5)	85		(7)	147		(8)	39
(6)	957						
√	1,042		√	888		√	249

Prepayments			Property, Plant and Equipment			Accumulated Depreciation		
√	112		√	7,710			3,769	√
(9)	67		(2)	1,568	1,574 (4)	(4) 481	517	(3)
√	179		√	7,704			3,805	√

Other Assets			Accounts Payable			Short-Term Borrowing		
√	610			540	√		121	√
		40 (10)		56	(11)		325	(12)
√	570			596	√		446	√

15.11 a. continued.

Current Portion Long-Term Debt		
	110 √	
(13) 110	84 (14)	
	84 √	

Advances from Customers	
	619 √
	42 (15)
	661 √

Other Current Liabilities		
		1,485 √
(16) 49		
		1,436 √

Long-Term Debt	
	1,418 √
(14) 84	
	1,334 √

Deferred Tax Liability	
	352 √
	12 (17)
	364 √

Other Noncurrent Liabilities	
	715 √
	4 (18)
	719 √

Common Stock	
	119 √
	119 √

Unrealized Holding Gain on Marketable Securities	
	-- √
	85 (5)
	85 √

Retained Earnings	
	1,188 √
	324 (1)
	1,512 √

Additional Paid-in Capital	
	48 √
	48 √

Treasury Stock	
√ 14	
(19) 98	
√ 112	

15.11 a. continued.

    a.   T-account work sheet for 2009.

	Cash	
√	465	

	Operations		
(1)	101	286	(4)
(3)	560	25	(7)
(15)	182	74	(8)
(16)	390	30	(9)
(18)	4	44	(11)

	Investing		
(4)	1,697	2,821	(2)
		17	(6)
		35	(10)

	Financing		
(12)	1	84	(13)
(17)	230		
(19)	2		
(20)	5		
√	221		

Marketable Securities			Accounts Receivable			Inventories	
√	1,042		√	888		√	249
(5)	7		(7)	25		(8)	74
(6)	17						
√	1,066		√	913		√	323

Prepayments			Property, Plant and Equipment			Accumulated Depreciation		
√	179		√	7,704			3,805	√
(9)	30		(2)	2,821	1,938 (4)	(4)	527	560 (3)
√	209		√	8,587			3,838	√

15.11 a. continued.

Other Assets	
√ 570	
(10) 35	
√ 605	

Accounts Payable	
	596 √
(11) 44	
	552 √

Short-Term Borrowing	
	446 √
	1(12)
	447 √

Current Portion Long-Term Debt	
	84 √
(13) 84	89(14)
	89 √

Advances from Customers	
	661 √
	182(15)
	843 √

Other Current Liabilities	
	1,436 √
	390(16)
	1,826 √

Long-Term Debt	
	1,334 √
(14) 89	230(17)
	1,475 √

Deferred Tax Liability	
	364 √
	4(18)
	368 √

Other Noncurrent Liabilities	
	719 √
	2(19)
	721 √

Common Stock	
	119 √
	1(20)
	120 √

Additional Paid-in Capital	
	48 √
	4(20)
	52 √

Unrealized Holding Gain on Marketable Securities	
	85 √
	7 (5)
	92 √

Retained Earnings	
	1,512 √
	101 (1)
	1,613 √

Treasury Stock	
√ 112	
√ 112	

15.11 continued.

b. **Comparative Statement of Cash Flows for Airlines Corporation**
(Amounts in Millions)

	2009	2008
Operations:		
Net Income	$ 101	$ 324
Depreciation Expense	560	517
Deferred Income Taxes	4	12
Gain on Sale of Property, Plant and Equipment	(286)	(106)
(Increase) Decrease in Accounts Receivable	(25)	(147)
(Increase) Decrease in Inventories	(74)	(39)
(Increase) Decrease in Prepayments	(30)	(67)
Increase (Decrease) in Accounts Payable	(44)	56
Increase (Decrease) in Advances from Customers	182	42
Increase (Decrease) in Other Current Liabilities	390	(49)
Cash Flow from Operations	$ 778	$ 543
Investing:		
Sale of Property, Plant and Equipment	$ 1,697	$ 1,199
Acquisition of Property, Plant and Equipment	(2,821)	(1,568)
Acquisition of Marketable Securities	(17)	(957)
(Increase) Decrease in Other Noncurrent Assets	(35)	40
Cash Flow from Investing	$(1,176)	$ (1,286)
Financing:		
Increase in Short-Term Borrowing	$ 1	$ 325
Increase in Long-Term Borrowing	230	--
Increase in Common Stock	5	--
Decrease in Long-Term Borrowing	(84)	(110)
Acquisition of Treasury Stock	--	(98)
Increase in Other Noncurrent Liabilities	2	4
Cash Flow from Financing	$ 154	$ 121
Net Change in Cash	$ (244)	$ (622)
Cash, January 1	465	1,087
Cash, December 31	$ 221	$ 465

15.11 continued.

c. During 2008, cash flow from operations exceeded net income primarily because of the noncash expense for depreciation. Cash flows from operations and from the sale of property, plant and equipment were sufficient to finance capital expenditures. Airlines Corporation used the excess cash flow as well as cash from additional short-term borrowing to repay long-term debt and reacquire treasury stock. It invested the remaining excess cash flow in short-term marketable securities. Although the balance in the cash account declined during 2008, the combined balance in cash and marketable securities actually increased.

Net income declined in 2009 relative to 2008 but cash flow from operations increased. The increase occurred because Airlines Corporation received increased cash advances from customers and stretched its other current liabilities. Cash flow from operations and from the sale of property, plant and equipment were insufficient to finance capital expenditures. Airlines Corporation increased long-term borrowing and decreased the balance in its cash account to finance these capital expenditures.

One additional item to note for Airlines Corporation is the significant turnover of aircraft each year. The airline sold older aircraft at a gain and replaced them with newer aircraft.

15.13   (Breda Enterprises, Inc.; preparing a statement of cash flows.)

BREDA ENTERPRISES, INC.
Statement of Cash Flows
For the Year Ended December 31, 2009

Operations:		
Net Income (1)...	$ 90,000	
Adjustments for Noncash Transactions:		
Decrease in Merchandise Inventory (3)..................	4,000	
Increase in Accounts Payable (3)............................	12,000	
Loss on Sale of Equipment (4).................................	13,000	
Depreciation Expense (4)...	42,000	
Amortization of Leasehold Asset (5).......................	5,000	
Loss on Conversion of Bonds (8)	15,000	
Increase in Accounts Receivable (Net) (2).............	(10,600)	
Increase in Notes Receivable (2)	(15,000)	
Increase in Interest Receivable (2) [(.08 x		
$15,000) x (1/6)]..	(200)	
Decrease in Advances from Customers (2)............	(2,700)	
Realized Gain on Marketable Securities (7)............	(4,600)	
Interest Expense Greater than Cash Paid for Interest = Amortization of Bond Premium (8)	(1,500)	
Cash Flow from Operations...		$ 146,400
Investing:		
Sale of Equipment (4)..	$ 25,000	
Sale of Marketable Securities (7)............................	9,100	
Purchase of Equipment (4) ($31,000 + $38,000 − $26,000)	(43,000)	
Cash Flow from Investing..		(8,900)
Financing:		
Reduction of Lease Liability (5)..............................	$ (2,400)	
Dividends (6)...	(24,000)	
Cash Flow from Financing		(26,400)
Change in Cash		$ 111,100

15.15　(Canned Soup Company; interpreting the statement of cash flows.) (Based on financial statements of Campbell Soup Company.)

a.　Canned uses suppliers and other creditors to finance its working capital needs. Consumer foods is a mature industry in the United States, so Canned's modest growth rate does not require large incremental investments in accounts receivable and inventories.

b.　(1)　Capital expenditures have declined slightly each year, suggesting little need to add productive capacity.

　　(2)　Depreciation expense is a growing percentage of acquisitions of property, plant and equipment, suggesting slower growth in manufacturing capacity.

　　(3)　Substantial trading in marketable securities each year. Mature, profitable firms tend to accumulate cash beyond their operating needs and invest in marketable securities until they need cash.

　　(4)　Acquisition of another business in Year 8. Firms in mature industries grow by acquiring other firms. Canned financed this acquisition in part by selling marketable securities.

c.　(1)　Increases in long-term debt approximately equal repayments of long-term debt, particularly for Year 7 and Year 8. Mature firms tend to roll over debt as long as they remain in the no-growth phase.

　　(2)　Canned repurchased a portion of its common stock with excess cash.

　　(3)　Dividends have grown in line with increases in net income and represent approximately a 37% payout rate relative to net income.

15.17　(Cypress Corporation; interpreting the statement of cash flows.)

a.　Although net income increased between 2011 and 2013, the firm increased accounts receivable and inventories to support this growth. It stretched its creditors somewhat to finance the buildup of accounts receivable and inventories, but not sufficiently to keep cash from operations from decreasing.

b.　The principal factors causing cash flow from operations to increase in 2014 is an increase in net income. Inventories decreased and the firm stretched its payable somewhat as well. The principal factors causing the increased cash flow from operations in 2015 are increased and decreased accounts receivable and decreased inventories, partially offset by decreases in accounts payable and other liabilities.

c. The firm has repaid both short- and long-term debt, likely reducing its debt service payments. It invested excess cash in marketable securities. It also substantially increased its dividend. Even with these actions, cash on the balance sheet increased significantly, particularly in 2015.

CHAPTER 16

SYNTHESIS OF FINANCIAL REPORTING

Exercises and Problems: Answers and Solutions

16.1   (Identifying accounting principles.)

    a.   FIFO cost flow assumption.

    b.   Allowance method.

    c.   Equity method.

    d.   Capital or financing lease method.

    e.   Weighted-average cost flow assumption.

    f.   Effective interest method.

    g.   Cash flow hedge.

    h.   Market value method.

    i.   Percentage-of-completion method.

    j.   Allowance method.

    k.   Fair value hedge.

    l.   Operating lease method.

    m.   FIFO cost flow assumption.

    n.   Market value method for securities available for sale.

    o.   Straight line method.

    p.   FIFO cost flow assumption.

    q.   Operating lease method.

    r.   LIFO cost flow assumption.

16.1 continued.

  s. Capital or financing lease method.

  t. LIFO cost flow assumption.

16.3 (Chicago Corporation; comprehensive review problem.)

  a.

Balance, December 31, 2008.	$ 100,000
Provision for 2009..	120,000
Less Balance, December 31, 2009...	(160,000)
Write-offs during 2009..	$ 60,000

  b.

	LIFO	FIFO
Beginning Inventory...	$ 1,500,000	$ 1,800,000
Purchases...	5,300,000	5,300,000
Available for Sale..	$ 6,800,000	$ 7,100,000
Less Ending Inventory	(1,800,000)	(1,700,000)
Cost of Goods Sold	$ 5,000,000	$ 5,400,000
Net Sales..	$13,920,000	$ 13,920,000
Less Cost of Goods Sold..................................	(5,000,000)	(5,400,000)
Gross Profit...	$ 8,920,000	$ 8,520,000

  c. The quantity of inventory increased because the LIFO ending inventory is larger than the LIFO beginning inventory. The acquisition costs of the inventory items decreased because the FIFO ending inventory is less than the FIFO beginning inventory despite an increase in quantity during the year.

  d. None of the companies declared dividends during 2009 because the changes (increases) in the investment accounts equal the amounts recognized as Chicago Corporation's equity in the earnings of these companies.

  e.

Investment in Chicago Finance Corporation.............	1,800,000
Investment in Rosenwald Company	125,000
Investment in Hutchinson Company.........................	75,000
Equity in Earnings of Chicago Finance Cor-poration...	1,800,000
Equity in Earnings of Rosenwald Company........	125,000
Equity in Earnings of Hutchinson Company......	75,000

Assets	=	Liabilities	+	Shareholders' Equity	(Class.)
+1,800,000				+1,800,000	IncSt → RE
+125,000				+125,000	IncSt → RE
+75,000				+75,000	IncSt → RE

16.3 continued.

f. $\$4,000,000/40 = \$100,000$.

g.

Cash		400,000	
Accumulated Depreciation		800,000	
Machinery and Equipment			1,000,000
Gain on Sale of Machinery and Equipment			200,000

Assets	=	Liabilities	+	Shareholders' Equity	(Class.)
+400,000				+200,000	IncSt → RE
+800,000					
−1,000,000					

h.

Interest Expense		288,000	
Bonds Payable (= \$3,648,000 − \$3,600,000)......			48,000
Cash (= .06 × \$4,000,000)...................................			240,000

Assets	=	Liabilities	+	Shareholders' Equity	(Class.)
−240,000		+48,000		−288,000	IncSt → RE

i. Effective interest rate × $\$3,600,000 = \$288,000$. The effective interest rate = 8%. Chicago Corporation issued these bonds for less than their face value because the coupon rate of 6% is less than the market interest rate at the time of issue of 8%.

j. Difference between book and taxable depreciation = $\$150,000/.30 = \$500,000$.

Because the Deferred Tax Liability account increased, tax depreciation must be $500,000 larger than depreciation for financial reporting.

k.

Cash		1,000,000	
Treasury Shares...			400,000
Additional Paid-in Capital			600,000

Assets	=	Liabilities	+	Shareholders' Equity	(Class.)
+1,000,000				+400,000	ContriCap
				+600,000	ContriCap

16.3 continued.

l. Acquisition Cost... $1,250,000
   Less Carrying Value .... (750,000)
   Accumulated Amortization .... $ 500,000

Because the patent is being amortized at the rate of $125,000 per year, the patent was acquired four years before the balance sheet date (= $500,000/$125,000).

m. If Chicago Corporation owns less than 20% of the common stock of Hutchinson Company, it must use the market-value method. Chicago Corporation would show the Investment in Hutchinson account at its market value of $125,000 (= $100,000 + $25,000) and show a $25,000 amount in the Unrealized Holding Gain on Investment in Securities account in Accumulated Other Comprehensive Income in the shareholders' equity section of the balance sheet. Hutchinson Company did not declare dividends during the year. Thus, net income of Chicago Corporation would decrease by the $75,000 equity in Hutchinson Company's earnings during 2009 recognized under the equity method. Consolidated retained earnings would, therefore, be $75,000 less than as now stated. In the statement of cash flows, there would be $75,000 smaller net income and no subtraction of $75,000 for the equity in earnings of Hutchinson Company.

n. Capitalized Lease Obligation ($1,100,000 –
     $1,020,000)... 80,000
   Interest Expense 90,000
      Cash.. 170,000

Assets	= Liabilities	+	Shareholders' Equity	(Class.)
−170,000	−80,000		−90,000	IncSt → RE

Amortization of Leased Property Rights.................. 150,000
    Accumulated Amortization 150,000

Assets	= Liabilities	+	Shareholders' Equity	(Class.)
−150,000			−150,000	IncSt → RE

Total expense would be $240,000 (= $90,000 + $150,000).

o. The income statement would show a $200,000 loss from the price decline, and retained earnings would be $200,000 less than as shown. The Inventories account would be shown at $1,600,000 instead of $1,800,000. There would be an addback for the loss on the statement of cash flows because the loss did not use cash.

16.3 continued.

p. Basic earnings per share = ($4,400,000 − $120,000)/1,600,000 = $2.675.

Fully diluted earnings per share = $4,400,000/(1,600,000 + ?) = $2.20.

The number of common shares that would be issued is 400,000.

q.

	Cash		
√	200,000		

	Operations		
(1)	4,400,000	100,000	(3)
(11)	1,000,000	300,000	(4)
(12)	125,000	1,800,000	(5)
(13)	150,000	125,000	(6)
(15)	60,000	75,000	(7)
(16)	130,000	200,000	(9)
(17)	50,000	20,000	(14)
(18)	260,000		
(19)	48,000		
(22)	170,000		

	Investing		
(9)	400,000	100,000	(8)
		1,700,000	(10)

	Financing		
(23)	1,000,000	2,200,000	(2)
		968,000	(20)
		80,000	(21)
√	325,000		

	Accounts Receivable	
√	500,000	
(3)	100,000	
√	600,000	

	Merchandise Inventory	
√	1,500,000	
(4)	300,000	
√	1,800,000	

16.3 q. continued.

Prepayments	
√ 200,000	
√ 200,000	

Investments in Chicago Finance Corporation	
√ 2,200,000	
(5) 1,800,000	
√ 4,000,000	

Investment in Rosenwald Corporation	
√ 900,000	
(6) 125,000	
√ 1,025,000	

Investment in Hutchinson Corporation	
√ 100,000	
(7) 75,000	
√ 175,000	

Land	
√ 400,000	
(8) 100,000	
√ 500,000	

Building	
√ 4,000,000	
√ 4,000,000	

Merchandise and Equipment	
√ 7,300,000	
(10) 1,700,000	1,000,000 (9)
√ 8,000,000	

Property Rights under Lease	
√ 1,500,000	
√ 1,500,000	

Accumulated Depreciation and Amortization	
	3,800,000 √
(9) 800,000	1,000,000 (11)
	4,000,000 √

Patent	
√ 875,000	
	125,000 (12)
√ 750,000	

Goodwill	
√ 1,125,000	
√ 1,125,000	

Accounts Payable	
	400,000 √
	150,000 (13)
	550,000 √

Advances from Customers	
	660,000 √
(14) 20,000	
	640,000 √

Salaries Payable	
	240,000 √
	60,000 (15)
	300,000 √

16.3 q. continued.

Income Taxes Payable		
	300,000	√
	130,000	(16)
	430,000	√

Rent Received in Advance		
	0	√
	50,000	(17)
	50,000	√

Other Current Liabilities		
	200,000	√
	260,000	(18)
	460,000	√

Bonds Payable		
	3,600,000	√
	48,000	(19)
	3,648,000	√

Equipment Mortgage Payable			
		1,300,000	√
(20)	968,000		
		332,000	√

Capitalized Lease Obligation			
		1,100,000	√
(21)	80,000		
		1,020,000	√

Deferred Tax Liability		
	1,400,000	√
	170,000	(22)
	1,570,000	√

Convertible Preferred Stock		
	2,000,000	√
	2,000,000	√

Common Stock		
	2,000,000	√
	2,000,000	√

Additional Paid-in Capital		
	2,400,000	√
	600,000	(23)
	3,000,000	√

Retained Earnings			
		2,800,000	√
(2)	2,200,000	4,400,000	(1)
		5,000,000	√

Treasury Stock			
√	1,400,000		
		400,000	(23)
√	1,000,000		

16.5   (Scania, Inc.; recasting financial statements to proposed reporting format.)

a.
Schedule 16.1
SCANIA, INC.
Recast Statement of Financial Position
(Amounts in Millions)

	December 31,	
	2006	2005
Business Assets and Liabilities		
Short-Term Operating Assets:		
Cash	SEK 1,126	SEK 1,106
Short-Term Investments Comprising Cash and Cash Equivalents	8,808	493
Accounts Receivable, Net	SEK 19,025	SEK 18,377
Inventories	10,100	9,949
Total Short-Term Operating Assets	SEK 39,059	SEK 29,925
Short-Term Operating Liabilities:		
Current Interest-Bearing Liabilities	SEK (16,350)	SEK (9,351)
Current Provisions	(1,125)	(962)
Accrued Expenses and Deferred Income	(7,283)	(6,836)
Advance Payments from Customers	(449)	(593)
Trade Payables	(6,011)	(4,901)
Other Current Liabilities	(1,939)	(2,021)
Total Short-Term Operating Liabilities	SEK (33,157)	SEK (24,664)
Net Short-Term Operating Assets	SEK 5,902	SEK 5,261
Long-Term Operating Assets:		
Intangible Noncurrent Assets	SEK 2,464	SEK 2,698
Tangible Noncurrent Assets	17,130	16,715
Lease Assets	9,666	9,883
Holdings in Associated Companies and Joint Ventures	173	96
Long-Term Interest-Bearing Receivables	16,599	15,543
Other Long-Term Receivables	1,023	1,393
Total Long-Term Operating Assets	SEK 47,055	SEK 46,328
Long-Term Operating Liabilities:		
Provisions for Pensions	SEK (3,605)	SEK (3,458)
Other Noncurrent Provisions	(1,473)	(1,310)
Accrued Expenses and Deferred Income	(1,861)	(2,126)
Other Noncurrent Liabilities	(536)	(621)
Total Long-Term Operating Liabilities	SEK (7,475)	SEK (7,515)
Net Long-Term Operating Liabilities	SEK 39,580	SEK 38,813

16.5 a. continued.

Net Short-Term and Long-Term Operating Assets	SEK 45,482	SEK 44,074
Short-Term Investing Assets:		
Short-Term Investments	SEK 911	SEK 1,194
Net Business Assets and Liabilities	SEK 46,393	SEK 45,268

Financing

Noncurrent Interest-Bearing Liabilities	SEK (17,918)	SEK (19,323)

Income Taxes

Short-Term Tax Assets	SEK 370	SEK 206
Short-Term Tax Liabilities	(946)	(645)
Long-Term Deferred Tax Assets	649	565
Long-Term Tax Assets	34	0
Long-Term Deferred Tax Liabilities	(2,278)	(2,140)
Long-Term Other Tax Liabilities	(170)	(195)
Total Income Tax Assets, Net	SEK (2,341)	SEK (2,209)
Net Assets and Liabilities	SEK 26,134	SEK 23,736

Equity

Share Capital	SEK 2,000	SEK 2,263
Contributed Capital	1,120	1,120
Hedge Reserve	87	(83)
Accumulated Exchange Rate Differences	243	903
Retained Earnings	22,679	19,524
Minority (Noncontrolling) Interest	5	9
Total Shareholders' Equity	SEK 26,134	SEK 23,736

16.5 continued.

b.

Schedule 16.2
SCANIA, INC.
Recast Statement of Comprehensive Income
(Amounts in Millions)

Year Ended December 31:	2006	2005	2004
Business Income			
Net Sales	SEK 70,738	SEK 63,328	SEK 56,788
Cost of Goods Sold	(52,255)	(47,835)	(42,528)
Research and Development..	(3,023)	(2,484)	(1,987)
Expenses:			
Selling Expenses	(6,016)	(5,829)	(5,343)
Administrative Expenses...	(1,189)	(858)	(789)
Share of Income of Associated Companies and Joint Ventures	5	8	8
Operating Income:			
Vehicles and Service	SEK 8,260	SEK 6,330	SEK 6,149
Interest and Lease Income...	SEK 3,527	SEK 3,518	SEK 3,427
Interest and Depreciation Expense	(2,608)	(2,575)	(2,572)
Other Income	232	178	134
Other Expenses	(179)	(138)	(132)
Selling and Administrative Expenses	(416)	(374)	(318)
Bad Debt Expenses	(63)	(80)	(89)
Operating Income:			
Customer Finance	SEK 493	SEK 529	SEK 450
Other Operating Interest Income	SEK 632	SEK 679	SEK 346
Net Operating Income	SEK 9,385	SEK 7,538	SEK 6,945
Other Financial Income	SEK 142	SEK 299	SEK 96
Other Financial Expense	(81)	(206)	(127)
Net Investing Income	SEK 61	SEK 93	SEK (31)
Net Business Income	SEK 9,446	SEK 7,631	SEK 6,914
Financing			
Interest Expense	SEK (863)	SEK (866)	SEK (638)
Income Taxes			
Income Tax Expense	SEK (2,644)	SEK (2,100)	SEK (1,960)
Net Income Consolidated Group	SEK 5,939	SEK 4,665	SEK 4,316
Minority (Noncontrolling) Interest	0	0	(2)
Scania Shareholders' Interest	SEK 5,939	SEK 4,665	SEK 4,314

16.5 b. continued.

Other Comprehensive
Income:

Hedge Reserve......................	SEK	170	SEK	(83)	SEK	0
Exchange Rate Differ- ences.................................		(660)		1,303		(250)
Total Other Compre- hensive Income........	SEK	(490)	SEK	1,220	SEK	(250)
Comprehensive Income.........	SEK	4,959	SEK	5,885	SEK	4,064

c.

Schedule 16.3
SCANIA, INC.
Recast Statement of Cash Flows
(Amounts in Millions)

Year Ended December 31:	2006	2005	2004
Business Cash Flows			
Operating Cash Flows			
Cash Collected from Revenues:			
Net Sales...............................	SEK 70,738	SEK 63,328	SEK 56,788
Interest and Lease Income...............................	3,527	3,518	3,427
Other Income........................	232	178	134
Interest Income	632	679	346
Share of Income in Associ- ated Companies and Joint Ventures.................	5	8	8
Plus Decrease (Less In- crease) in Receivables....	8	439	(1,664)
Less Increase in Net Investments in Credit Portfolio.............................	(3,514)	(1,410)	(478)
Cash Received from Rev- enues	SEK 71,628	SEK 66,740	SEK 58,561
Cash Disbursed for Manu- facturing Costs:			
Cost of Goods Sold	SEK(52,255)	SEK(47,835)	SEK(42,528)
Less Increase (Plus De- crease) in Inventories.....	(627)	284	(959)
Plus Increase in Taxes Payable	1,276	646	864
Cash Disbursed for Manu- facturing Costs....................	SEK(51,606)	SEK(46,905)	SEK(42,623)

Odd-numbered Solutions

16.5 c. continued.

Cash Disbursed for Other Operating Expenses:			
Research and Development Expenses	SEK (3,023)	SEK (2,484)	SEK (1,987)
Selling Expenses:			
Vehicles and Service	(6,016)	(5,829)	(5,343)
Administrative Expenses:			
Vehicles and Service	(1,189)	(858)	(789)
Interest and Depreciation Expense: Customer Finance	(2,608)	(2,575)	(2,572)
Selling and Administrative Expenses: Customer Finance	(416)	(374)	(318)
Bad Debt Expense	(63)	(80)	(89)
Other Expenses	(179)	(138)	(132)
Plus Items Not Affecting Cash Flow	3,236	2,953	2,386
Plus Increase in Pensions	96	124	250
Plus Increase (Less Decrease) in Other Liabilities and Provisions	1,126	(731)	356
Cash Disbursed for Other Operating Expenses	SEK (9,036)	SEK (9,992)	SEK (8,238)
Cash Received (Repaid) from Current Operating Borrowing	SEK 8,827	SEK 912	SEK (207)
Cash Disbursed for Acquisitions/Divestments of Businesses	SEK 0	SEK (205)	SEK (49)
Cash Disbursed for Net Investments in Noncurrent Assets	SEK (3,810)	SEK (3,597)	SEK (2,798)
Total Operating Cash Flows	SEK 16,003	SEK 6,953	SEK 4,646

Investing Cash Flows

Cash Received from Investments (Net):			
Other Financial Income	SEK 142	SEK 299	SEK 96
Other Financial Expense	(81)	(206)	(127)
Cash Disbursed for Short-Term Investments Comprising Cash and Cash Equivalents	(8,315)	(23)	(50)
Cash Disbursed for Investments	SEK (8,254)	SEK 70	SEK (81)
Total Business Cash Flows	SEK 7,749	SEK 7,023	SEK 4,565

16.5 c. continued.

Financing Cash Flows

Cash Disbursed for Interest Expense	SEK	(863)	SEK	(866)	SEK (638)
Change in Debt Financing.....		7,591		62	(1,264)
Less Change in Current Operating Borrowing...........		(8,827)		(912)	207
Total Financing Cash Flows	SEK	(2,099)	SEK	(1,716)	SEK (1,695)

Income Tax Cash Flows

Cash Disbursed for Income Taxes.....................	SEK	(2,552)	SEK	(2,450)	SEK (1,784)

Equity Cash Flows

Cash Disbursed for Dividends	SEK	(3,000)	SEK	(3,000)	SEK (1,200)
Effect of Exchange Rate Changes..............................	SEK	(78)	SEK	130	SEK (10)
Net Change in Cash...............	SEK	20	SEK	(13)	SEK (124)
Cash, Beginning of Year		1,106		1,119	1,243
Cash, End of Year..................	SEK	1,126	SEK	1,106	SEK 1,119

This page is intentionally left blank

APPENDIX

TIME VALUE OF CASH FLOWS

Questions, Exercises, and Problems: Answers and Solutions

A.1   See the text or the glossary at the end of the book.

A.3   In simple interest, only the principal sum earns interest. In compound interest, interest is earned on the principal plus amounts of interest not paid or withdrawn.

A.5   The timing of the first payment for an annuity due is *now* (at the beginning of the first period) while that for an ordinary annuity is at the *end* of the first period. The future value of an annuity due is computed as of one year after the final payment, but for an ordinary annuity is computed as of the time of the last payment.

A.7   Present values increase when interest rates decrease and present values decrease when interest rates increase, regardless of the time period.

A.9   The formula assumes that the growth [represented by the parameter g in the formula $1/(r-g)$] continues forever. That is a long time. The formula assumes also that the discount and growth rates remain constant. In our experience, more harm results from assuming the growth persists forever than from the other assumptions.

A.11   a. $150,000 X .62741 = $94,112.

          b. $150,000 X .54027 = $81,041.

A.13   a.   ¥45,000,000/10.63663 = ¥4.23 million.

          b.   ¥45,000,000/12.29969 = ¥3.66 million.

A.15   a.   £145,000/4.62288 = £31,366.

          b.   £145,000/4.11141 = £35,268.

Odd-numbered Solutions

A.17   (Effective interest rates.)

    a.   12% per period; 5 periods.

    b.   6% per period; 10 periods.

    c.   3% per period; 20 periods.

    d.   1% per period; 60 periods.

A.19   a. $100 x .30832 = $30.83.

    b. $250 x .53063 = $132.66.

    c. $1,000 x .78757 = $787.57.

A.21   a. $1,000(1.00 + .94340) + $2,000(4.21236 − .94340) + $2,500(6.80169 − 4.21236) = $14,955.

    b. $1,000(1.00 + .92593) + $2,000(3.99271 − .92593) + $2,500(6.24689 − 3.99271) = $13,695.

    c. $1,000(1.00 + .90909) + $2,000(3.79079 − .90909) + $2,500(5.75902 − 3.79079) = $12,593.

A.23   a. $3,000/(.06 − .02) = $75,000.

    b. $3,000/(.08 − .02) = $50,000.

    c.   [$3,000/(.06 − .02)] x .79209 = $59,406.75.

    d.   [$3,000/(.08 − .02)] x .73503 = $36,751.50.

A.25   7.00%. Note that $100,000/$55,307 = 1.80809. See Table 4, 2-period row and observe 1.80809 in the 7% column.

A.27   a. $16\% = (\$67,280/\$50,000)^{1/2} - 1.$

    b.

Year (1)	Carrying Value Start of Year (2)	Interest for Year = (2) X .16 (3)	Amount (Reducing) Increasing Carrying Value (4)	Carrying Value End of Year = (2) + (3) + (4) (5)
1	$ 50,000	$ 8,000		$ 58,000
2	58,000	9,280	$ (67,280)	-0-

A.29 a. Terms of sale of 2/10, net/30 on a $100 gross invoice price, for example, mean that the interest rate is 2/98 for a 20-day period, because if the discount is not taken, a charge of $2 is levied for the use of $98. The $98 is used for 20 days (= 30 − 10), so the number of compounding periods in a year is 365/20 = 18.25. The expression for the exact rate of interest implied by 2/10, net 30 is $(1 + 2/98)^{(365/20)} - 1 = 1.020408^{18.25} - 1 = 44.59\%$.

b. Table 1 can be used. Use the 2% column and the 18-period row to see that the rate implied by 2/10, net 30 must be at least 42.825% (= 1.42825 − 1).

$30,000 + ($10,000/.01) = $1,030,000.

A.31 Present value of future proceeds = .72845($35,000) + C = $35,000; where C represents the present value of the foregone interest payments. Table 2, 16-period row, 2% column = .72845.

C = $35,000 − $25,495.75 = $9,504.25.

A.33 Present value of deposit = $3.00.

Present value of $3.00, recorded 20 periods, have discounted at .50% per period = $3.00 x .90506 = $2.72.

Loss of $.28 (= $3.00 − $2.72) in foregone interest vs. Loss of $1.20 in price.

Net advantage of returnables is $.92.

A.35 $600/12 = $50 saved per month. $2,000/$50 = 40.0.

Present value of annuity of $1 discounted at 1% for 50 periods = 39.19612.

The present value of the annuity is $40 when the annuity lasts between 51 and 52 periods. Oberweis Dairy will recoup its investment in a bit more than four years.

A.37   (Friendly Loan Company; find implicit interest rate; truth-in lending laws reduce the type of deception suggested by this problem.)

The effective interest rate is 19.86% and must be found by trial and error. The time line for this problem is:

	+$6,000	−$2,000	−$2,000	−$2,000	−$2,000	−$2,000
End of Year	0	1	2	3	4	5

which is equivalent, at least in terms of the implied interest rate, to:

	+$3	−$1	−$1	−$1	−$1	−$1
End of Year	0	1	2	3	4	5

Scanning Table 4, 5-period column, one finds the factor 2.99061, which is approximately 3.00, in the 20% column, so one can easily see that the implied interest rate is about 20% per year.

A.39   (Lynch Company/Bages Company; computation of present value of cash flows; untaxed acquisition, no change in tax basis of assets.)

a. $440,000 = $390,000 + $50,000 = $700,000 − $260,000.

b. $3,745,966 = $440,000 x 8.51356; see Table 4, 20-period column, 10% row.

A.41   (Valuation of intangibles with perpetuity formulas.)

a. $50 million = $4 million/.08.

b.   Increase.

c. $66 2/3 million = $4 million/(.08 − .02).

d.   Increase.

e.   Decrease.

A.43 (Gulf Coast Manufacturing; choosing between investment alternatives.)

Basic Data Repeated from Problem

	Lexus	Mercedes-Benz
Initial Cost at the Start of 2008	$60,000	$45,000
Initial Cost at the Start of 2011		48,000
Trade-in Value		
End of 2010		23,000
End of 2013 [Note A]	16,000	24,500
Estimated Annual Cash Operating Costs, Except Major Servicing	4,000	4,500
Estimated Cash Cost of Major Servicing		
End of 2011	6,500	
End of 2009 and End of 2012		2,500

Present Value Computations

	Factor	Source [B]	Lexus	Mercedes-Benz
Initial Cost at the Start of 2008	1.00000		$60,000	$45,000
Initial Cost at the Start of 2011	0.75131	T[2, 3, .10]		36,063
Trade-in Value				
End of 2010	0.75131	T[2, 3, .10]		(17,280)
End of 2013 [Note A]	0.56447	T[2, 6, .10]	(9,032)	(13,830)
Estimated Annual Cash Operating Costs, Except Major Servicing	4.35526	T[4, 6, .10]	17,421	19,599
Estimated Cash Cost of Major Servicing				
End of 2011	0.68301	T[2, 4, .10]	4,440	
End of 2009 and End of 2012	0.82645	T[2, 2, .10]		2,066
	0.62092	T[2, 5, .10]		1,552
Sum of Present Values of All Costs............			$72,829	$73,170

Note A:
At this time, Lexus is 6 years old; second Mercedes-Benz is 3 years old.

[B]T[i,j,r] means Table i (= Table 2 or Table 4) from the back of the book, row j, interest rate r.

a. Strategy L, buying one Lexus has lower present value of costs, but the difference is so small that we'd encourage the CEO to go with his whim, whatever it may be. Also, the relatively new theory of real options will likely prefer Strategy M because it gives the owner more choices at the end of the third year.

b. Depreciation plays no role, so long as we ignore income taxes. Only cash flows matter.

A.45 (Fast Growth Start-Up Company; valuation involving perpetuity growth model assumptions. (Amounts in Millions)

We find the answer with trial and error, starting with 5 years of fast growth.

Growth Rate for Early Years of Fast Growth: 25%
Growth Rate for Steady State, Terminal Value: 4%
Discount Rate: 15%
Number of Years of Fast Growth: 5

End of Year	Free Cash Flow	Discount Factors from Table 2	Present Value End of Year 0
0	$ 100	1.00000	$ 100.0
1	125	0.86957	108.7
2	156	0.75614	118.1
3	195	0.65752	128.4
4	244	0.57175	139.6
5	305	0.49718	151.7
Terminal Value 5	2,885	0.49718	1,434.5

$305 x 1.04/(.15 − .04)

Total Valuation...................................... $ 2,181.1

Growth Rate for Early Years of Fast Growth: 25%
Growth Rate for Steady State, Terminal Value: 4%
Discount Rate: 15%
Number of Years of Fast Growth: 6

End of Year	Free Cash Flow	Discount Factors from Table 2	Present Value End of Year 0
0	$ 100	1.00000	$ 100.0
1	125	0.86957	108.7
2	156	0.75614	118.1
3	195	0.65752	128.4
4	244	0.57175	139.6
5	305	0.49718	151.7
6	381	0.43233	164.9
Terminal Value 6	3,607	0.43233	1,559.2

$381 x 1.04/(.15 − .04)

Total Valuation...................................... $ 2,470.7

A.45 continued.

Growth Rate for Early Years of Fast Growth: 25%
Growth Rate for Steady State, Terminal Value: 4%
Discount Rate: 15%
Number of Years of Fast Growth: 7

End of Year	Free Cash Flow	Discount Factors from Table 2	Present Value End of Year 0
0	$ 100	1.00000	$ 100.0
1	125	0.86957	108.7
2	156	0.75614	118.1
3	195	0.65752	128.4
4	244	0.57175	139.6
5	305	0.49718	151.7
6	381	0.43233	164.9
7	477	0.37594	179.3
Terminal Value 7	4,508	0.37594	1,694.8

Terminal Value
$477 x 1.04/(.15 − .04)

Total Valuation..................................... $ 2,785.6

We see that assuming a bit more than 6 years of fast growth, followed by the steady state justifies a market valuation (the so-called market cap) of $2.5 billion.

This page is intentionally left blank

This page is intentionally left blank

This page is intentionally left blank

This page is intentionally left blank

This page is intentionally left blank